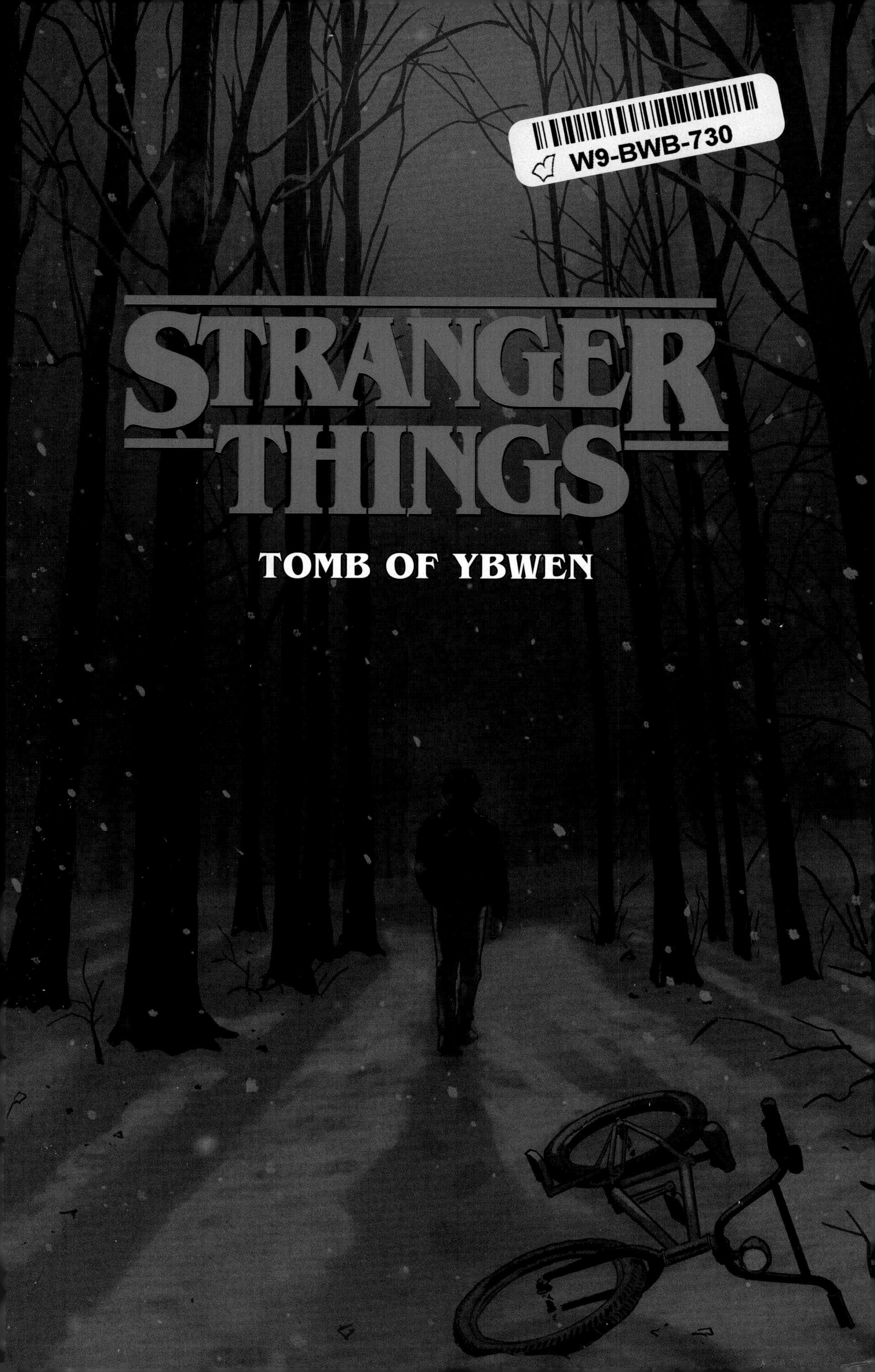
STRANGER THINGS
TOMB OF YBWEN

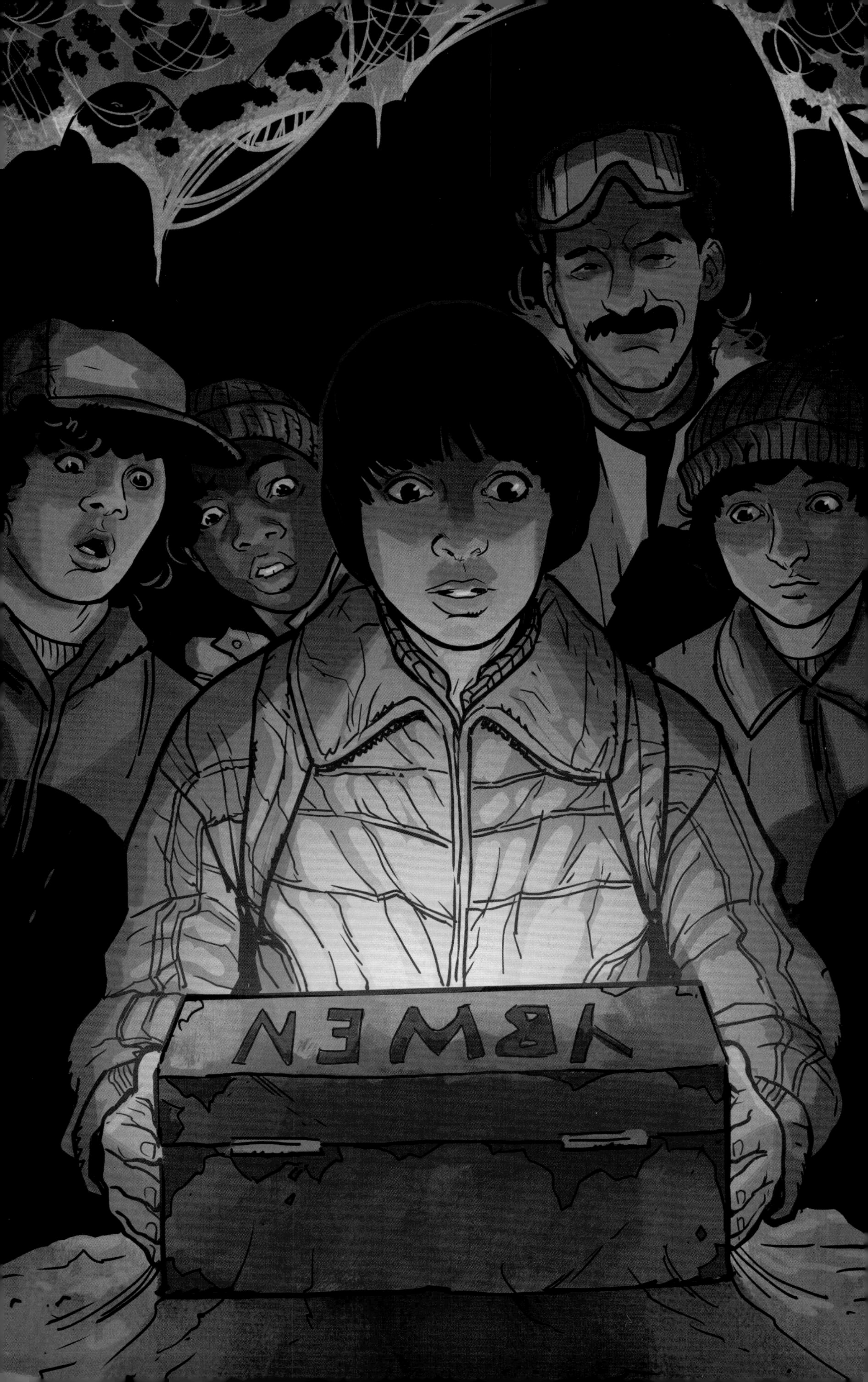

NETFLIX

STRANGER THINGS

TOMB OF YBWEN

script
GREG PAK

line art
DIEGO GALINDO

colors
FRANCESCO SEGALA

lettering
NATE PIEKOS OF BLAMBOT®

front cover art by
KYLE LAMBERT

chapter break art by
MARC ASPINALL

dark horse books

president and publisher
MIKE RICHARDSON

editor
SPENCER CUSHING

assistant editor
KONNER KNUDSEN

collection designer
PATRICK SATTERFIELD

digital art technician
SAMANTHA HUMMER

Special thanks to NETFLIX, CINDY CHANG, JOE LAWSON and KYLE LAMBERT.

Advertising Sales: ads@DarkHorse.com | ComicShopLocator.com

STRANGER THINGS: TOMB OF YBWEN, May 2022. Published by Dark Horse Comics LLC, 10956 SE Main Street, Milwaukie, Oregon 97222. Stranger Things™ & © 2021 Netflix. All rights reserved. Dark Horse Comics® and the Dark Horse logo are trademarks of Dark Horse Comics LLC, registered in various categories and countries. All rights reserved. No portion of this publication may be reproduced or transmitted, in any form or by any means, without the express written permission of Dark Horse Comics LLC. Names, characters, places, and incidents featured in this publication either are the product of the author's imagination or are used fictitiously. Any resemblance to actual persons (living or dead), events, institutions, or locales, without satiric intent, is coincidental.

This volume collects issue #1 through #4 of the Dark Horse comic book series
Stranger Things: Tomb of Ybwen.

Published by Dark Horse Books
A division of Dark Horse Comics LLC
10956 SE Main Street
Milwaukie, OR 97222

DarkHorse.com | Netflix.com

First edition: May 2022

Ebook ISBN: 978-1-50672-553-6
Trade Paperback ISBN: 978-1-50672-554-3

1 3 5 7 9 10 8 6 4 2
Printed in China

Library of Congress Cataloging-in-Publication Data

Names: Pak, Greg, author. | Galindo, Diego, 1978- artist. | Segala, Francesco, colourist. | Piekos, Nate, letterer.
Title: Tomb of Ybwen / script, Greg Pak ; line art, Diego Galindo ; colors, Francesco Segala ; lettering, Nate Piekos of Blambot.
Other titles: Stranger things (Television program)
Description: First edition. | Milwaukie, OR : Dark Horse Books, 2022. | Series: Stranger things ; vol. 5 | "This volume collects issue #1 through #4 of the Dark Horse comic book series Stranger Things: Tomb of Ybwen." | Summary: "It's January 1985–the Hawkins crew have survived their battle with the mind flayer, but Will and Joyce are still reeling from the recent death of Bob Newby. After he and Mr. Clarke discover a mysterious map Bob left in a box of old nerdy memorabilia, Will rallies the crew to investigate–but with a blizzard coming, they're afraid to follow"– Provided by publisher.
Identifiers: LCCN 2021049029 (print) | LCCN 2021049030 (ebook) | ISBN 9781506725543 (trade paperback) | ISBN 9781506725536 (ebook)
Subjects: LCGFT: Horror comics. | Science fiction comics.
Classification: LCC PN6728.S769 P35 2022 (print) | LCC PN6728.S769 (ebook) | DDC 741.5/973–dc23/eng/20211013
LC record available at https://lccn.loc.gov/2021049029
LC ebook record available at https://lccn.loc.gov/2021049030

NEIL HANKERSON executive vice president • TOM WEDDLE chief financial officer • DALE LaFOUNTAIN chief Information officer • TIM WIESCH vice president of licensing • MATT PARKINSON vice president of marketing VANESSA TODD-HOLMES vice president of production and scheduling • MARK BERNARDI vice president of book trade and digital sales • RANDY LAHRMAN vice president of product development • KEN LIZZI general counsel • DAVE MARSHALL editor in chief • DAVEY ESTRADA editorial director • CHRIS WARNER senior books editor • CARY GRAZZINI director of specialty projects • LIA RIBACCHI art director • MATT DRYER director of digital art and prepress • MICHAEL GOMBOS senior director of licensed publications • KARI YADRO director of custom programs • KARI TORSON director of international licensing

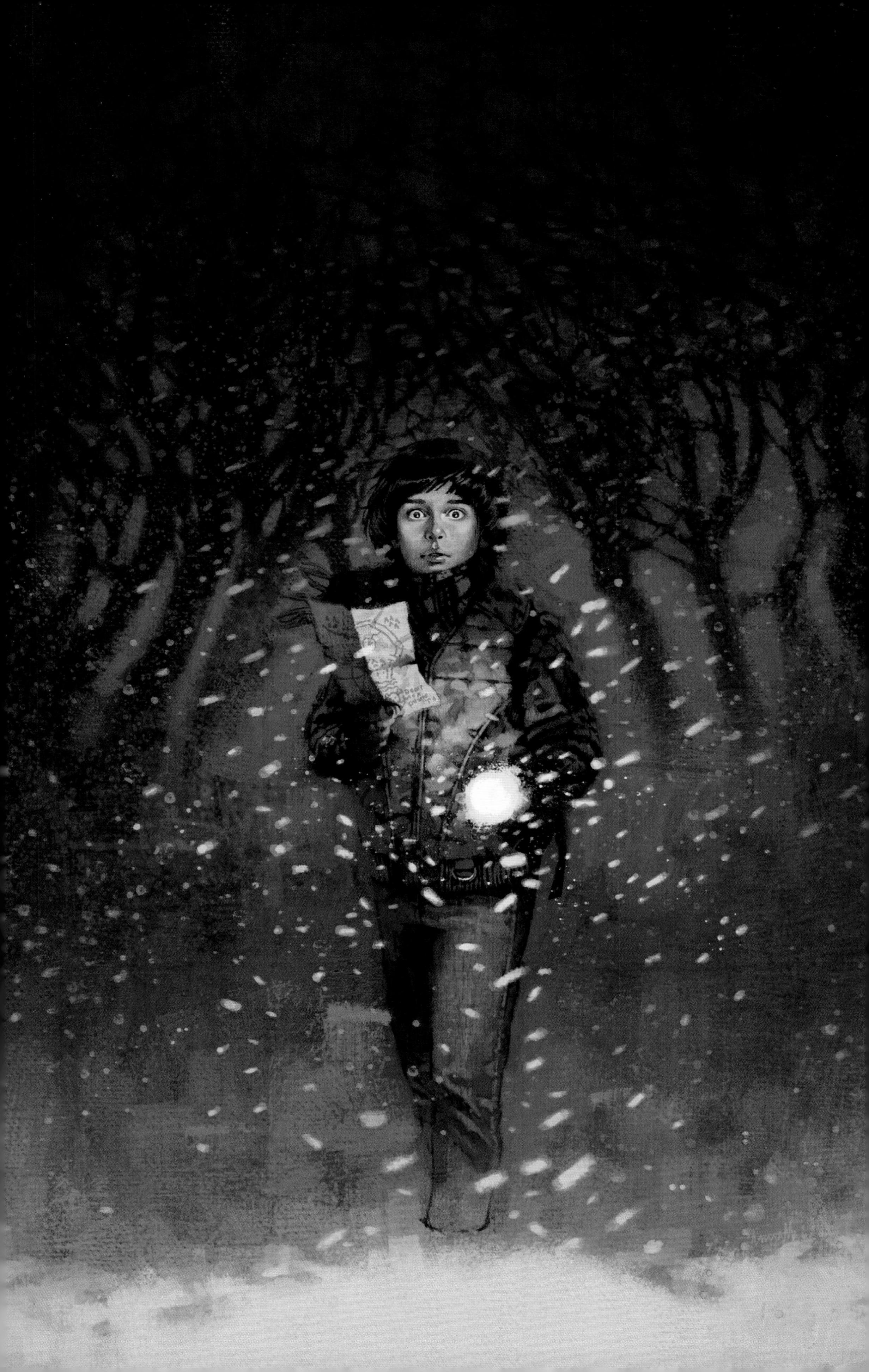

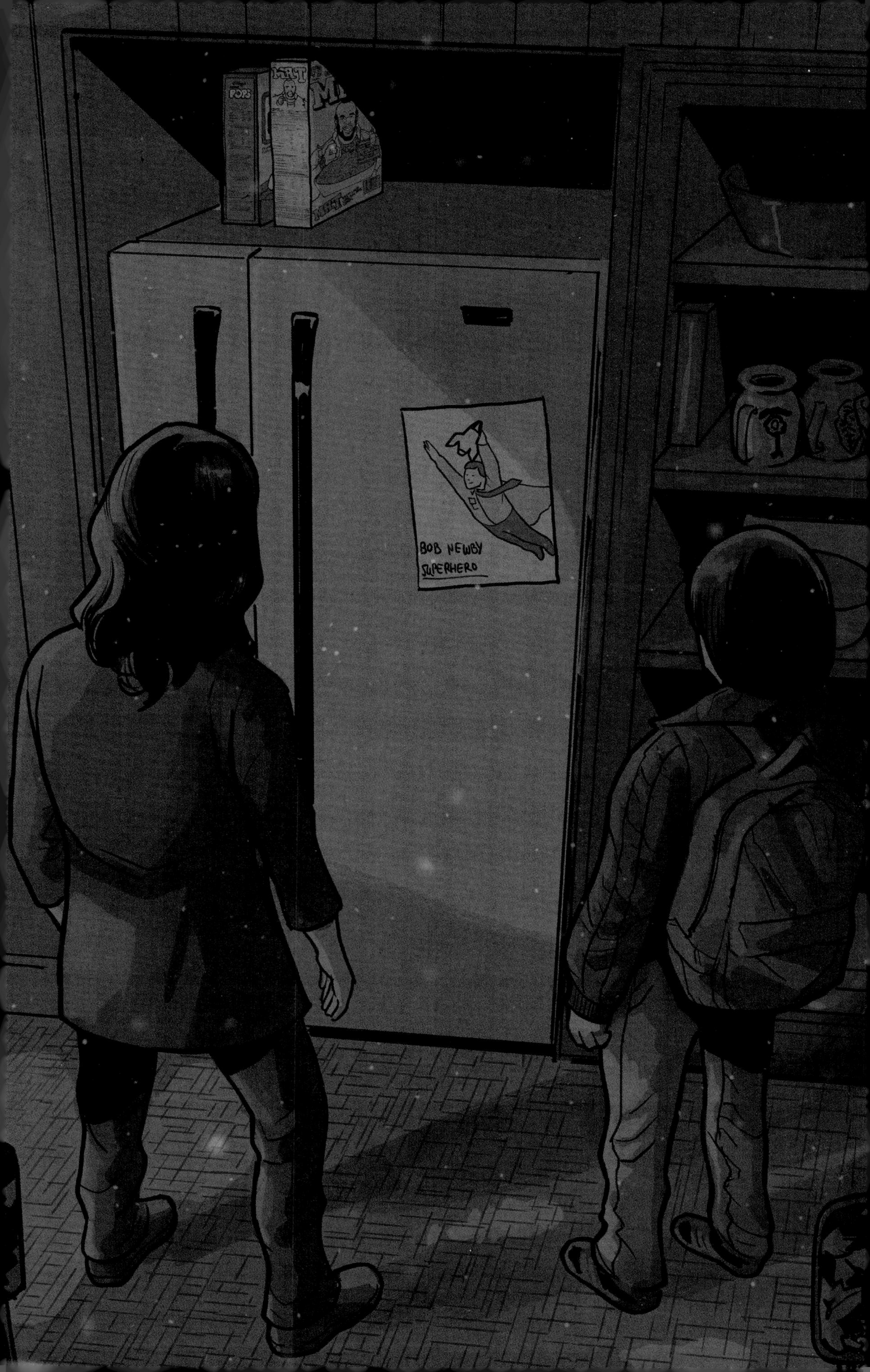
BOB NEWBY
SUPERHERO

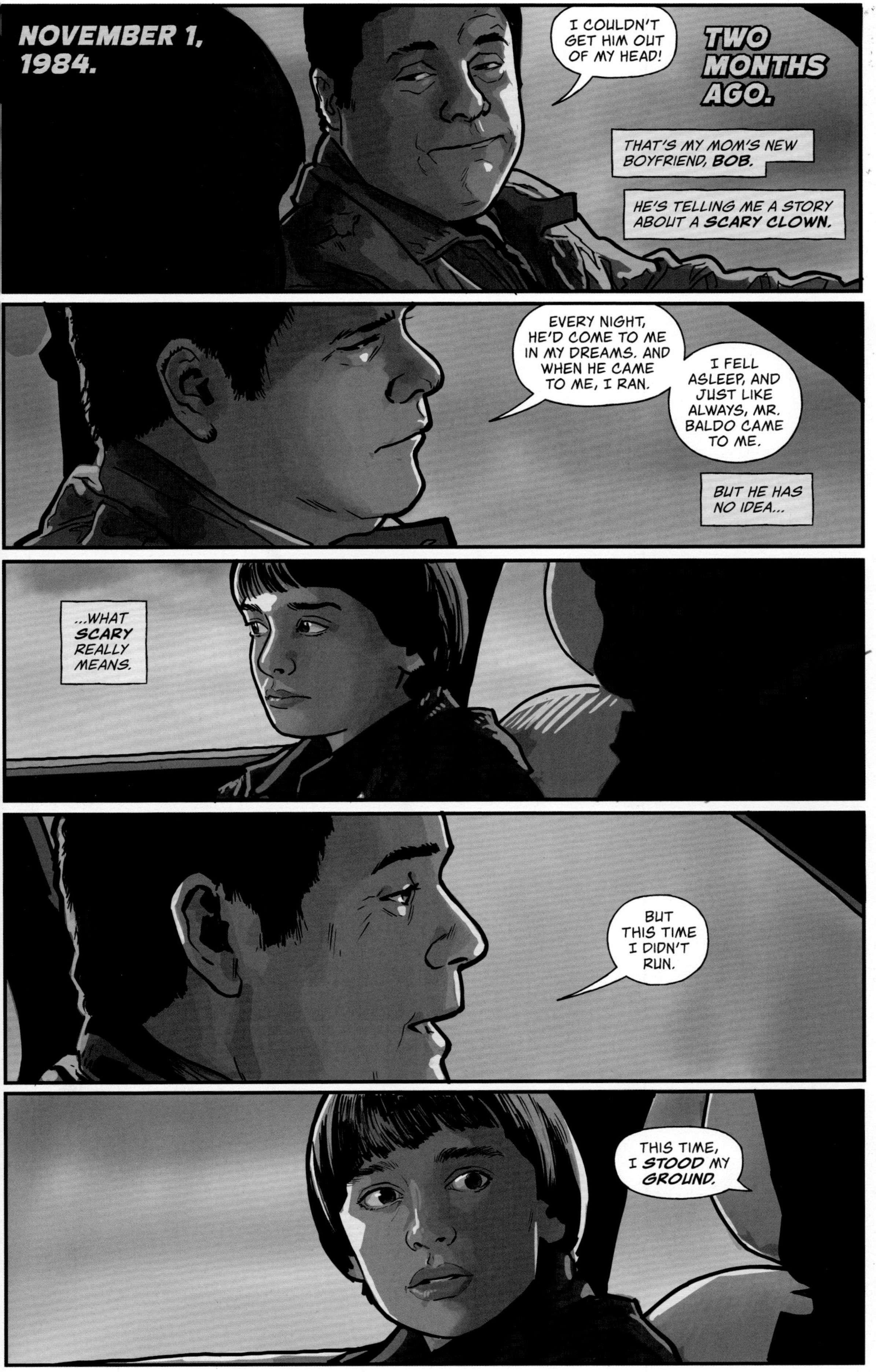
NOVEMBER 1, 1984.
I COULDN'T GET HIM OUT OF MY HEAD!
TWO MONTHS AGO.
THAT'S MY MOM'S NEW BOYFRIEND, BOB.
HE'S TELLING ME A STORY ABOUT A SCARY CLOWN.
EVERY NIGHT, HE'D COME TO ME IN MY DREAMS. AND WHEN HE CAME TO ME, I RAN.
I FELL ASLEEP, AND JUST LIKE ALWAYS, MR. BALDO CAME TO ME.
BUT HE HAS NO IDEA...
...WHAT SCARY REALLY MEANS.
BUT THIS TIME I DIDN'T RUN.
THIS TIME, I STOOD MY GROUND.

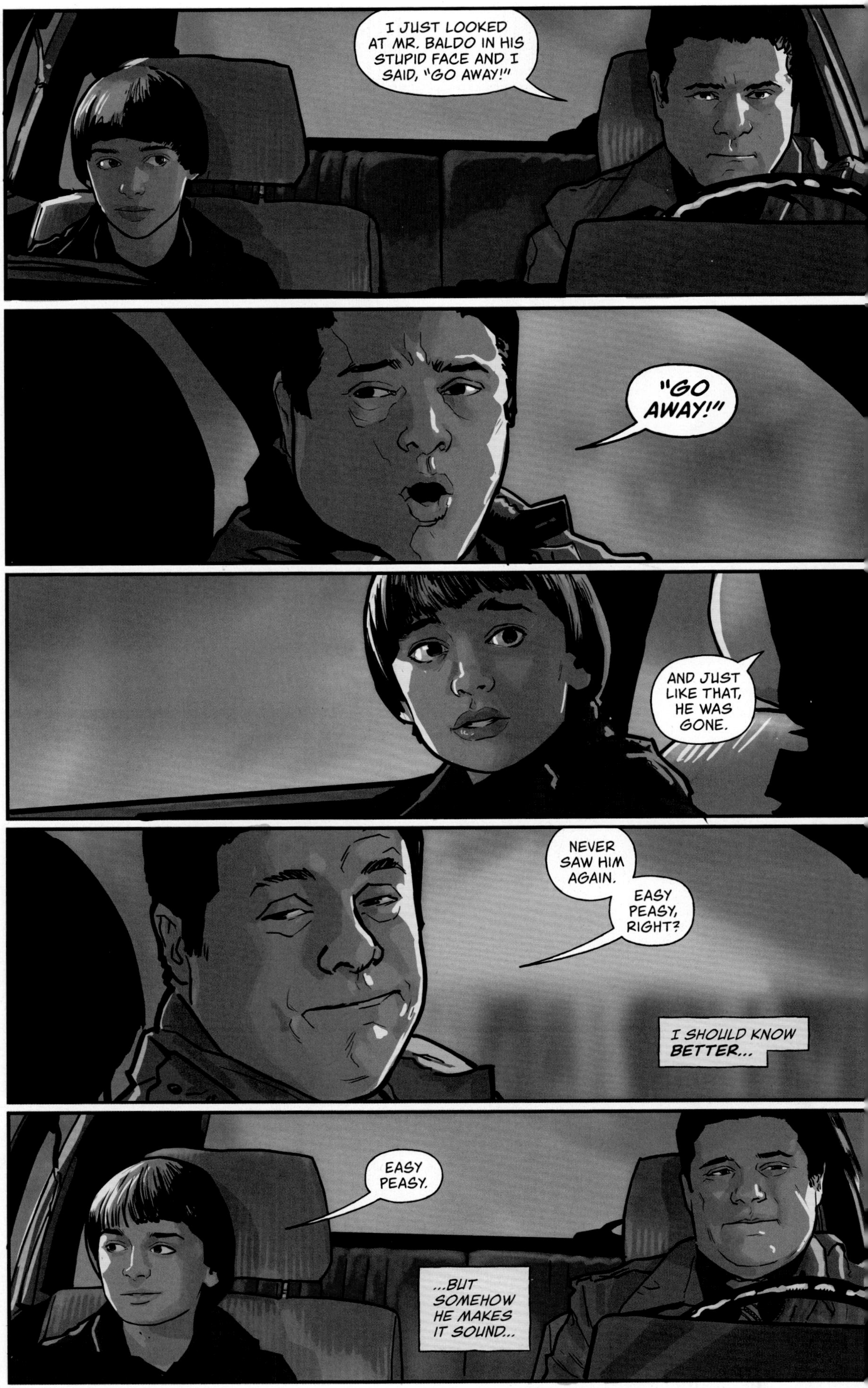
I JUST LOOKED AT MR. BALDO IN HIS STUPID FACE AND I SAID, "GO AWAY!"
"GO AWAY!"
AND JUST LIKE THAT, HE WAS GONE.
NEVER SAW HIM AGAIN.
EASY PEASY, RIGHT?
I SHOULD KNOW BETTER...
EASY PEASY.
...BUT SOMEHOW HE MAKES IT SOUND...

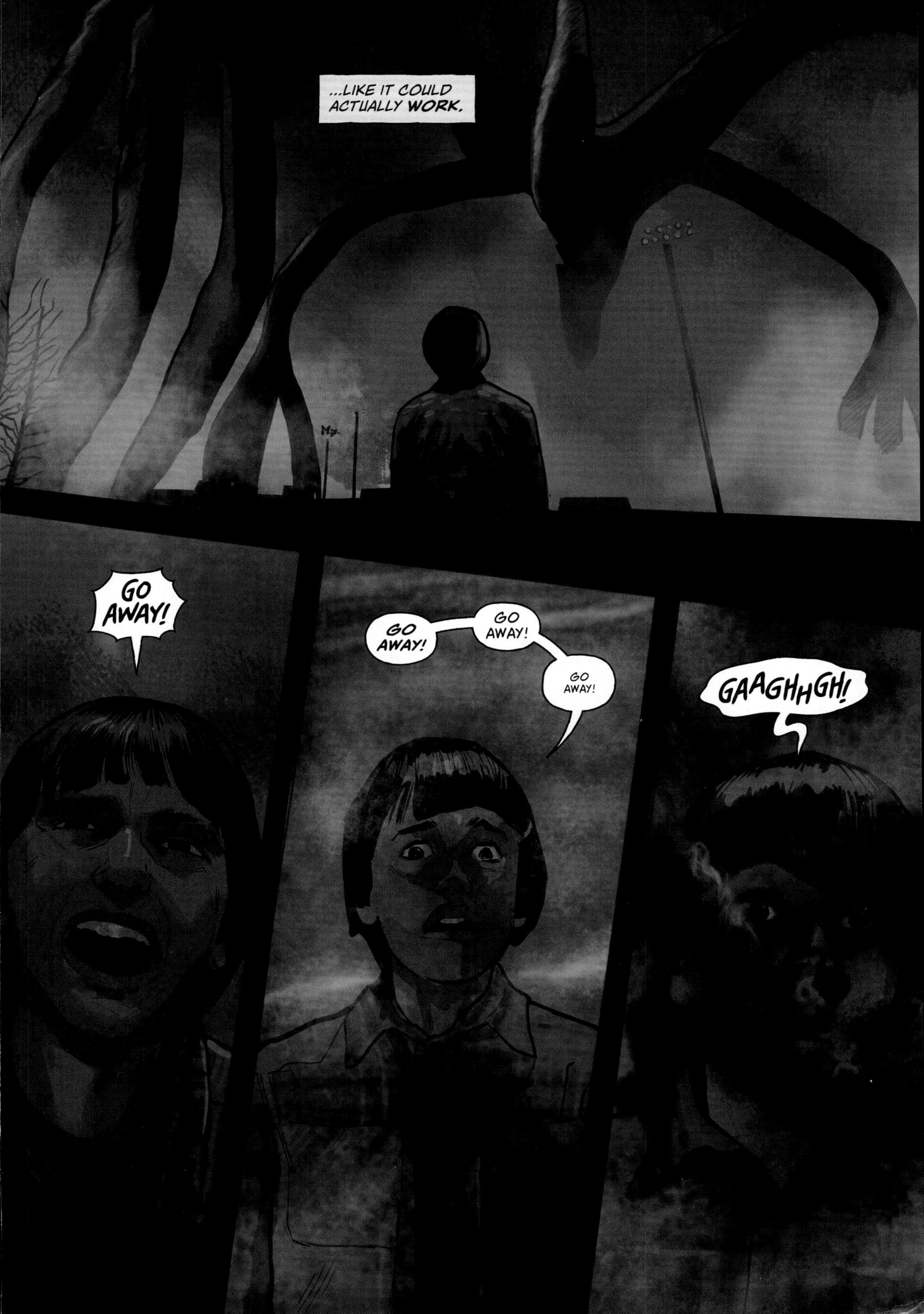
...LIKE IT COULD ACTUALLY WORK.
GO AWAY!
GO AWAY!
GO AWAY!
GO AWAY!
GAAGHHGH!

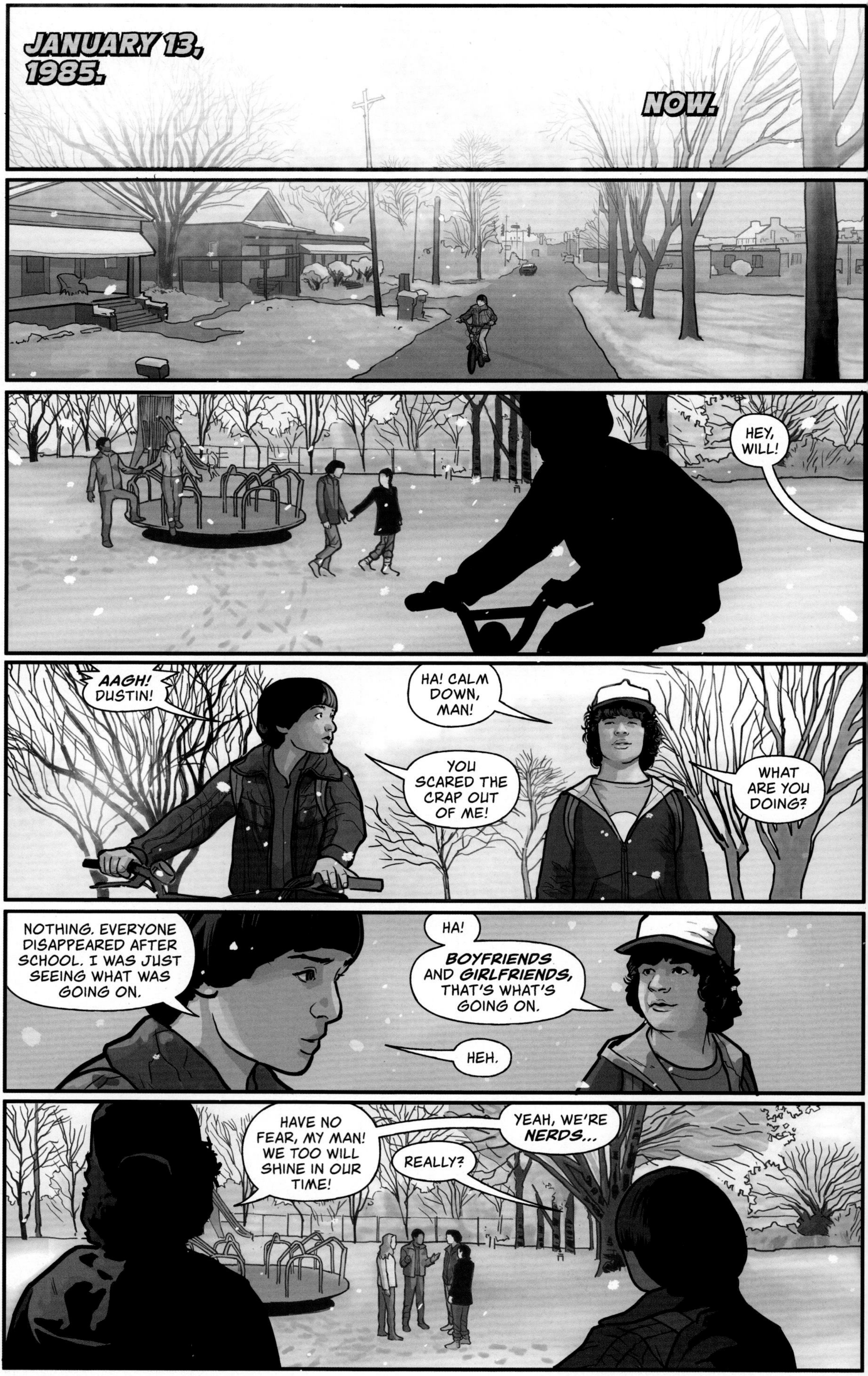
JANUARY 13, 1985.
NOW.
HEY, WILL!
AAGH! DUSTIN!
HA! CALM DOWN, MAN!
YOU SCARED THE CRAP OUT OF ME!
WHAT ARE YOU DOING?
NOTHING. EVERYONE DISAPPEARED AFTER SCHOOL. I WAS JUST SEEING WHAT WAS GOING ON.
HA!
BOYFRIENDS AND GIRLFRIENDS, THAT'S WHAT'S GOING ON.
HEH.
YEAH, WE'RE NERDS...
REALLY?
HAVE NO FEAR, MY MAN! WE TOO WILL SHINE IN OUR TIME!

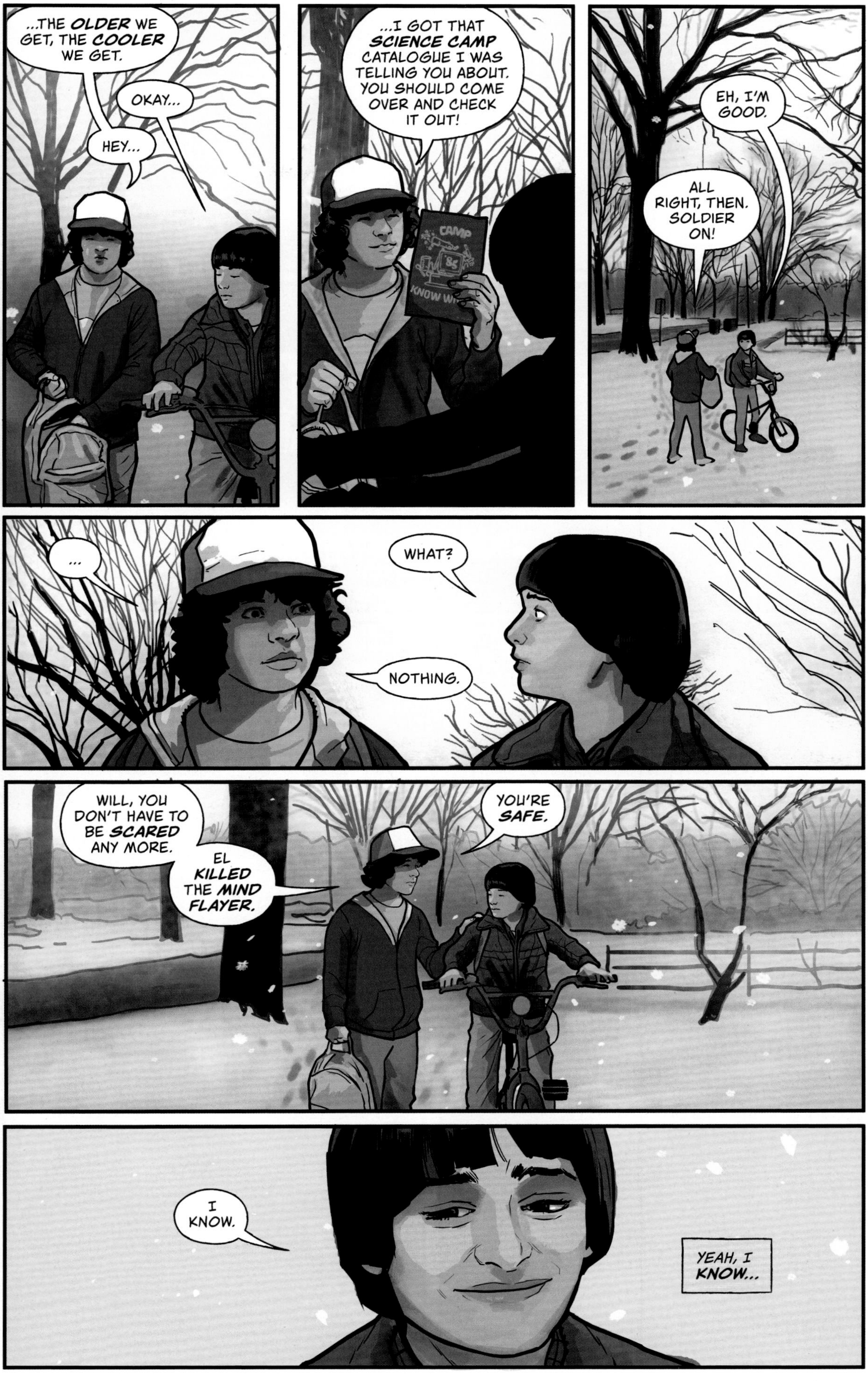
...THE OLDER WE GET, THE COOLER WE GET.
HEY...
OKAY...
...I GOT THAT SCIENCE CAMP CATALOGUE I WAS TELLING YOU ABOUT. YOU SHOULD COME OVER AND CHECK IT OUT!
CAMP '85
KNOW WH
EH, I'M GOOD.
ALL RIGHT, THEN. SOLDIER ON!
...
WHAT?
NOTHING.
WILL, YOU DON'T HAVE TO BE SCARED ANY MORE.
EL KILLED THE MIND FLAYER.
YOU'RE SAFE.
I KNOW.
YEAH, I KNOW...

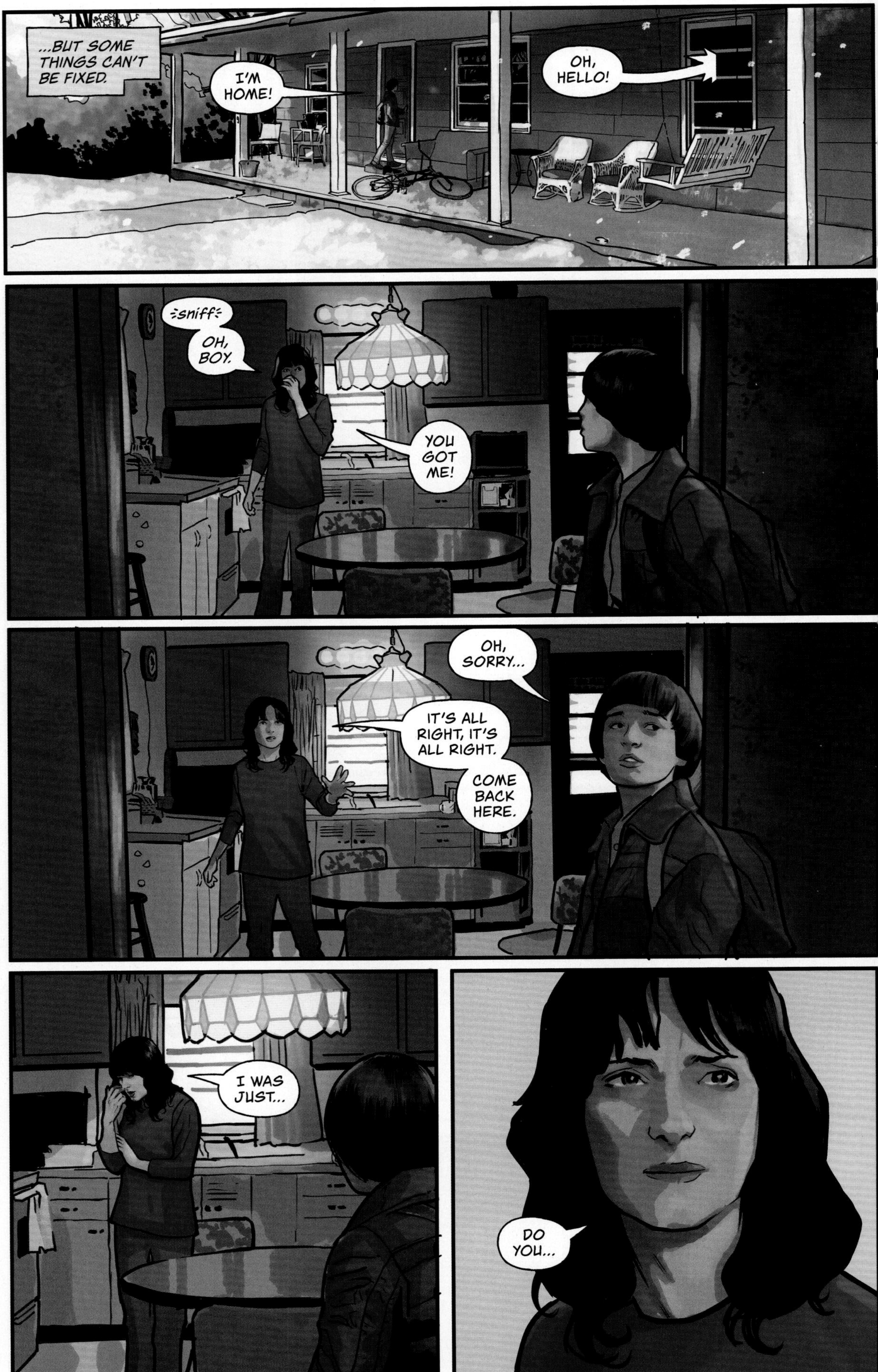
...BUT SOME THINGS CAN'T BE FIXED.
I'M HOME!
OH, HELLO!
=sniff=
OH, BOY.
YOU GOT ME!
OH, SORRY...
IT'S ALL RIGHT, IT'S ALL RIGHT.
COME BACK HERE.
I WAS JUST...
DO YOU...

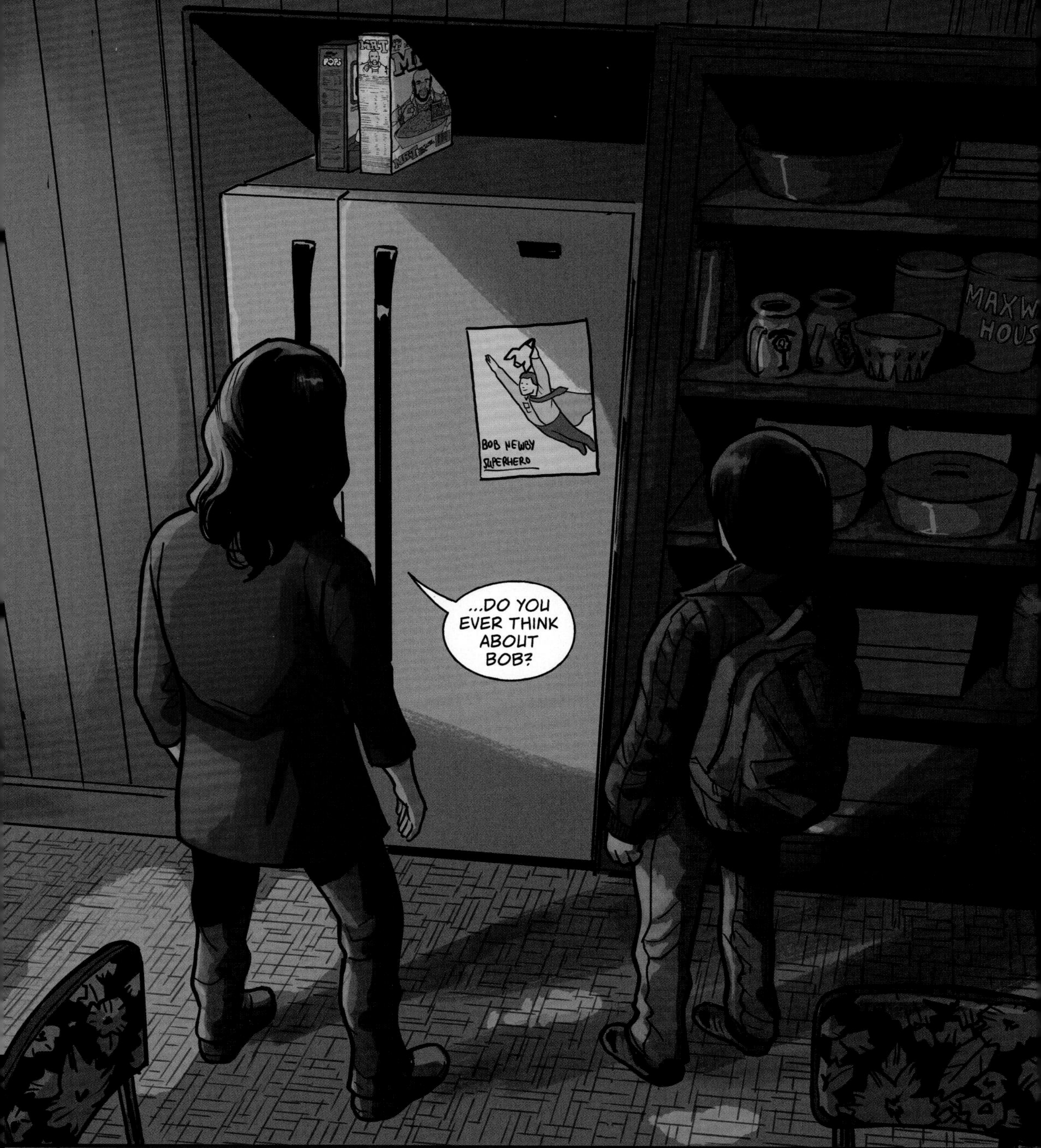
BOB NEWBY
SUPERHERO
...DO YOU EVER THINK ABOUT BOB?

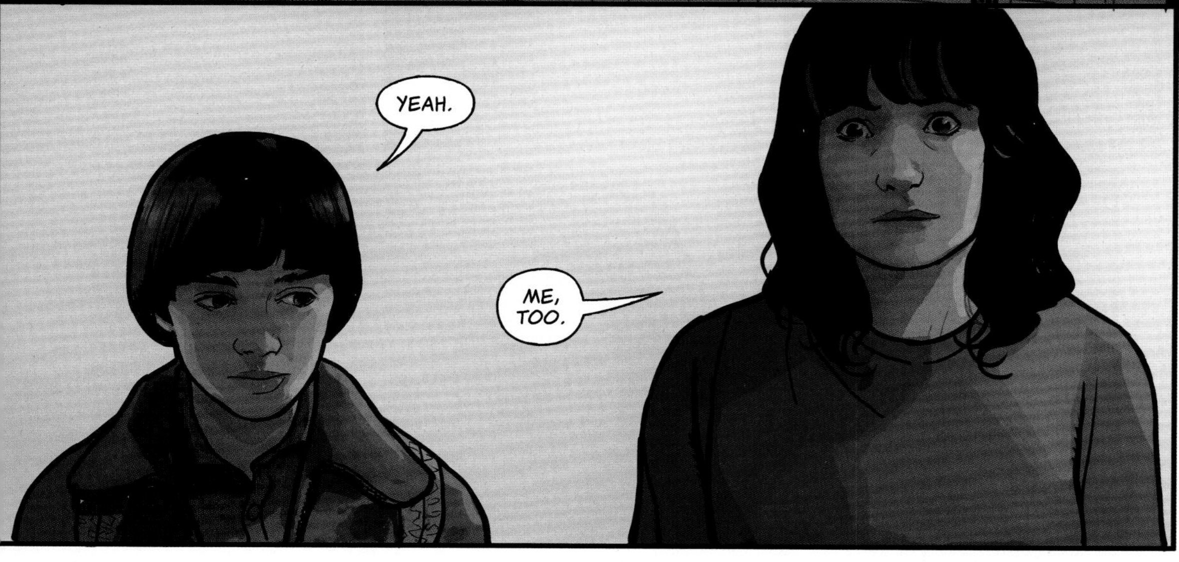
YEAH.
ME, TOO.

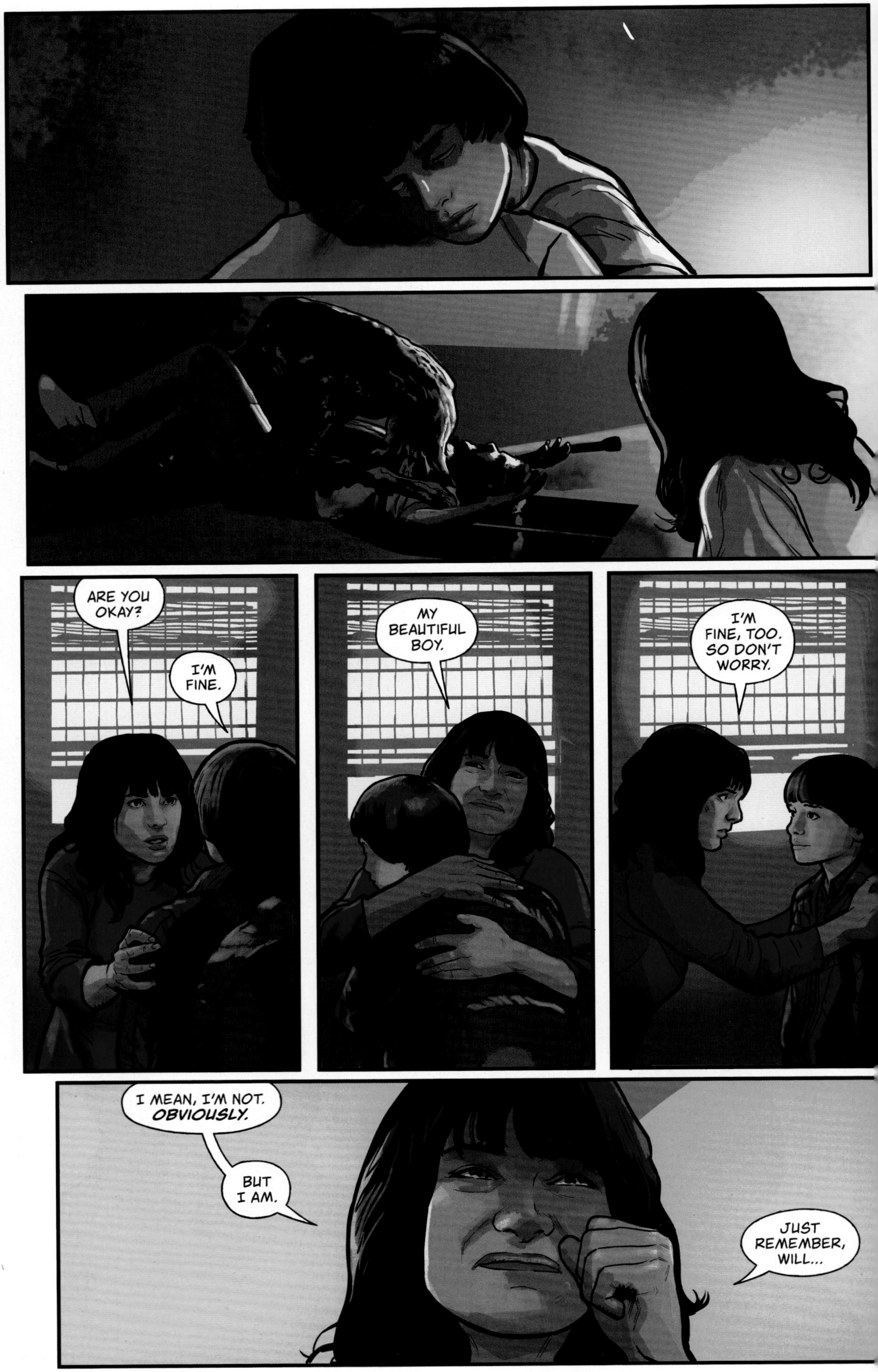
ARE YOU OKAY?
I'M FINE.
MY BEAUTIFUL BOY.
I'M FINE, TOO. SO DON'T WORRY.
I MEAN, I'M NOT. *OBVIOUSLY.*
BUT I AM.
JUST REMEMBER, WILL...

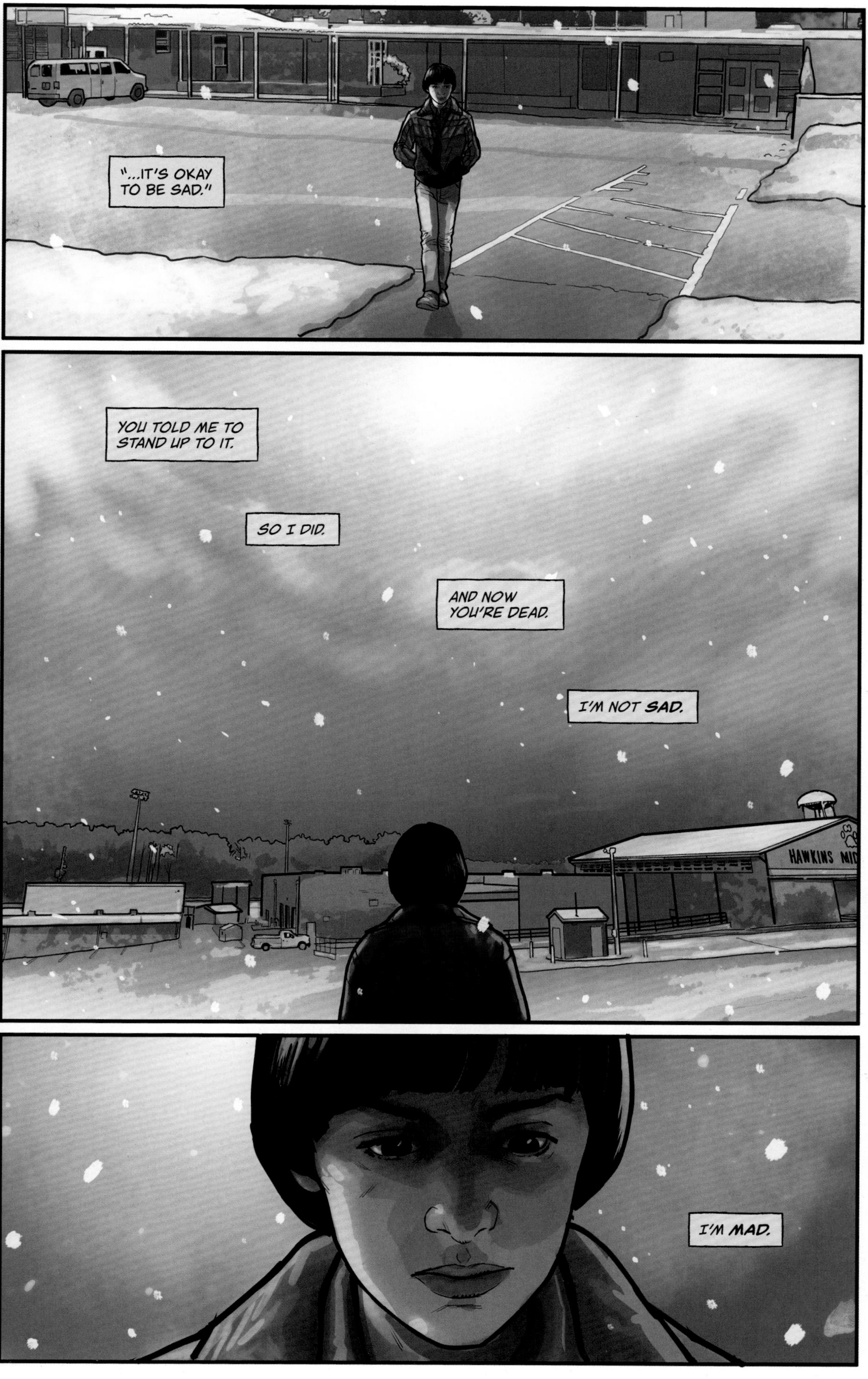
"...IT'S OKAY TO BE SAD."
YOU TOLD ME TO STAND UP TO IT.
SO I DID.
AND NOW YOU'RE DEAD.
I'M NOT SAD.
HAWKINS
I'M MAD.

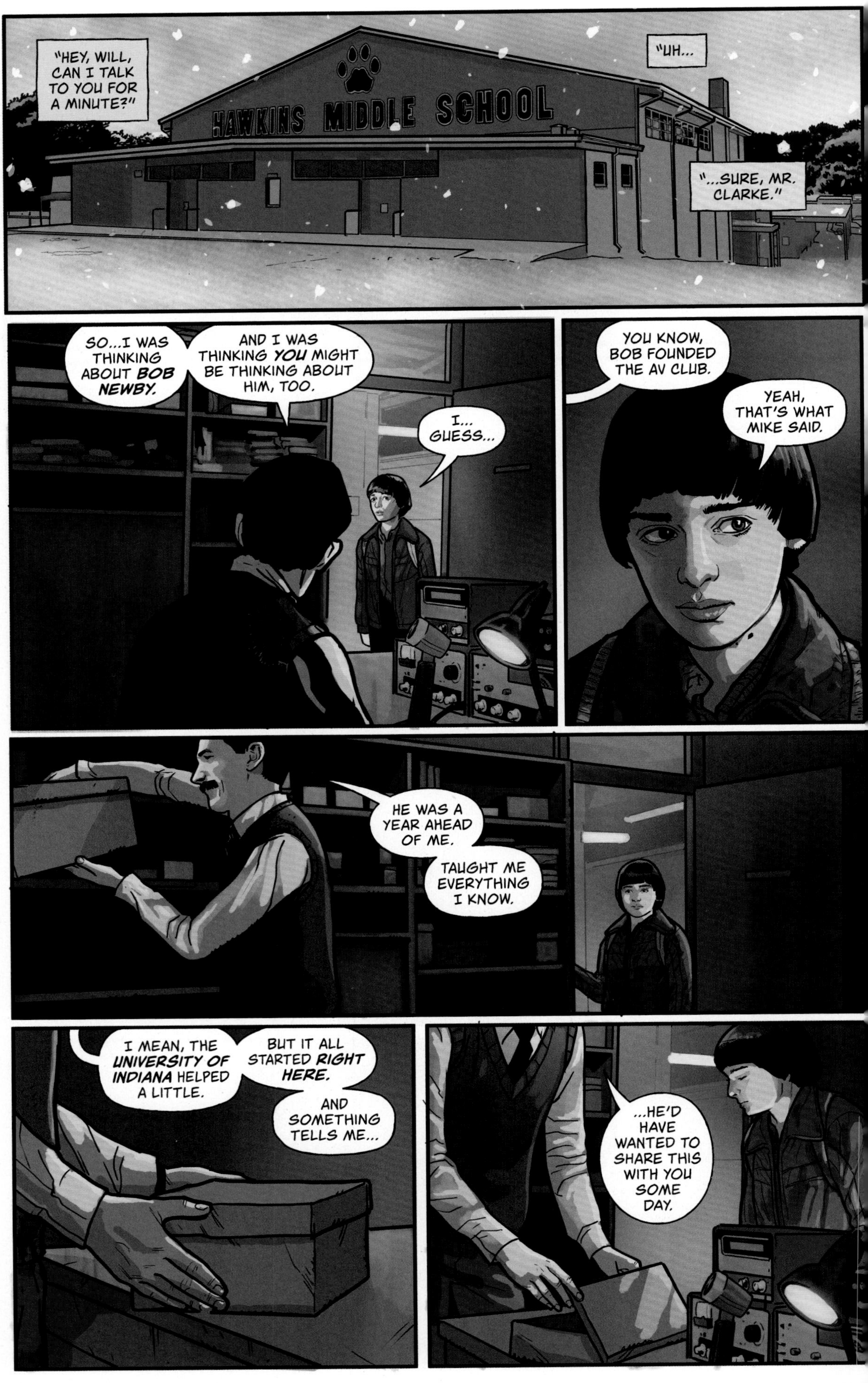
"HEY, WILL, CAN I TALK TO YOU FOR A MINUTE?"
"UH...
"...SURE, MR. CLARKE."
HAWKINS MIDDLE SCHOOL
SO...I WAS THINKING ABOUT BOB NEWBY.
AND I WAS THINKING YOU MIGHT BE THINKING ABOUT HIM, TOO.
I... GUESS...
YOU KNOW, BOB FOUNDED THE AV CLUB.
YEAH, THAT'S WHAT MIKE SAID.
HE WAS A YEAR AHEAD OF ME.
TAUGHT ME EVERYTHING I KNOW.
I MEAN, THE UNIVERSITY OF INDIANA HELPED A LITTLE.
BUT IT ALL STARTED RIGHT HERE.
AND SOMETHING TELLS ME...
...HE'D HAVE WANTED TO SHARE THIS WITH YOU SOME DAY.

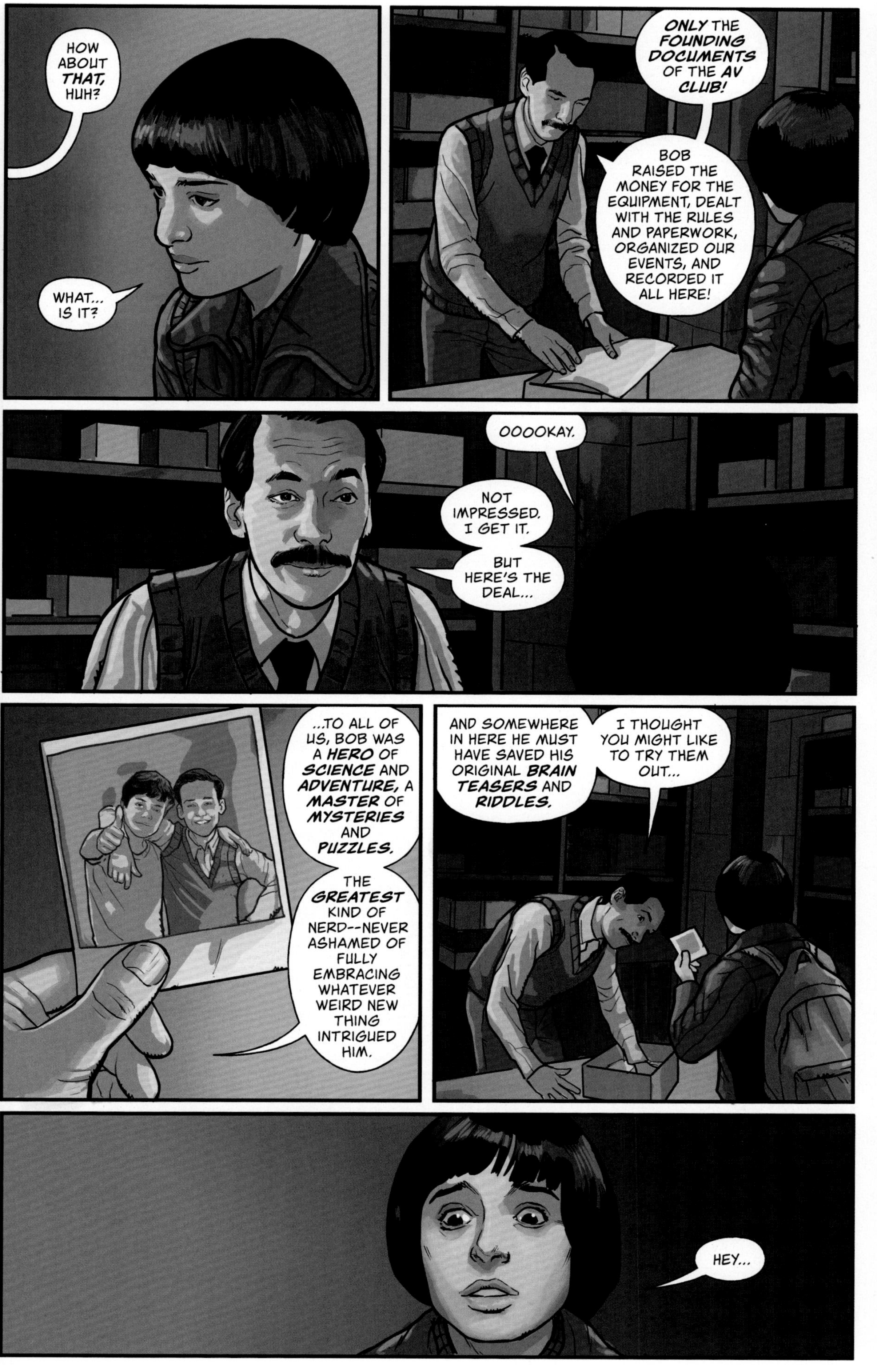
HOW ABOUT THAT, HUH?
WHAT... IS IT?
ONLY THE FOUNDING DOCUMENTS OF THE AV CLUB!
BOB RAISED THE MONEY FOR THE EQUIPMENT, DEALT WITH THE RULES AND PAPERWORK, ORGANIZED OUR EVENTS, AND RECORDED IT ALL HERE!
OOOOKAY.
NOT IMPRESSED. I GET IT.
BUT HERE'S THE DEAL...
...TO ALL OF US, BOB WAS A HERO OF SCIENCE AND ADVENTURE, A MASTER OF MYSTERIES AND PUZZLES.
THE GREATEST KIND OF NERD--NEVER ASHAMED OF FULLY EMBRACING WHATEVER WEIRD NEW THING INTRIGUED HIM.
AND SOMEWHERE IN HERE HE MUST HAVE SAVED HIS ORIGINAL BRAIN TEASERS AND RIDDLES.
I THOUGHT YOU MIGHT LIKE TO TRY THEM OUT...
HEY...

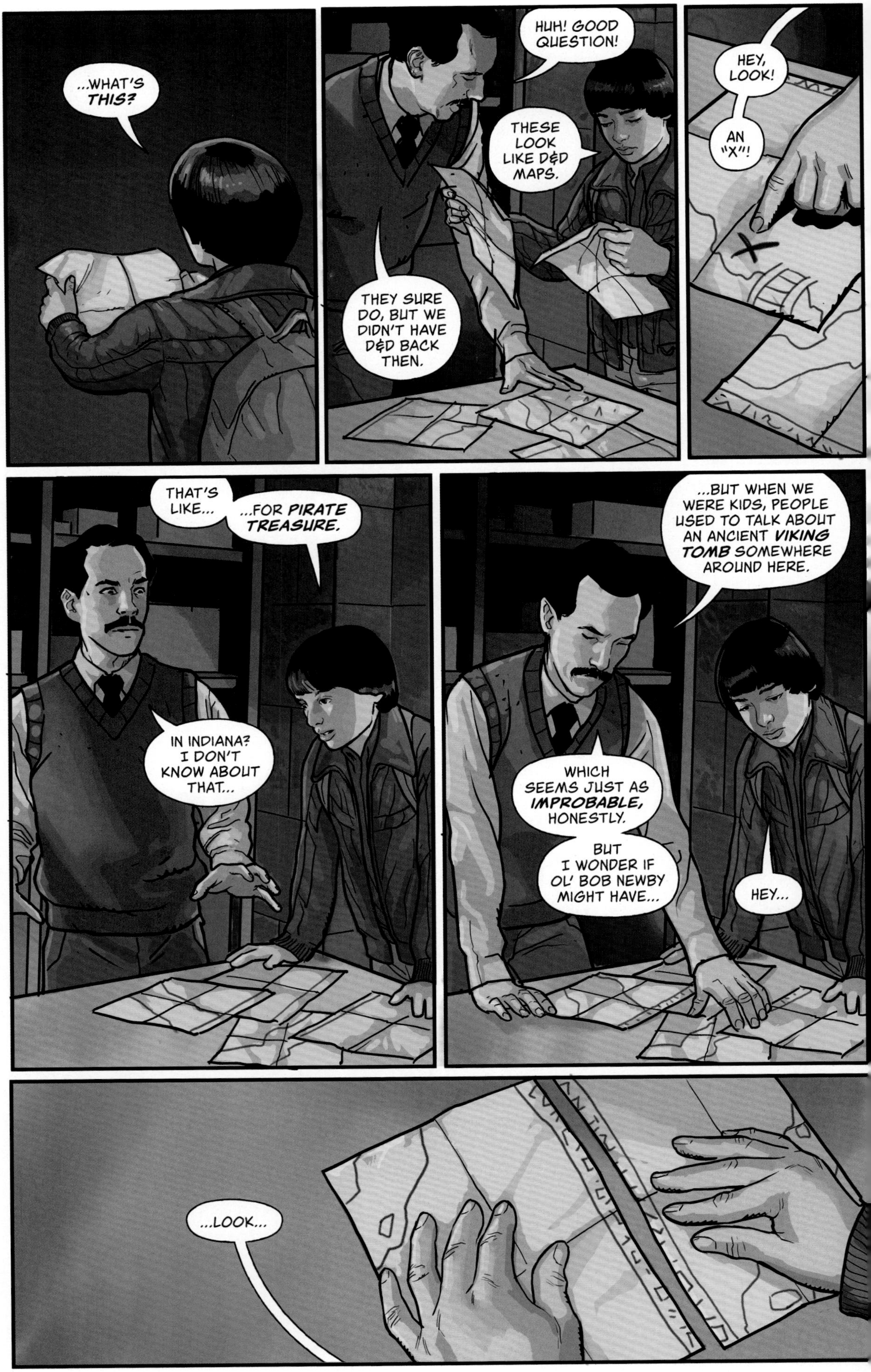
...WHAT'S *THIS?*
HUH! GOOD QUESTION!
THESE LOOK LIKE D&D MAPS.
THEY SURE DO, BUT WE DIDN'T HAVE D&D BACK THEN.
HEY, LOOK!
AN "X"!
THAT'S LIKE...
...FOR *PIRATE TREASURE.*
IN INDIANA? I DON'T KNOW ABOUT THAT...
...BUT WHEN WE WERE KIDS, PEOPLE USED TO TALK ABOUT AN ANCIENT *VIKING TOMB* SOMEWHERE AROUND HERE.
WHICH SEEMS JUST AS *IMPROBABLE,* HONESTLY.
BUT I WONDER IF OL' BOB NEWBY MIGHT HAVE...
HEY...
...LOOK...

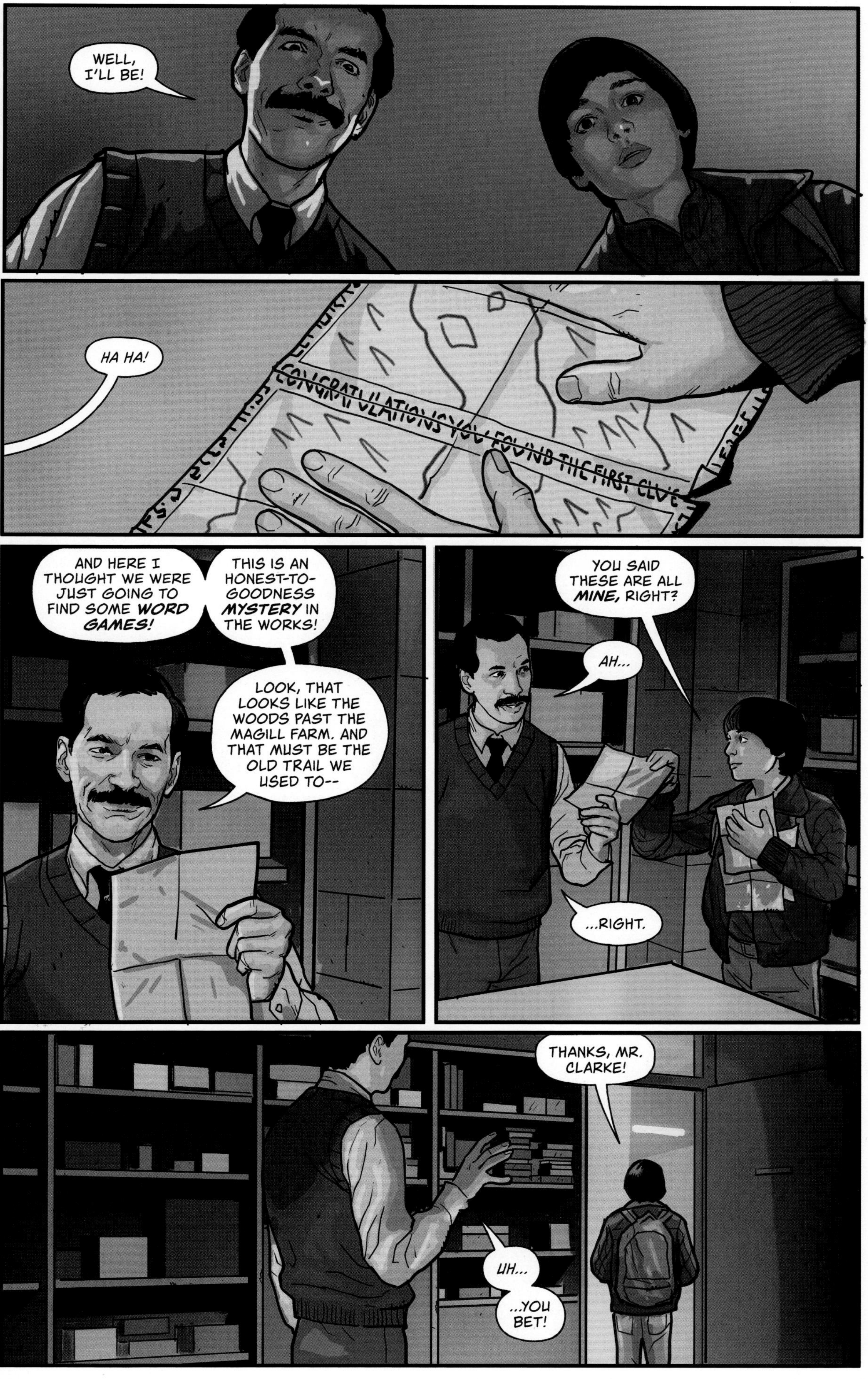
WELL, I'LL BE!
HA HA!
CONGRATULATIONS YOU FOUND THE FIRST CLUE
AND HERE I THOUGHT WE WERE JUST GOING TO FIND SOME *WORD GAMES!*
THIS IS AN HONEST-TO-GOODNESS *MYSTERY* IN THE WORKS!
LOOK, THAT LOOKS LIKE THE WOODS PAST THE MAGILL FARM. AND THAT MUST BE THE OLD TRAIL WE USED TO--
YOU SAID THESE ARE ALL *MINE,* RIGHT?
AH...
...RIGHT.
THANKS, MR. CLARKE!
UH...
...YOU BET!

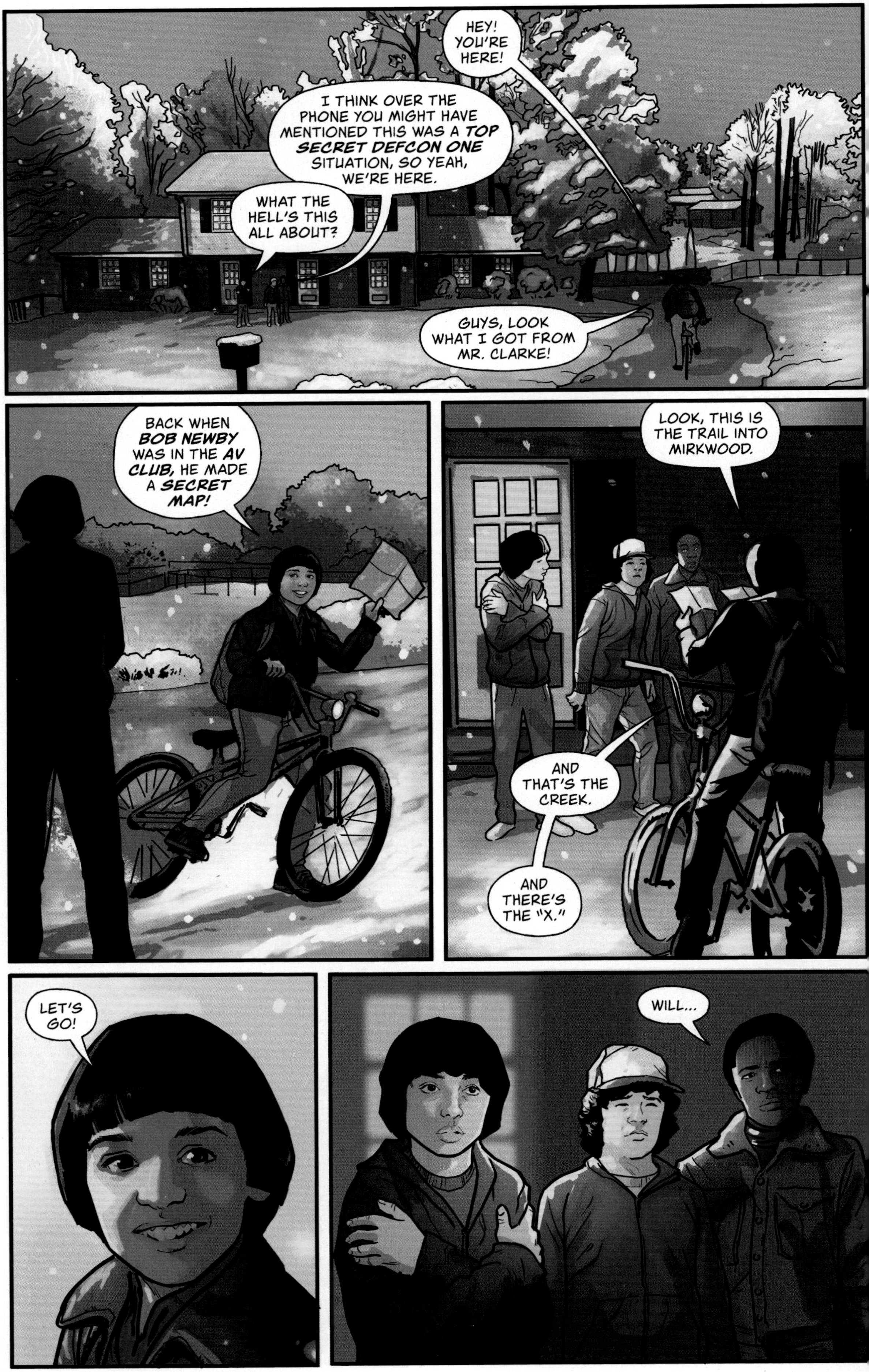
HEY! YOU'RE HERE!
I THINK OVER THE PHONE YOU MIGHT HAVE MENTIONED THIS WAS A TOP SECRET DEFCON ONE SITUATION, SO YEAH, WE'RE HERE.
WHAT THE HELL'S THIS ALL ABOUT?
GUYS, LOOK WHAT I GOT FROM MR. CLARKE!
BACK WHEN BOB NEWBY WAS IN THE AV CLUB, HE MADE A SECRET MAP!
LOOK, THIS IS THE TRAIL INTO MIRKWOOD.
AND THAT'S THE CREEK.
AND THERE'S THE "X."
LET'S GO!
WILL...

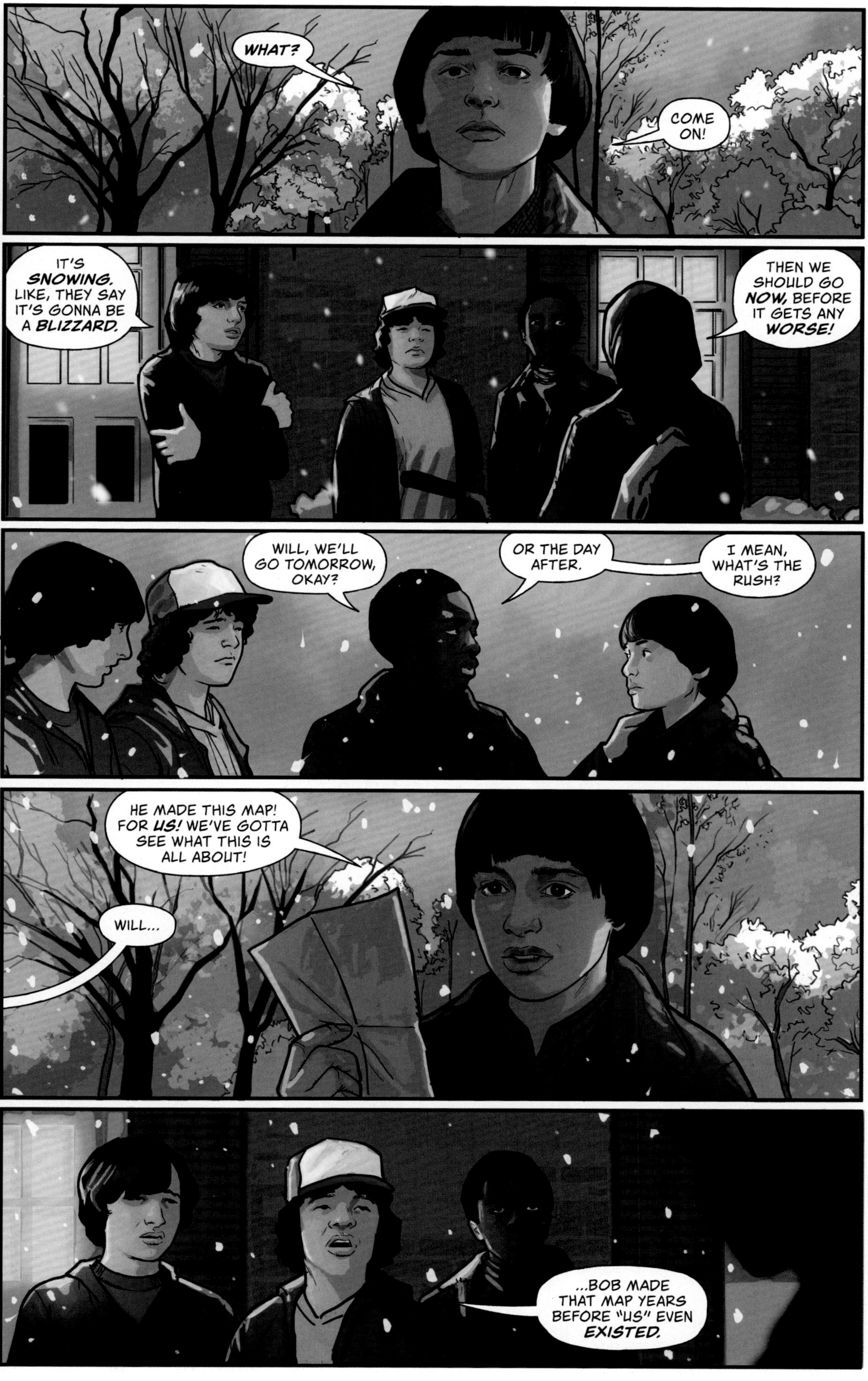
WHAT?
COME ON!
IT'S SNOWING. LIKE, THEY SAY IT'S GONNA BE A BLIZZARD.
THEN WE SHOULD GO NOW, BEFORE IT GETS ANY WORSE!
WILL, WE'LL GO TOMORROW, OKAY?
OR THE DAY AFTER.
I MEAN, WHAT'S THE RUSH?
HE MADE THIS MAP! FOR US! WE'VE GOTTA SEE WHAT THIS IS ALL ABOUT!
WILL...
...BOB MADE THAT MAP YEARS BEFORE "US" EVEN EXISTED.

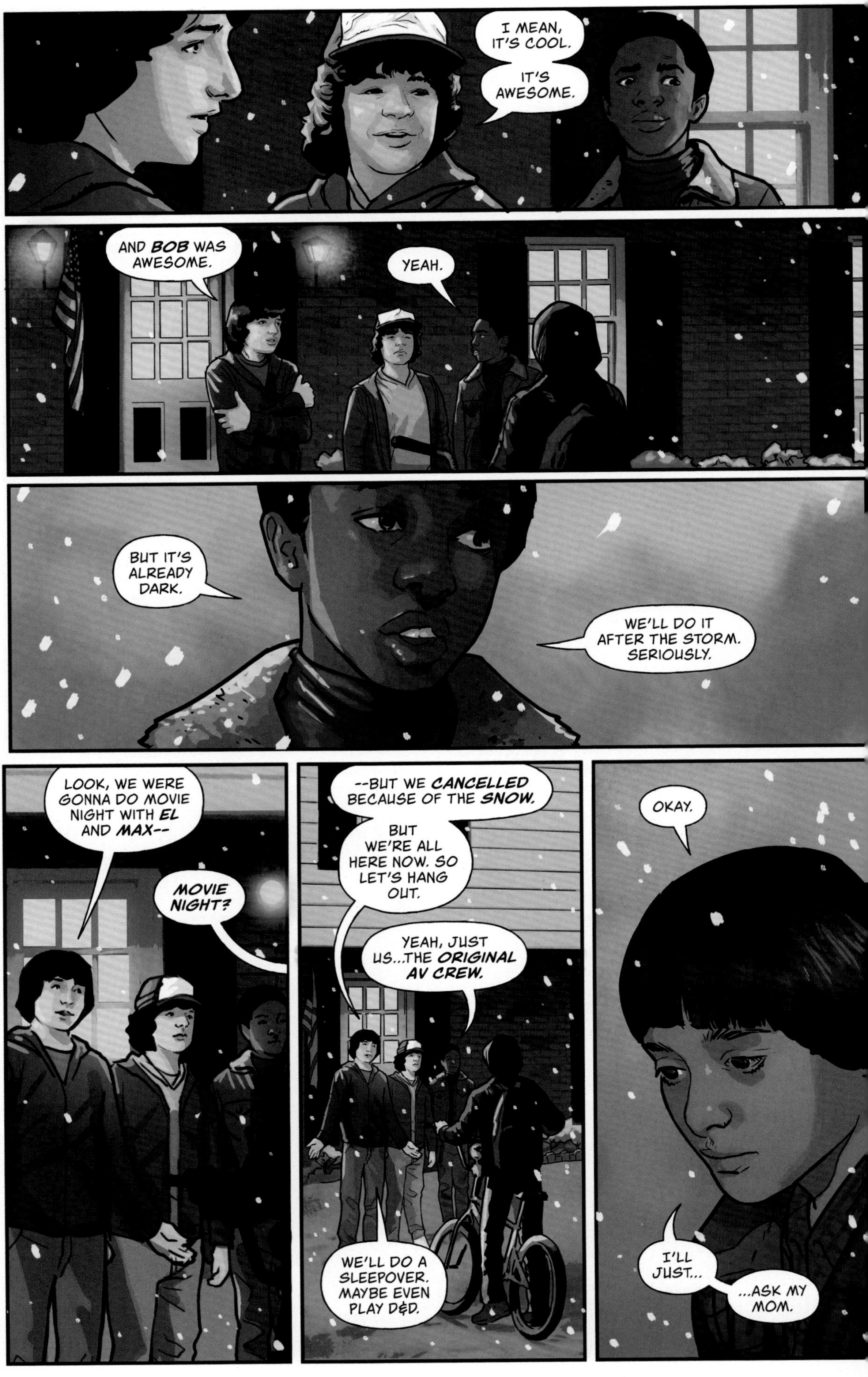
I MEAN, IT'S COOL.
IT'S AWESOME.
AND BOB WAS AWESOME.
YEAH.
BUT IT'S ALREADY DARK.
WE'LL DO IT AFTER THE STORM. SERIOUSLY.
LOOK, WE WERE GONNA DO MOVIE NIGHT WITH EL AND MAX--
MOVIE NIGHT?
--BUT WE CANCELLED BECAUSE OF THE SNOW.
BUT WE'RE ALL HERE NOW. SO LET'S HANG OUT.
YEAH, JUST US...THE ORIGINAL AV CREW.
WE'LL DO A SLEEPOVER. MAYBE EVEN PLAY D&D.
OKAY.
I'LL JUST...
...ASK MY MOM.

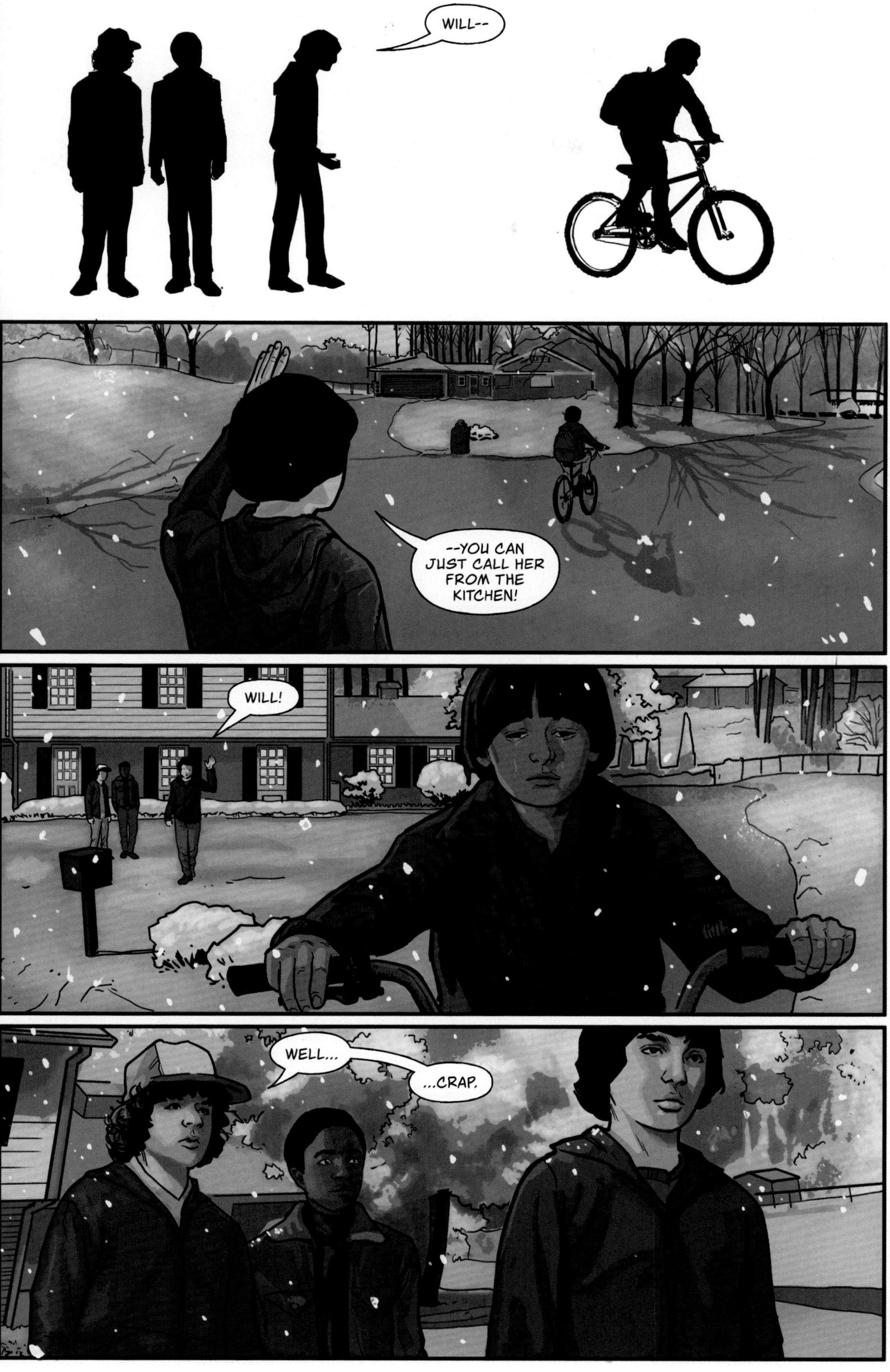
WILL--
--YOU CAN JUST CALL HER FROM THE KITCHEN!
WILL!
WELL...
...CRAP.

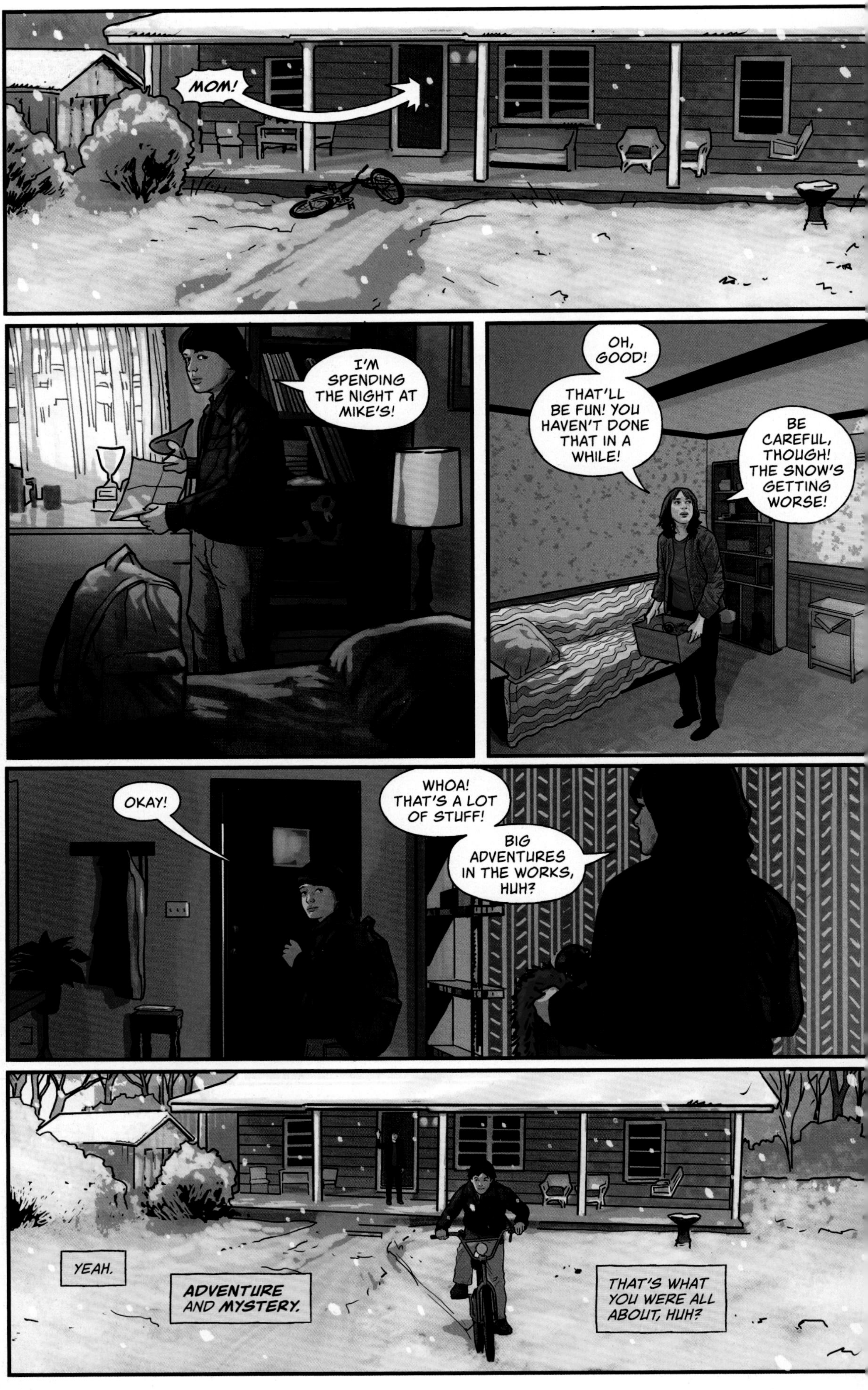
MOM!
I'M SPENDING THE NIGHT AT MIKE'S!
OH, GOOD!
THAT'LL BE FUN! YOU HAVEN'T DONE THAT IN A WHILE!
BE CAREFUL, THOUGH! THE SNOW'S GETTING WORSE!
OKAY!
WHOA! THAT'S A LOT OF STUFF!
BIG ADVENTURES IN THE WORKS, HUH?
YEAH.
ADVENTURE AND MYSTERY.
THAT'S WHAT YOU WERE ALL ABOUT, HUH?

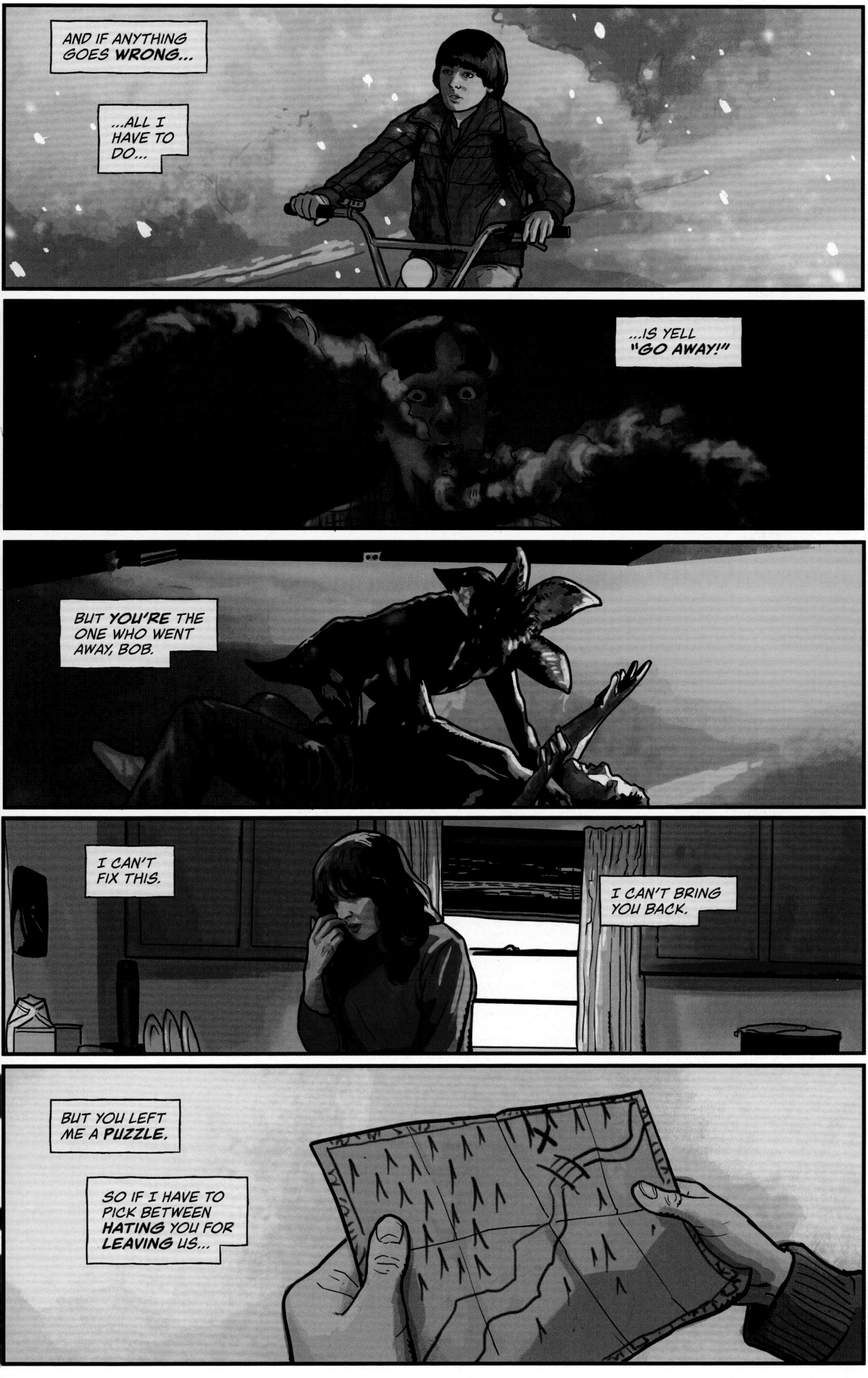
AND IF ANYTHING GOES **WRONG...**
...ALL I HAVE TO DO...
...IS YELL **"GO AWAY!"**
BUT **YOU'RE** THE ONE WHO WENT AWAY, BOB.
I CAN'T FIX THIS.
I CAN'T BRING YOU BACK.
BUT YOU LEFT ME A **PUZZLE.**
SO IF I HAVE TO PICK BETWEEN **HATING** YOU FOR **LEAVING** US...

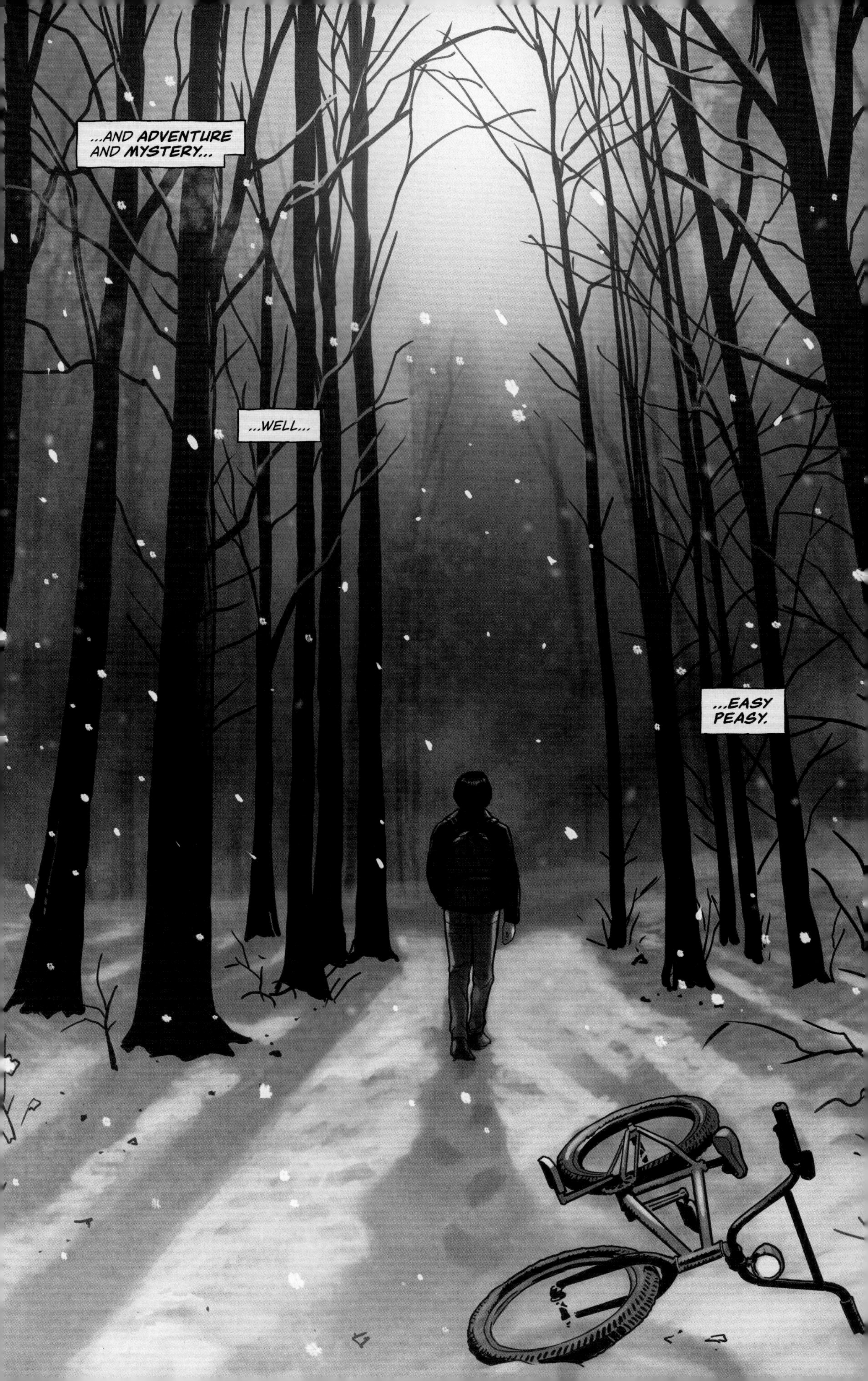
...AND ADVENTURE AND MYSTERY...
...WELL...
...EASY PEASY.

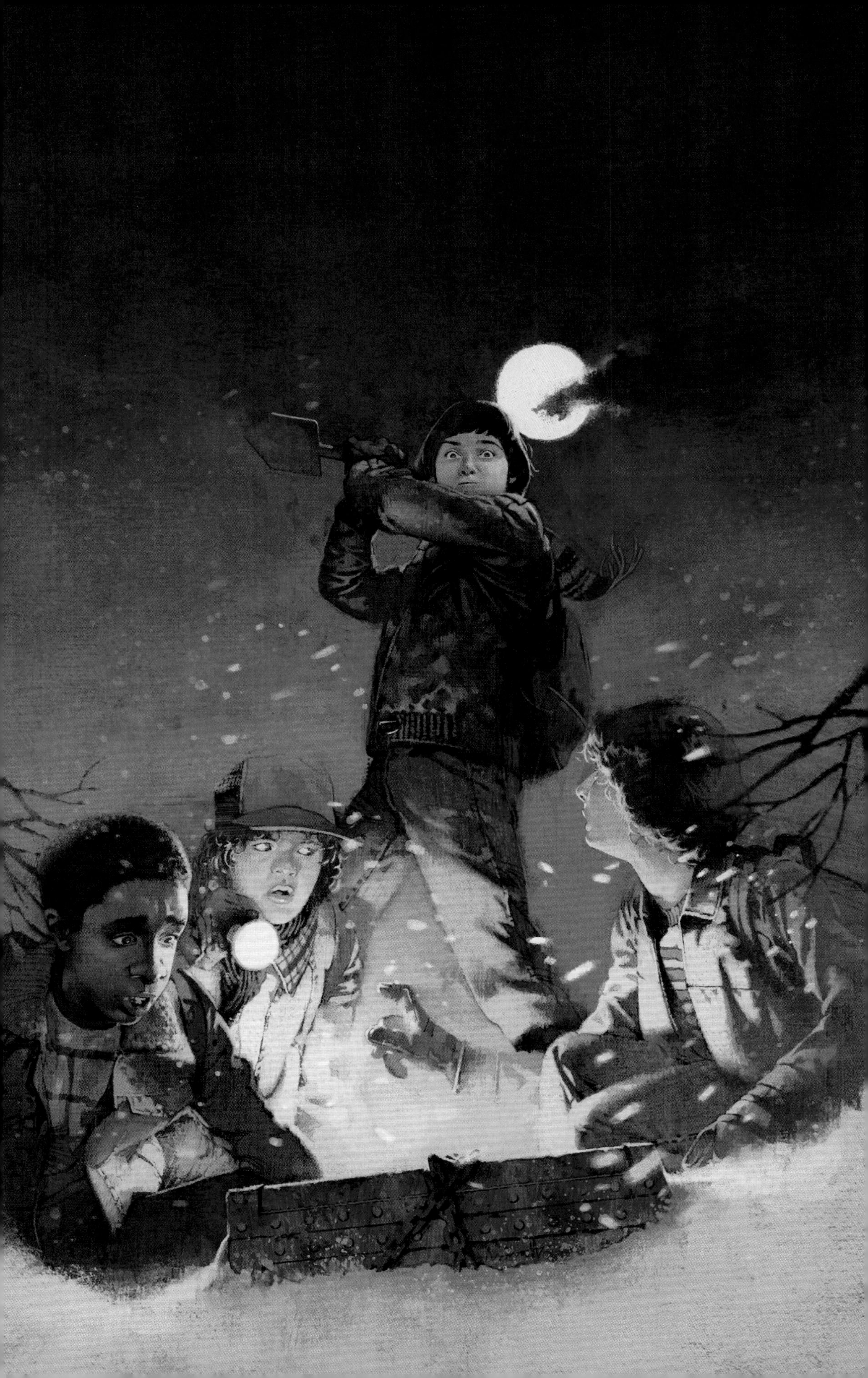

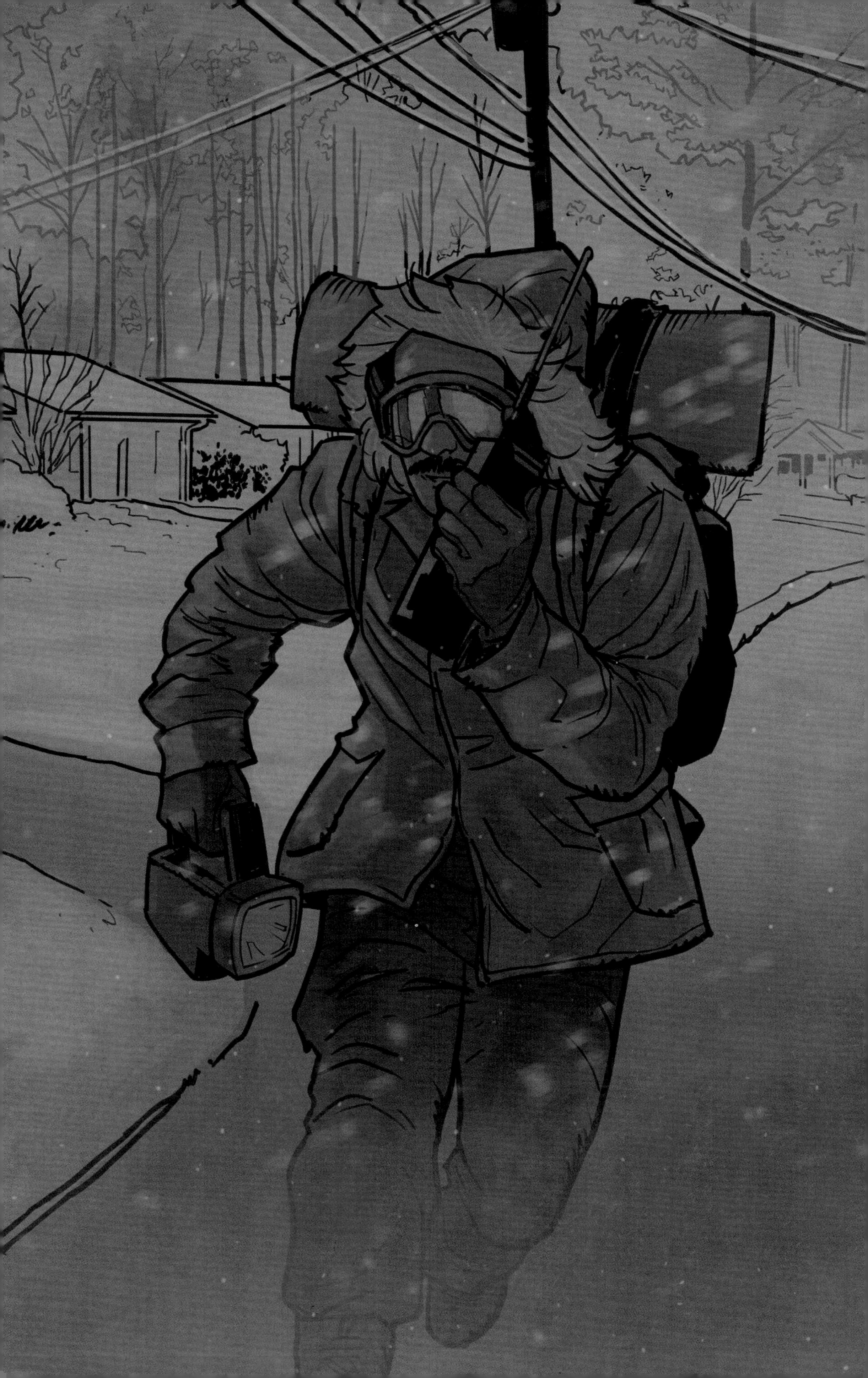

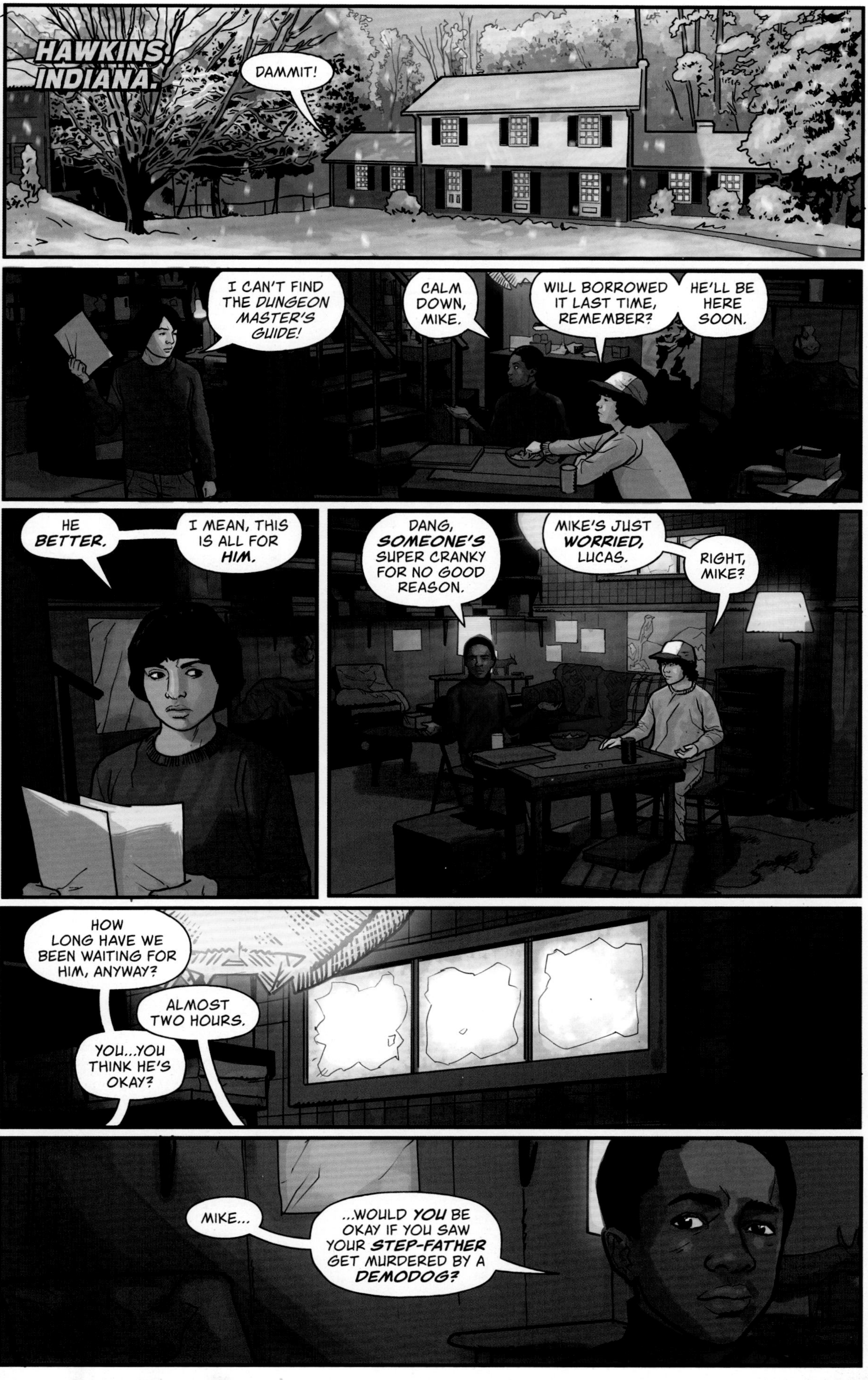
HAWKINS, INDIANA.
DAMMIT!
I CAN'T FIND THE DUNGEON MASTER'S GUIDE!
CALM DOWN, MIKE.
WILL BORROWED IT LAST TIME, REMEMBER?
HE'LL BE HERE SOON.
HE BETTER.
I MEAN, THIS IS ALL FOR HIM.
DANG, SOMEONE'S SUPER CRANKY FOR NO GOOD REASON.
MIKE'S JUST WORRIED, LUCAS.
RIGHT, MIKE?
HOW LONG HAVE WE BEEN WAITING FOR HIM, ANYWAY?
ALMOST TWO HOURS.
YOU...YOU THINK HE'S OKAY?
MIKE...
...WOULD YOU BE OKAY IF YOU SAW YOUR STEP-FATHER GET MURDERED BY A DEMODOG?

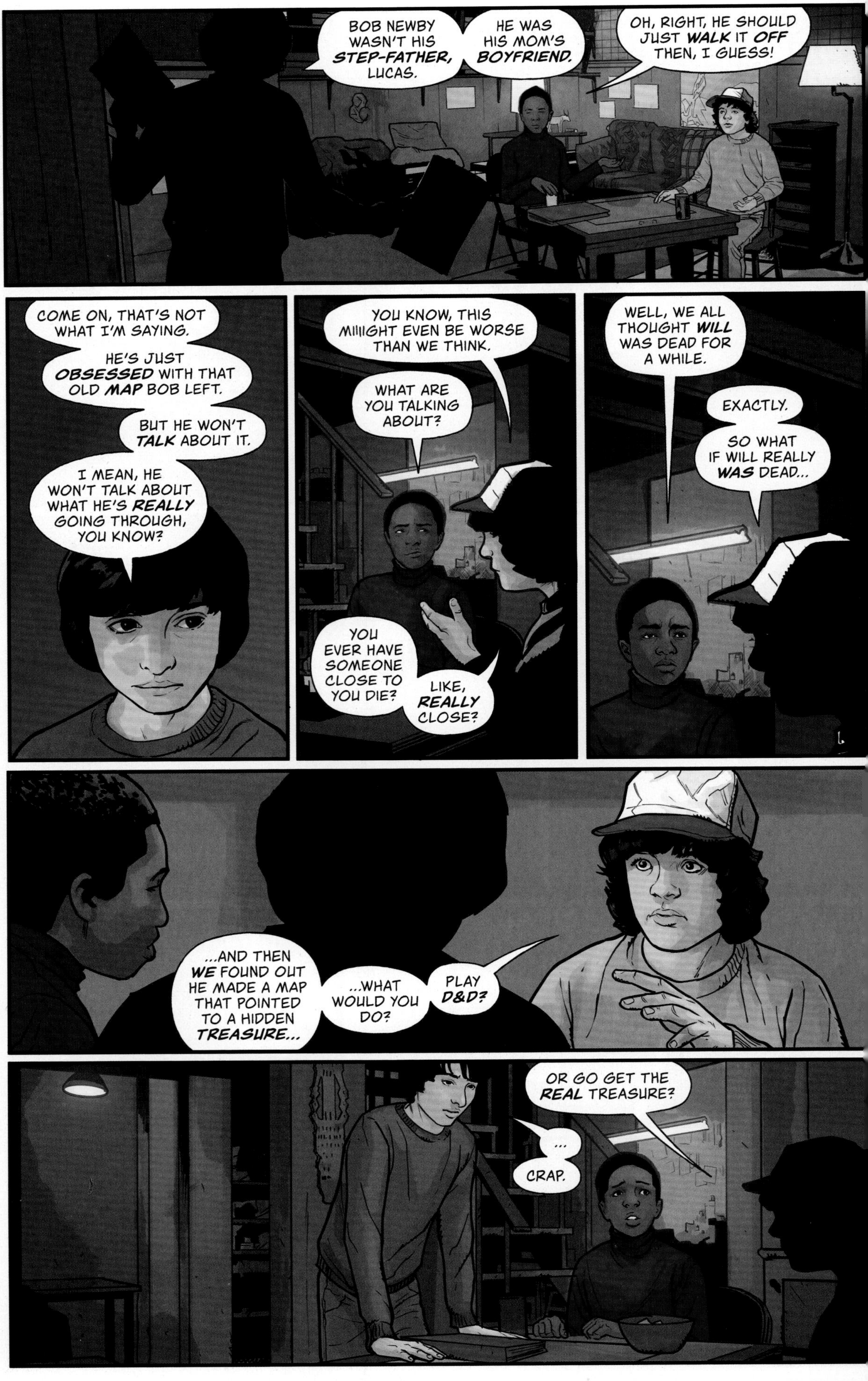

BOB NEWBY WASN'T HIS STEP-FATHER, LUCAS.
HE WAS HIS MOM'S BOYFRIEND.
OH, RIGHT, HE SHOULD JUST WALK IT OFF THEN, I GUESS!
COME ON, THAT'S NOT WHAT I'M SAYING.
HE'S JUST OBSESSED WITH THAT OLD MAP BOB LEFT.
BUT HE WON'T TALK ABOUT IT.
I MEAN, HE WON'T TALK ABOUT WHAT HE'S REALLY GOING THROUGH, YOU KNOW?
YOU KNOW, THIS MIIIIGHT EVEN BE WORSE THAN WE THINK.
WHAT ARE YOU TALKING ABOUT?
YOU EVER HAVE SOMEONE CLOSE TO YOU DIE?
LIKE, REALLY CLOSE?
WELL, WE ALL THOUGHT WILL WAS DEAD FOR A WHILE.
EXACTLY.
SO WHAT IF WILL REALLY WAS DEAD...
...AND THEN WE FOUND OUT HE MADE A MAP THAT POINTED TO A HIDDEN TREASURE...
...WHAT WOULD YOU DO?
PLAY D&D?
OR GO GET THE REAL TREASURE?
...
CRAP.

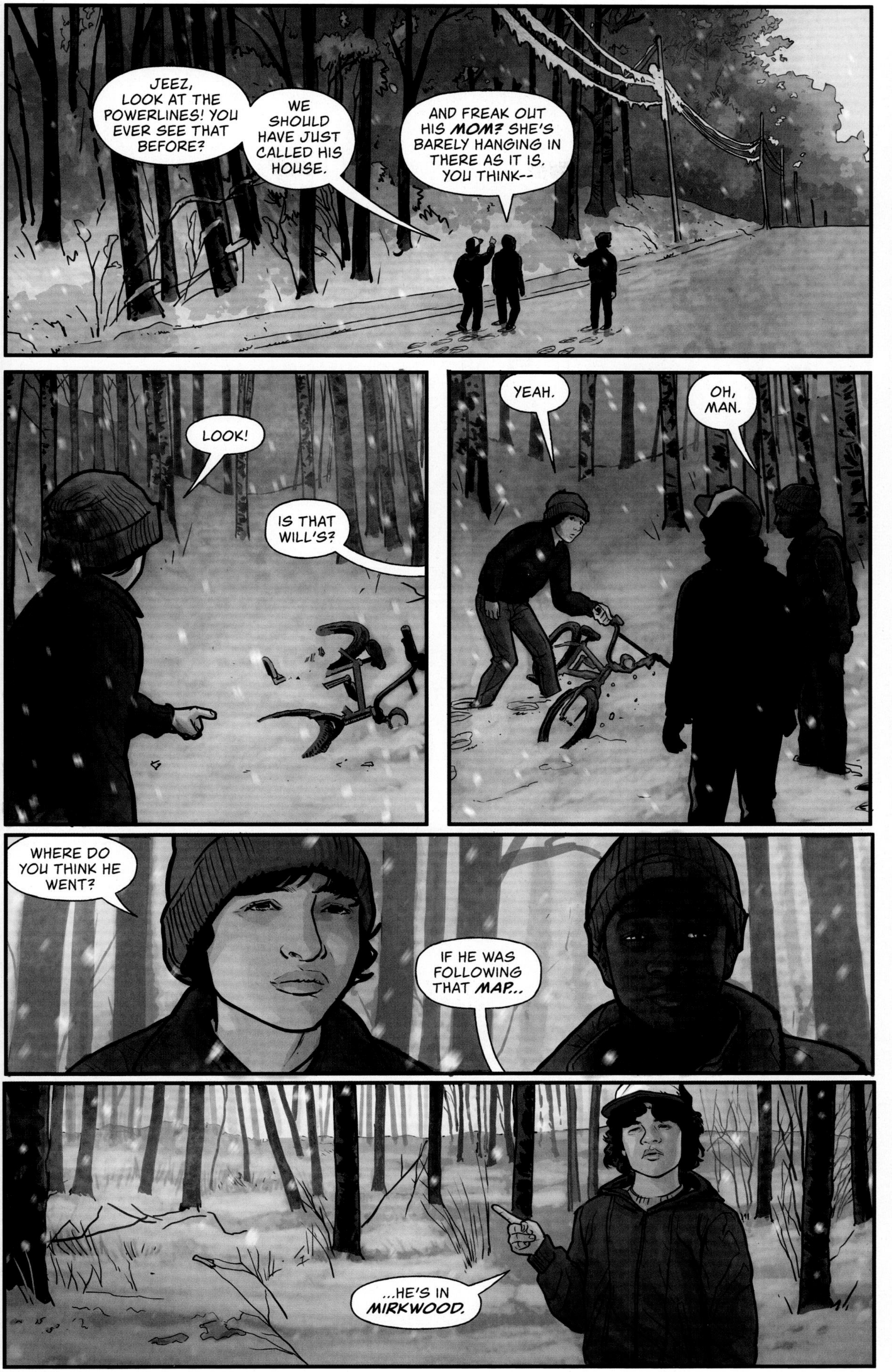
JEEZ, LOOK AT THE POWERLINES! YOU EVER SEE THAT BEFORE?
WE SHOULD HAVE JUST CALLED HIS HOUSE.
AND FREAK OUT HIS MOM? SHE'S BARELY HANGING IN THERE AS IT IS. YOU THINK--
LOOK!
IS THAT WILL'S?
YEAH.
OH, MAN.
WHERE DO YOU THINK HE WENT?
IF HE WAS FOLLOWING THAT MAP...
...HE'S IN MIRKWOOD.

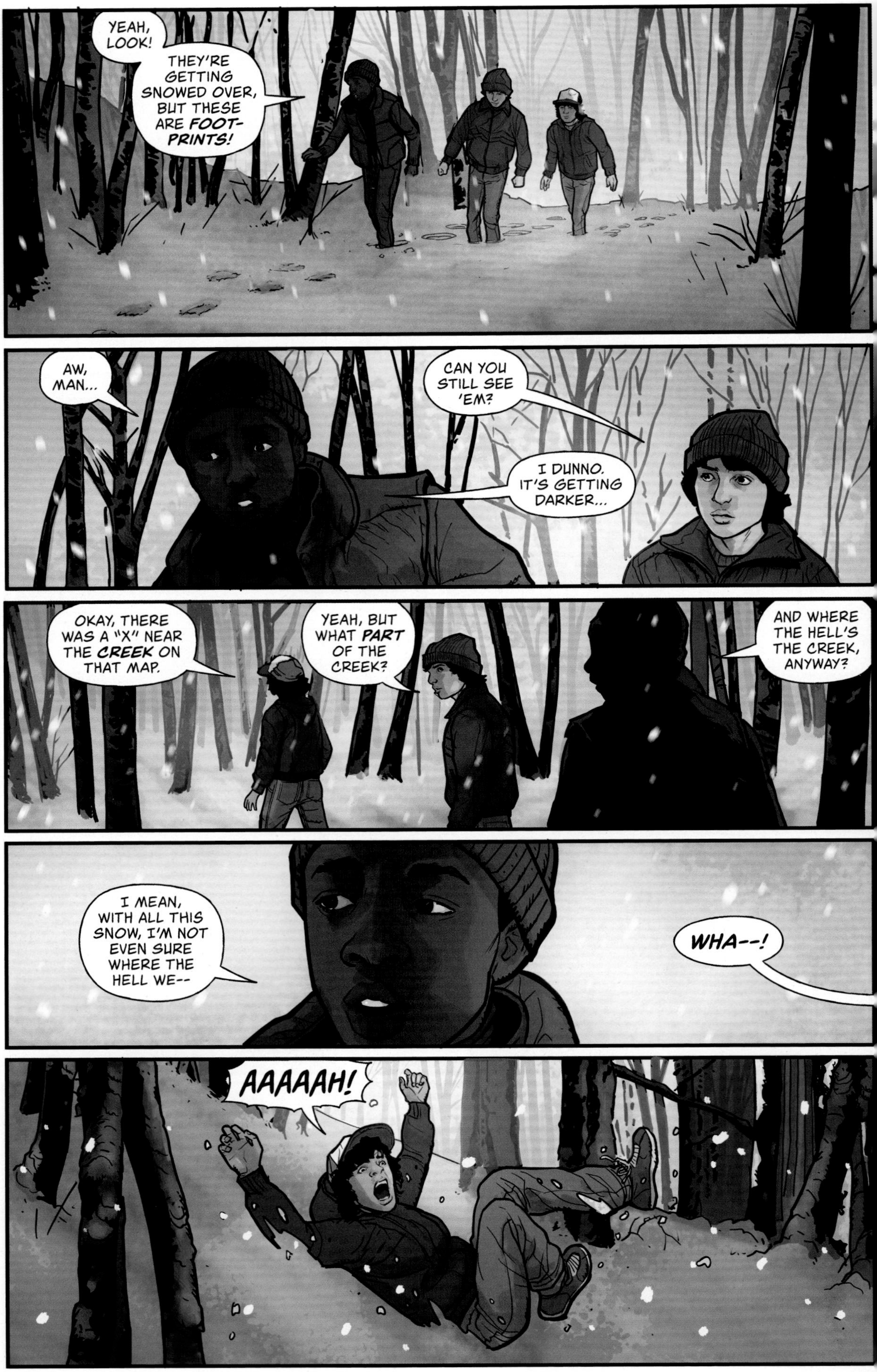
YEAH, LOOK!
THEY'RE GETTING SNOWED OVER, BUT THESE ARE FOOT-PRINTS!
AW, MAN...
CAN YOU STILL SEE 'EM?
I DUNNO. IT'S GETTING DARKER...
OKAY, THERE WAS A "X" NEAR THE CREEK ON THAT MAP.
YEAH, BUT WHAT PART OF THE CREEK?
AND WHERE THE HELL'S THE CREEK, ANYWAY?
I MEAN, WITH ALL THIS SNOW, I'M NOT EVEN SURE WHERE THE HELL WE--
WHA--!
AAAAAH!

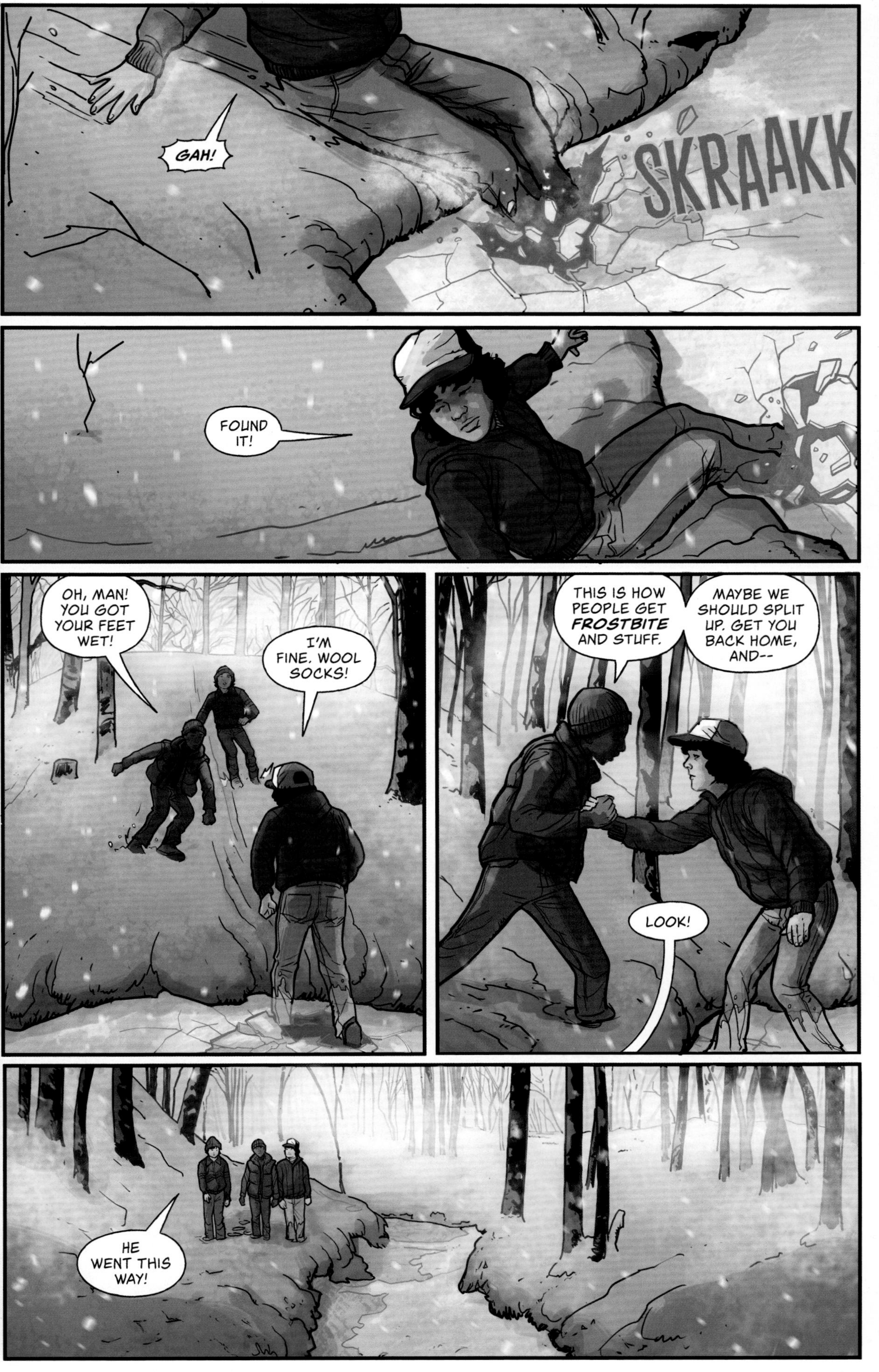
GAH!
SKRAAKK
FOUND IT!
OH, MAN! YOU GOT YOUR FEET WET!
I'M FINE. WOOL SOCKS!
THIS IS HOW PEOPLE GET *FROSTBITE* AND STUFF.
MAYBE WE SHOULD SPLIT UP. GET YOU BACK HOME, AND--
LOOK!
HE WENT THIS WAY!

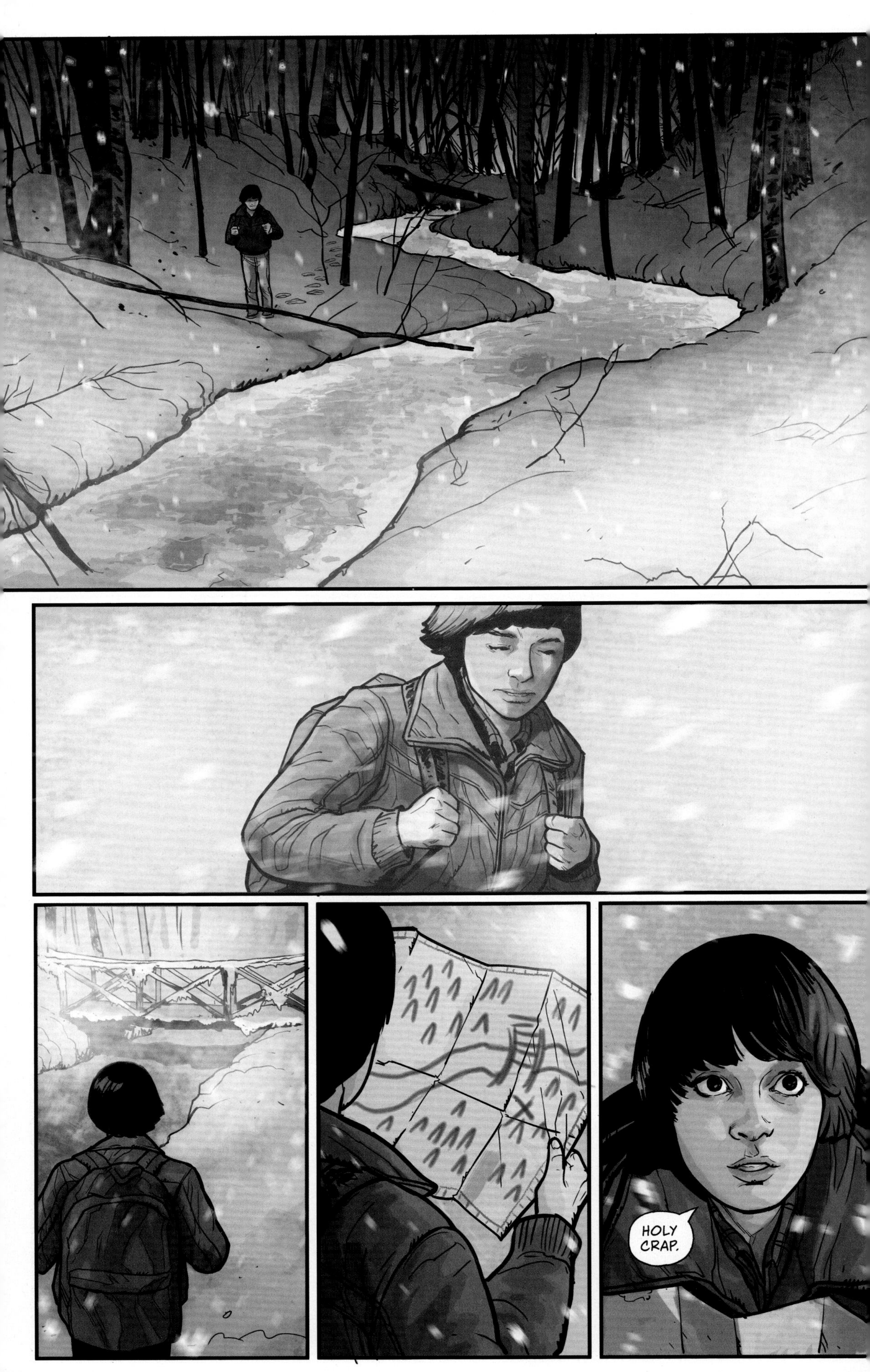
HOLY CRAP.

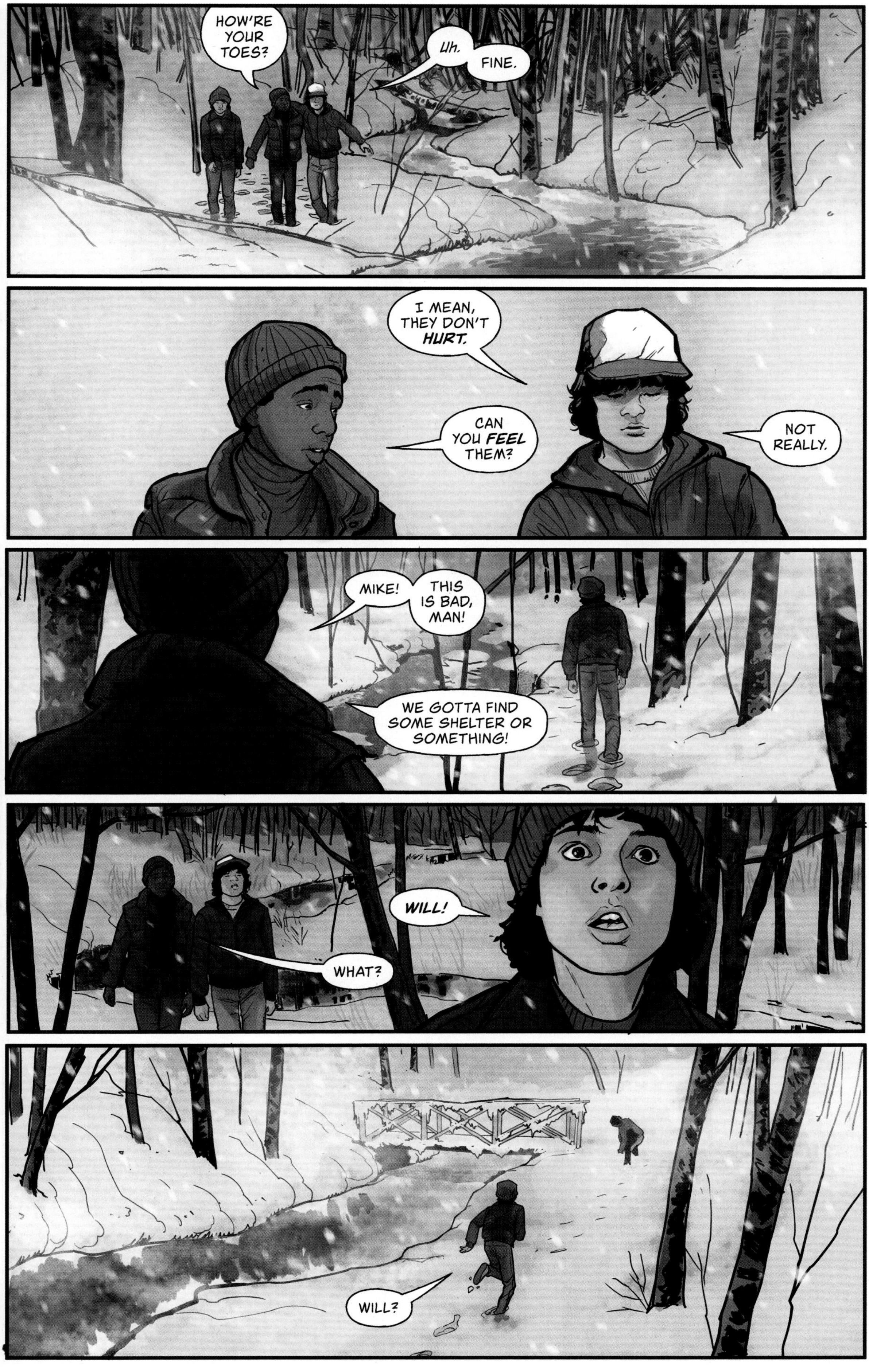
HOW'RE YOUR TOES?
UH.
FINE.
I MEAN, THEY DON'T HURT.
CAN YOU FEEL THEM?
NOT REALLY.
MIKE!
THIS IS BAD, MAN!
WE GOTTA FIND SOME SHELTER OR SOMETHING!
WILL!
WHAT?
WILL?

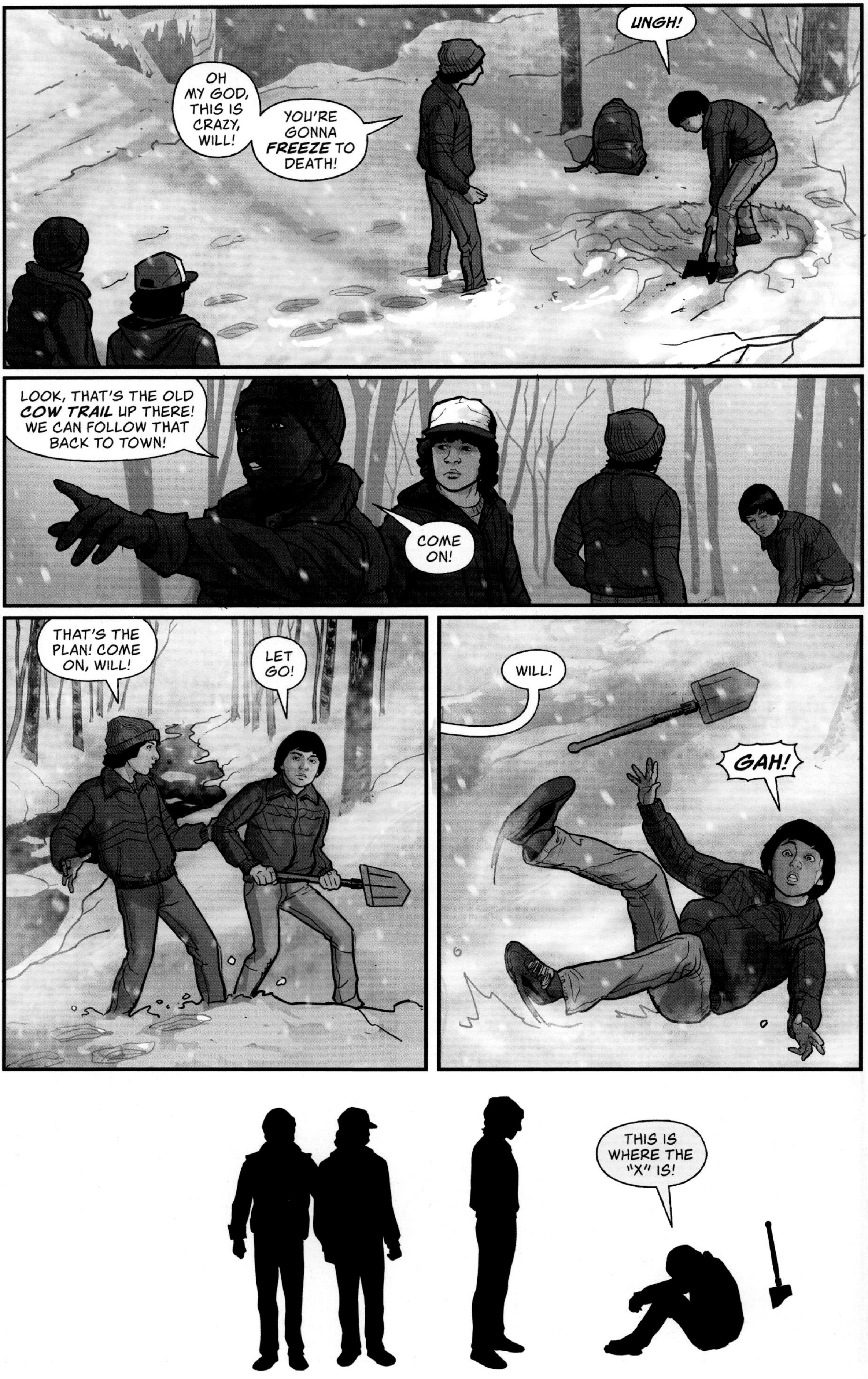
OH MY GOD, THIS IS CRAZY, WILL!
YOU'RE GONNA FREEZE TO DEATH!
UNGH!
LOOK, THAT'S THE OLD COW TRAIL UP THERE! WE CAN FOLLOW THAT BACK TO TOWN!
COME ON!
THAT'S THE PLAN! COME ON, WILL!
LET GO!
WILL!
GAH!
THIS IS WHERE THE "X" IS!

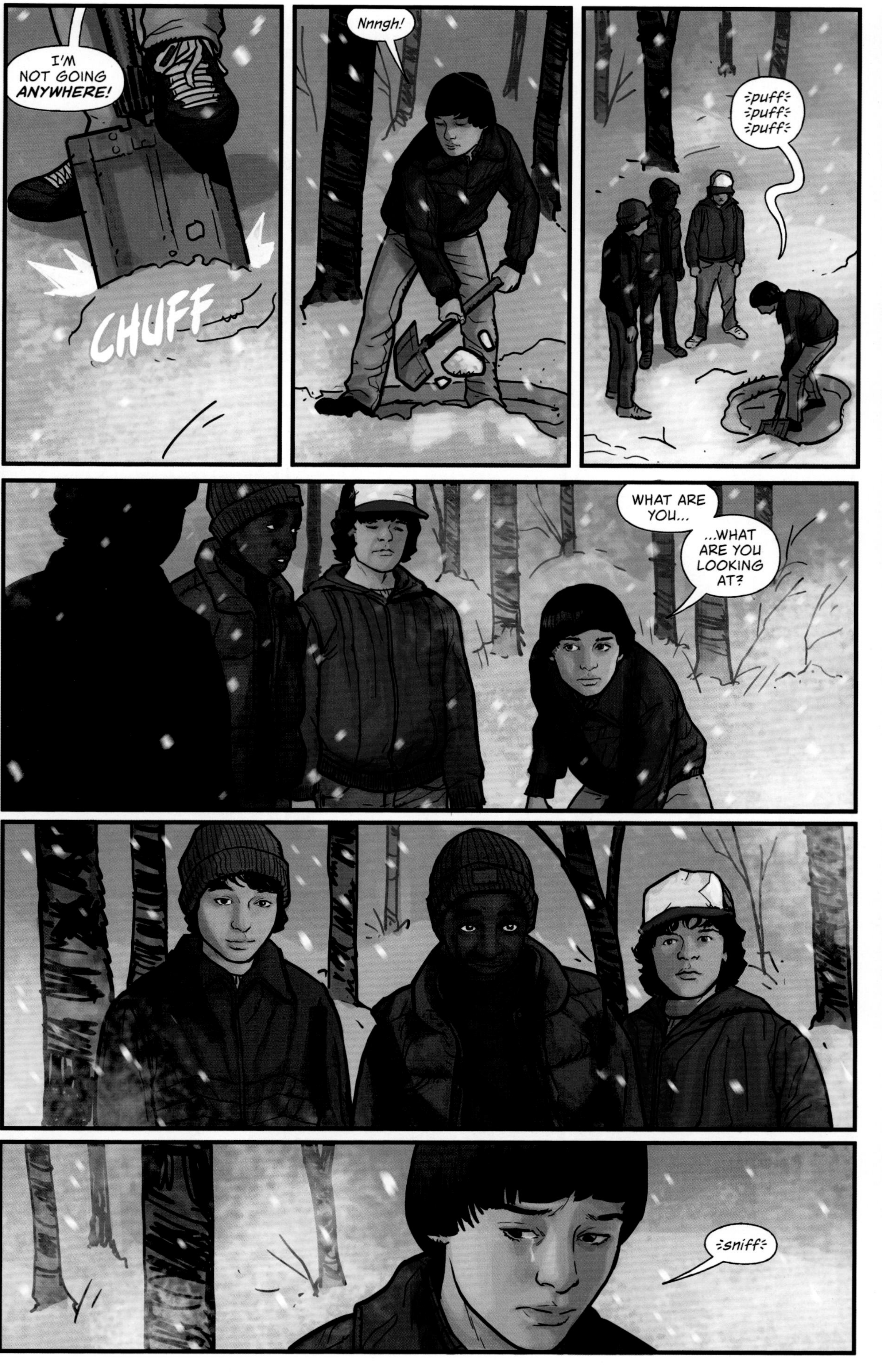
I'M NOT GOING ANYWHERE!
CHUFF
Nnngh!
puff puff puff
WHAT ARE YOU...
...WHAT ARE YOU LOOKING AT?
sniff

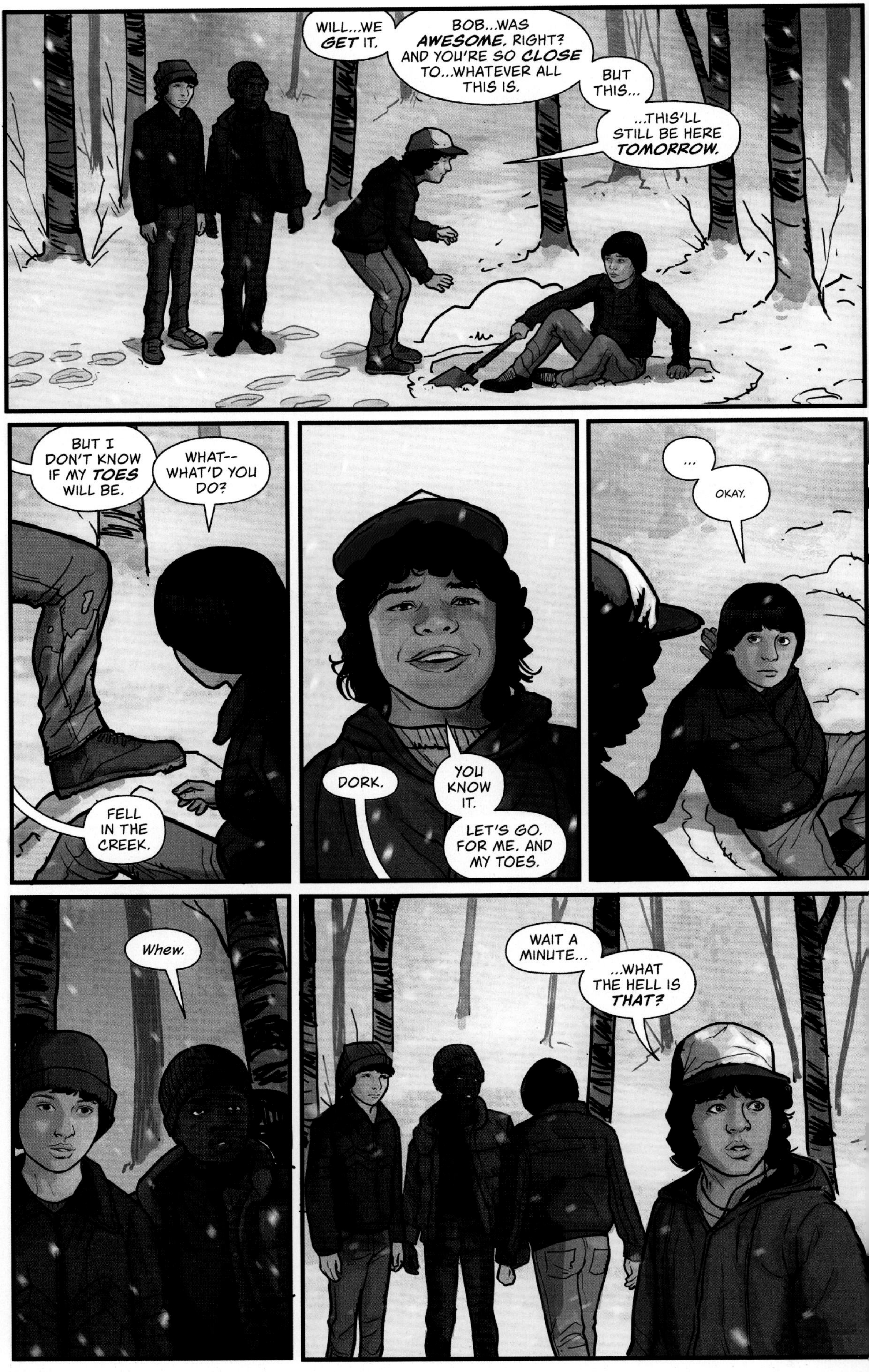
WILL...WE GET IT.
BOB...WAS AWESOME. RIGHT? AND YOU'RE SO CLOSE TO...WHATEVER ALL THIS IS.
BUT THIS...
...THIS'LL STILL BE HERE TOMORROW.
BUT I DON'T KNOW IF MY TOES WILL BE.
WHAT-- WHAT'D YOU DO?
FELL IN THE CREEK.
YOU KNOW IT.
DORK.
LET'S GO. FOR ME. AND MY TOES.
...
OKAY.
Whew.
WAIT A MINUTE...
...WHAT THE HELL IS THAT?

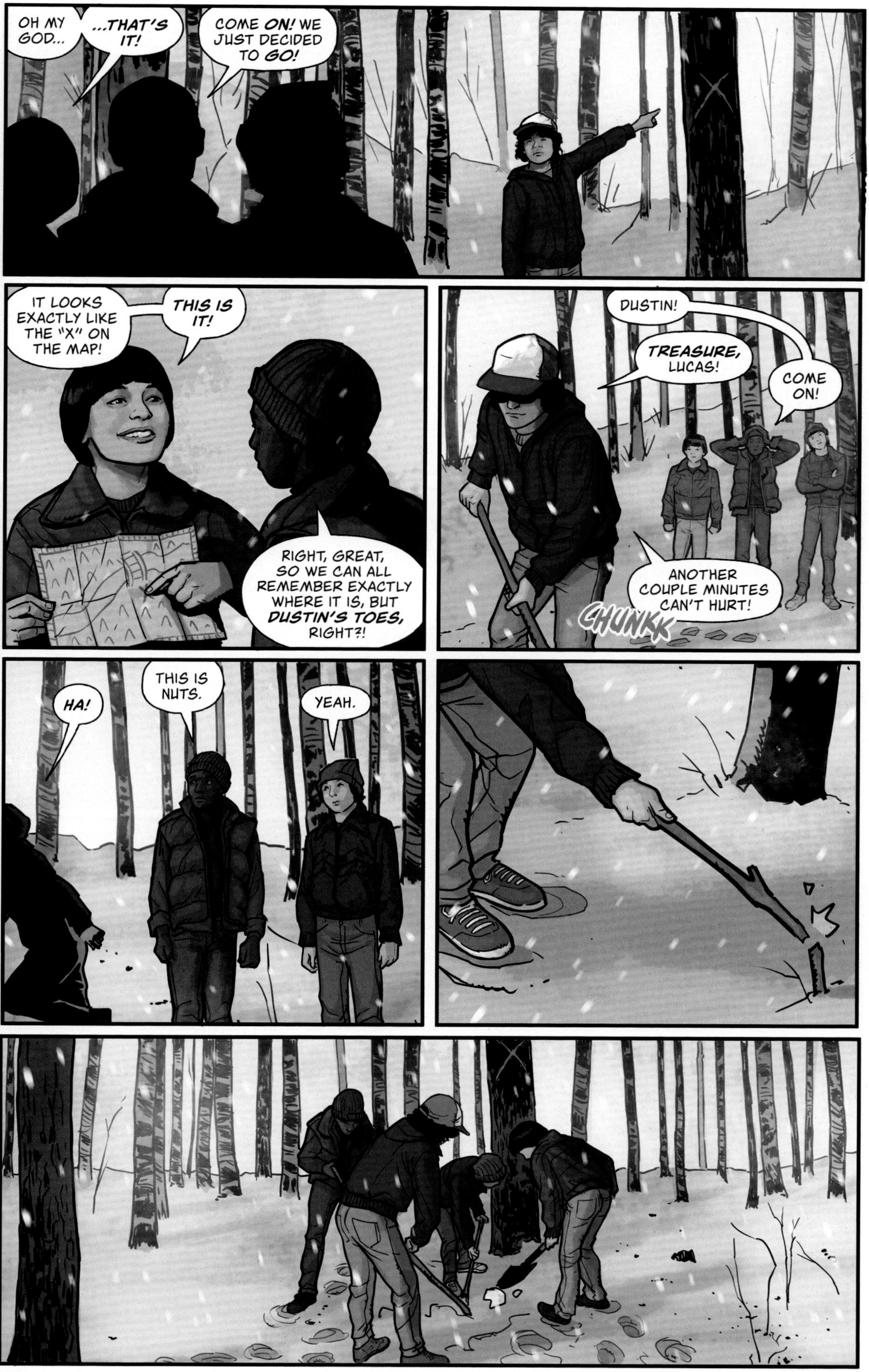
OH MY GOD...
...THAT'S IT!
COME ON! WE JUST DECIDED TO GO!
IT LOOKS EXACTLY LIKE THE "X" ON THE MAP!
THIS IS IT!
RIGHT, GREAT, SO WE CAN ALL REMEMBER EXACTLY WHERE IT IS, BUT DUSTIN'S TOES, RIGHT?!
DUSTIN!
TREASURE, LUCAS!
COME ON!
ANOTHER COUPLE MINUTES CAN'T HURT!
CHUNKK
HA!
THIS IS NUTS.
YEAH.

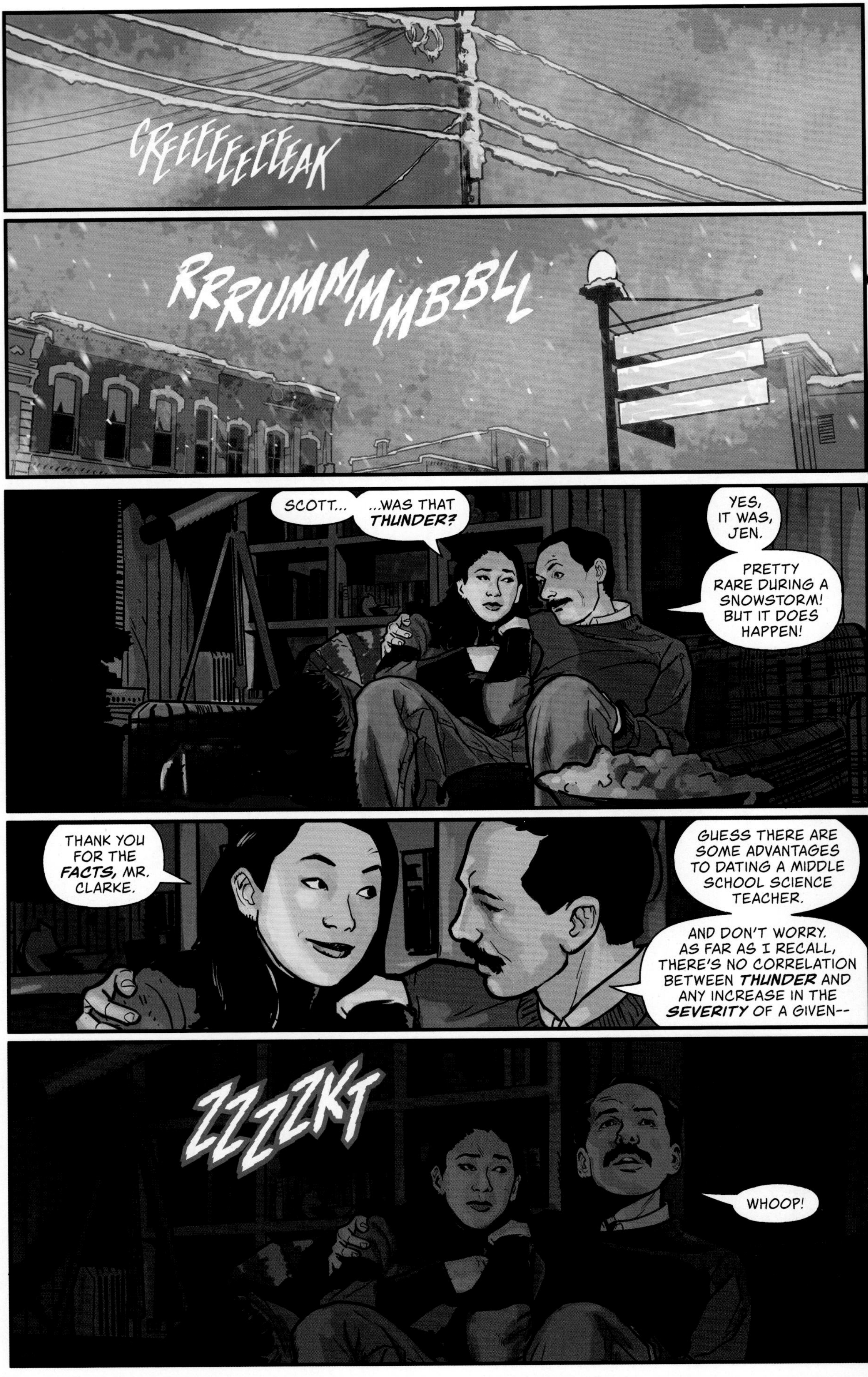
CREEEEEEEEEAK
RRRUMMMMBBLL
SCOTT...
...WAS THAT *THUNDER?*
YES, IT WAS, JEN.
PRETTY RARE DURING A SNOWSTORM! BUT IT DOES HAPPEN!
THANK YOU FOR THE *FACTS,* MR. CLARKE.
GUESS THERE ARE SOME ADVANTAGES TO DATING A MIDDLE SCHOOL SCIENCE TEACHER.
AND DON'T WORRY. AS FAR AS I RECALL, THERE'S NO CORRELATION BETWEEN *THUNDER* AND ANY INCREASE IN THE *SEVERITY* OF A GIVEN--
ZZZZKT
WHOOP!

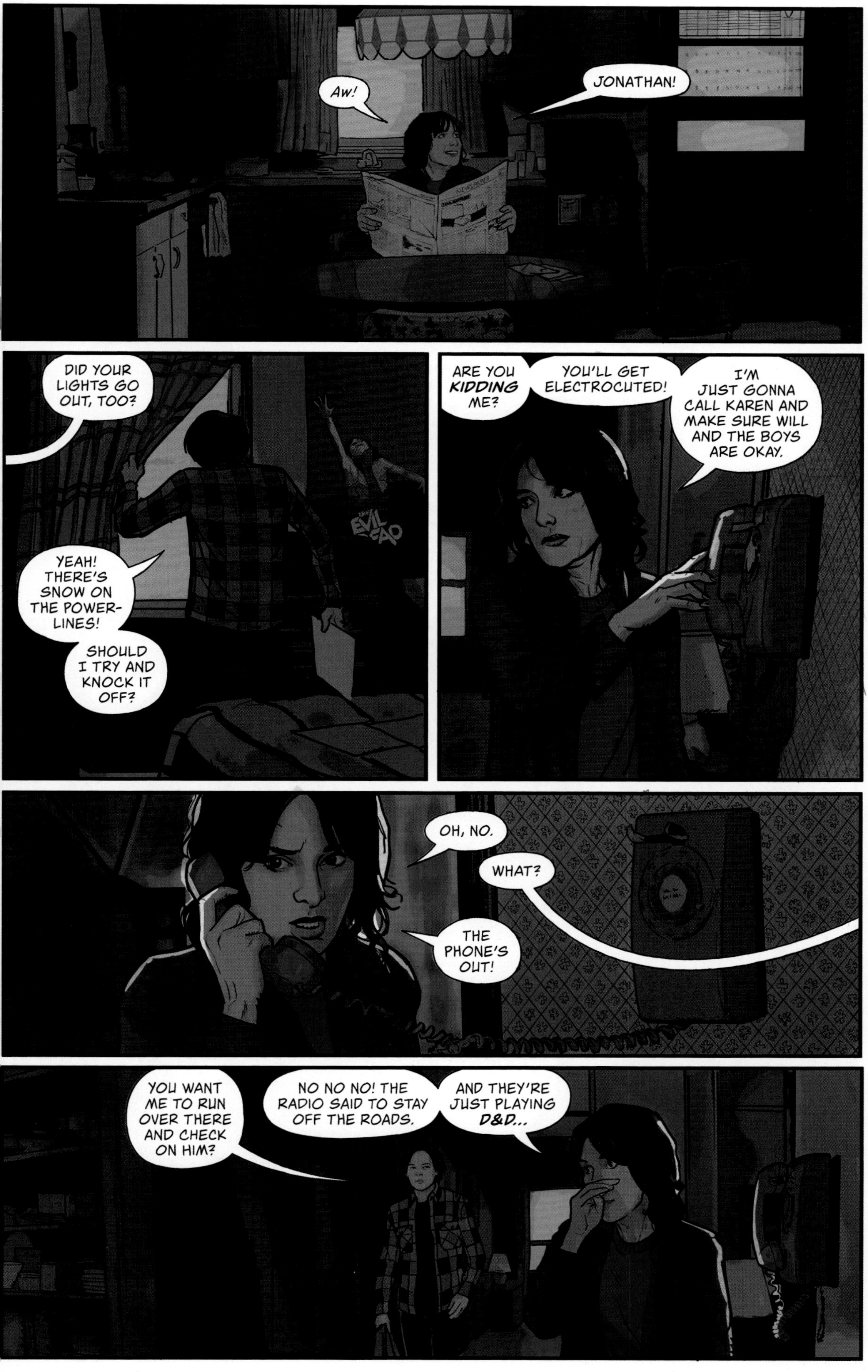
AW!
JONATHAN!
DID YOUR LIGHTS GO OUT, TOO?
YEAH! THERE'S SNOW ON THE POWER-LINES!
SHOULD I TRY AND KNOCK IT OFF?
ARE YOU *KIDDING* ME?
YOU'LL GET ELECTROCUTED!
I'M JUST GONNA CALL KAREN AND MAKE SURE WILL AND THE BOYS ARE OKAY.
OH, NO.
WHAT?
THE PHONE'S OUT!
YOU WANT ME TO RUN OVER THERE AND CHECK ON HIM?
NO NO NO! THE RADIO SAID TO STAY OFF THE ROADS.
AND THEY'RE JUST PLAYING *D&D*...

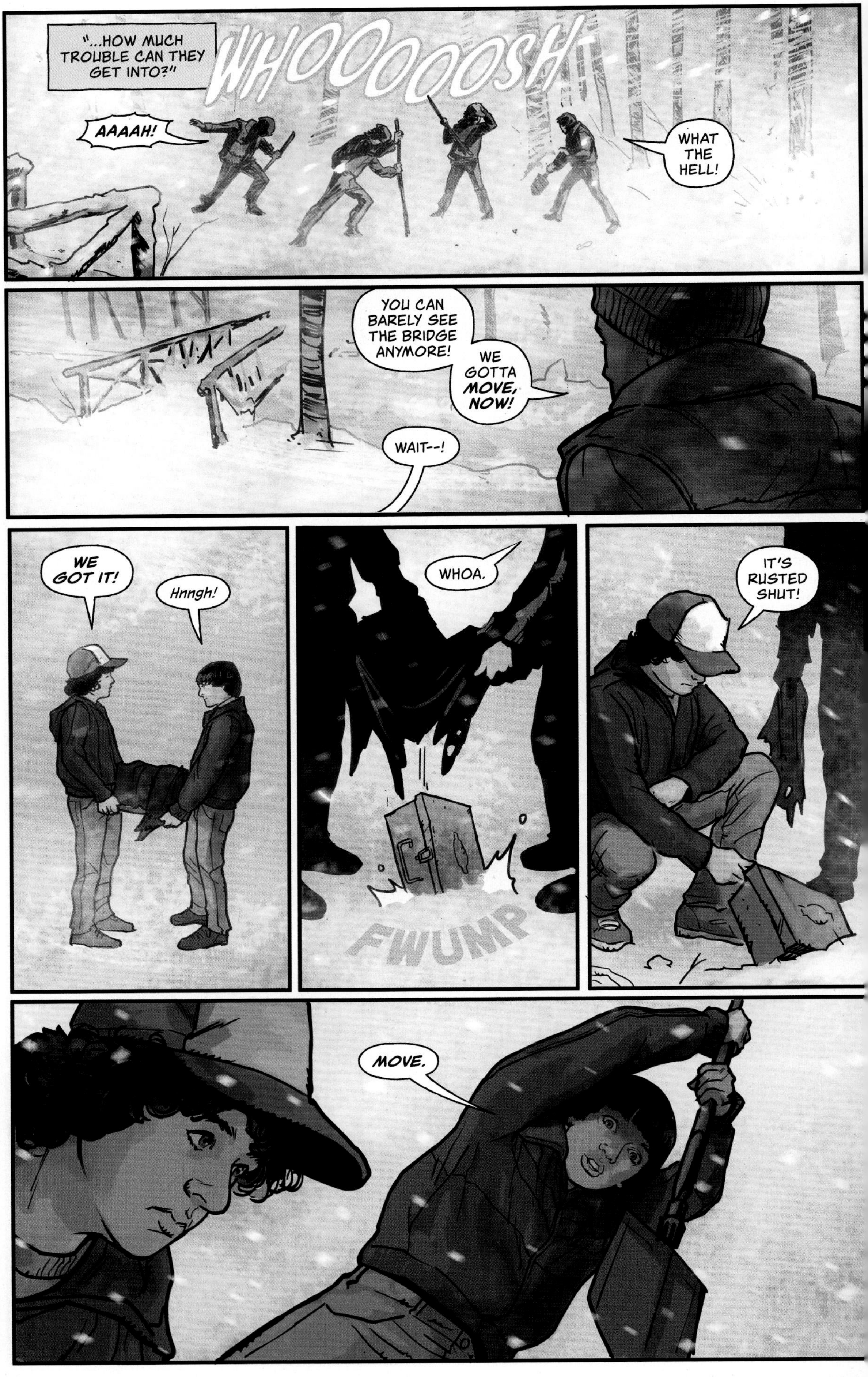
"...HOW MUCH TROUBLE CAN THEY GET INTO?"
WHOOOOOOSH
AAAAH!
WHAT THE HELL!
YOU CAN BARELY SEE THE BRIDGE ANYMORE!
WE GOTTA MOVE, NOW!
WAIT--!
WE GOT IT!
Hnngh!
WHOA.
FWUMP
IT'S RUSTED SHUT!
MOVE.

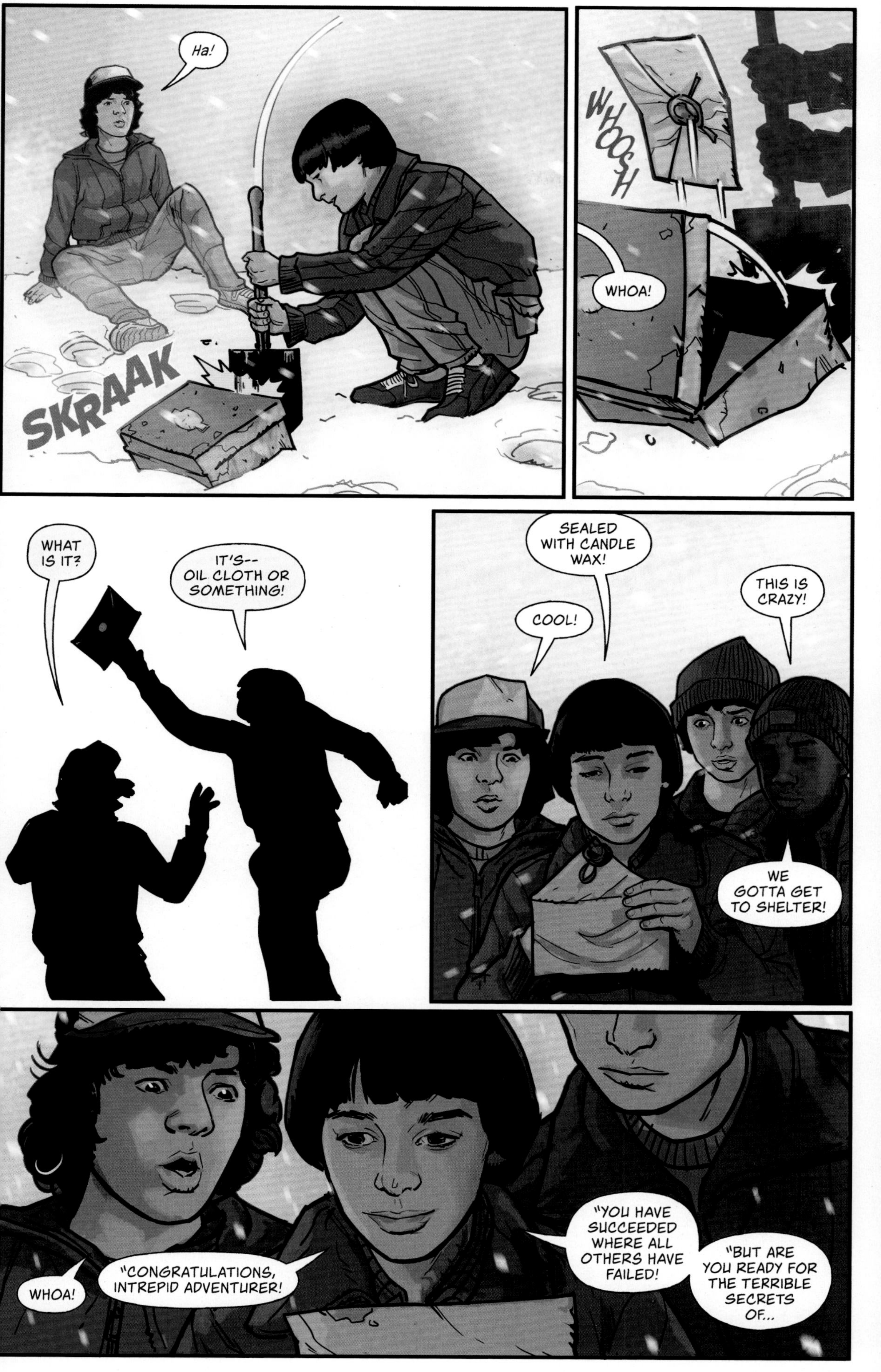
Ha!
SKRAAK
WHOOSH
WHOA!
WHAT IS IT?
IT'S-- OIL CLOTH OR SOMETHING!
SEALED WITH CANDLE WAX!
COOL!
THIS IS CRAZY!
WE GOTTA GET TO SHELTER!
WHOA!
"CONGRATULATIONS, INTREPID ADVENTURER!
"YOU HAVE SUCCEEDED WHERE ALL OTHERS HAVE FAILED!
"BUT ARE YOU READY FOR THE TERRIBLE SECRETS OF...

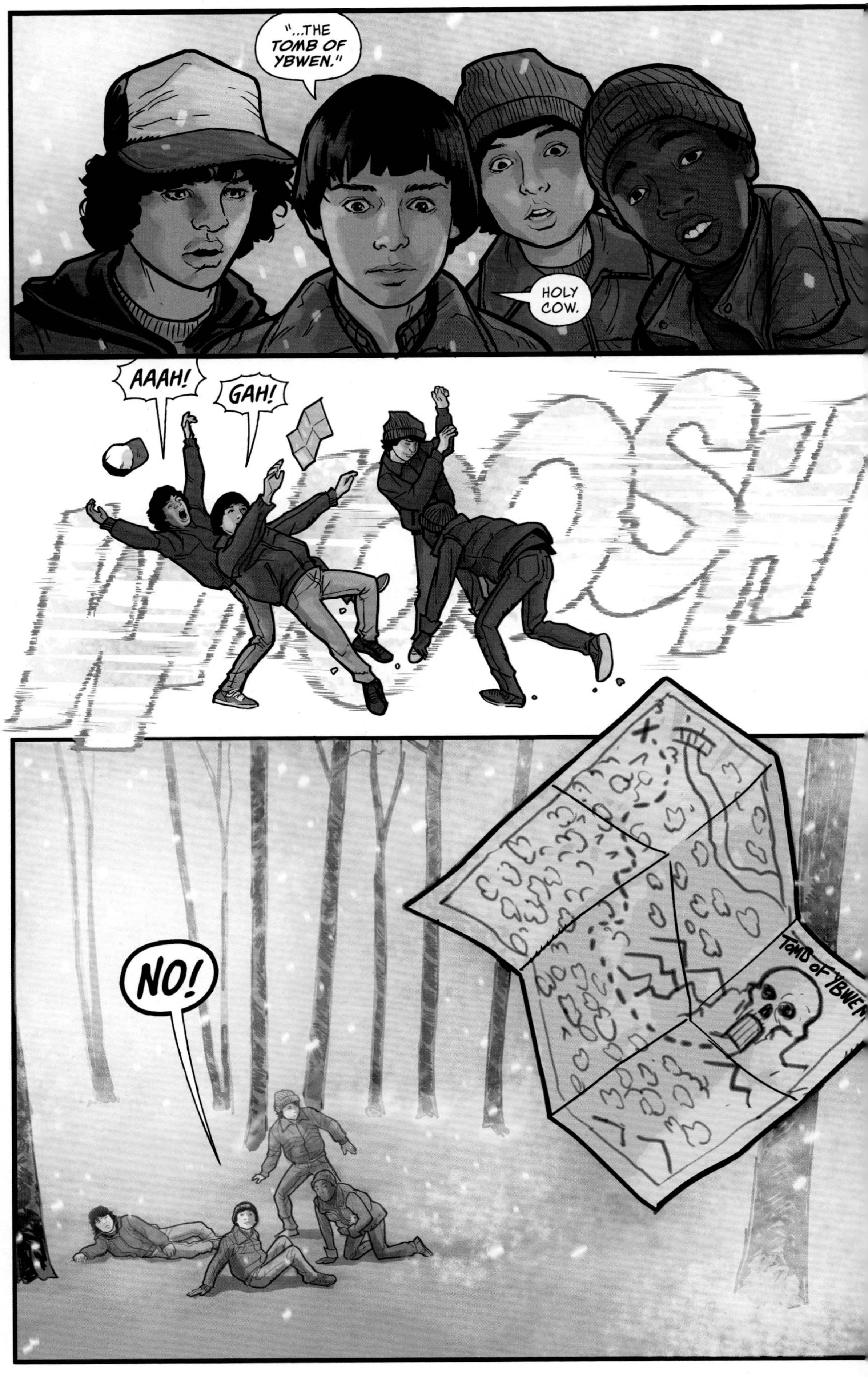
"...THE TOMB OF YBWEN."
HOLY COW.
AAAH!
GAH!
TOMB OF YBWEN
NO!

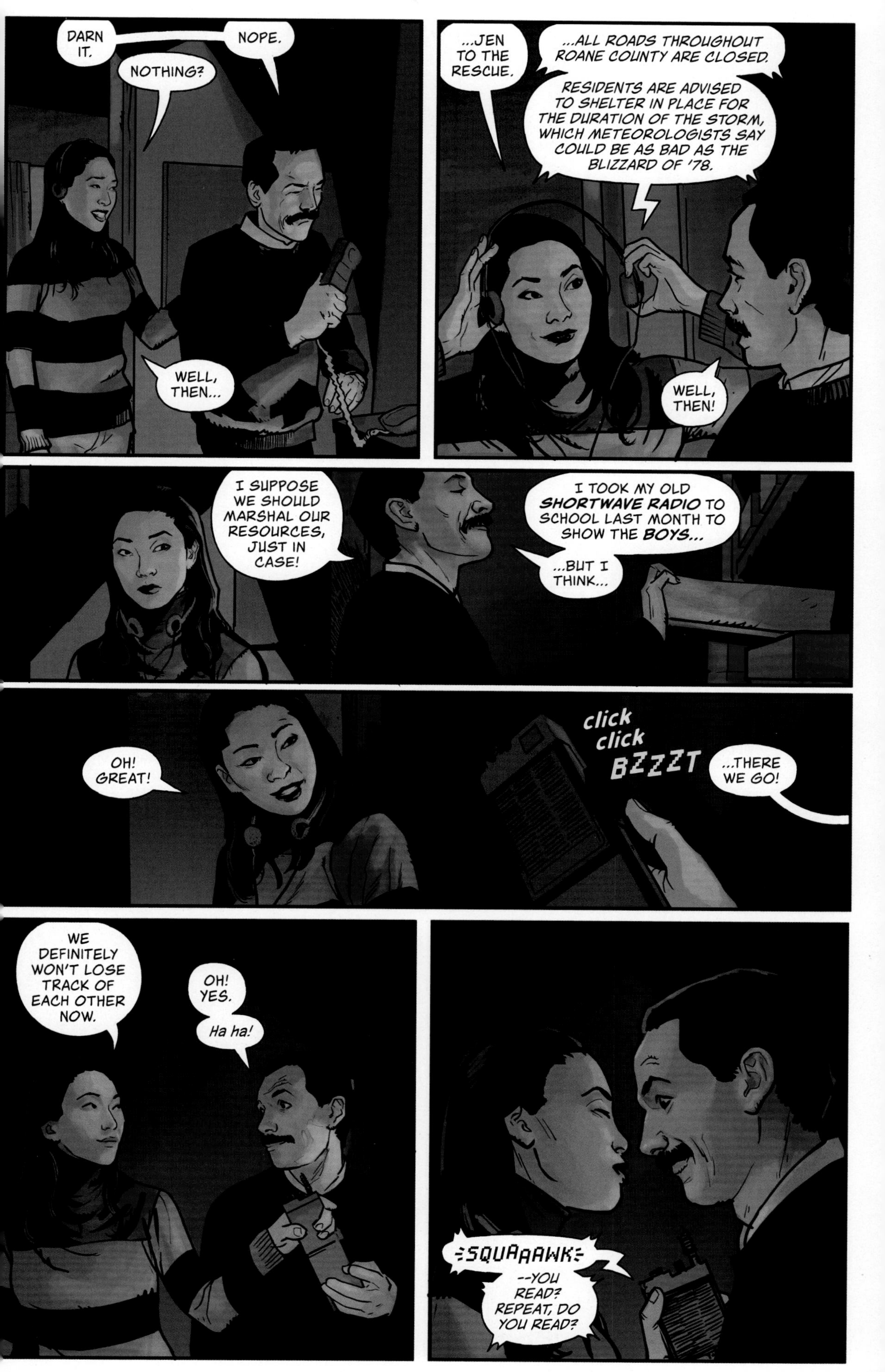
DARN IT.
NOTHING?
NOPE.
WELL, THEN...
...JEN TO THE RESCUE.
...ALL ROADS THROUGHOUT ROANE COUNTY ARE CLOSED.
RESIDENTS ARE ADVISED TO SHELTER IN PLACE FOR THE DURATION OF THE STORM, WHICH METEOROLOGISTS SAY COULD BE AS BAD AS THE BLIZZARD OF '78.
WELL, THEN!
I SUPPOSE WE SHOULD MARSHAL OUR RESOURCES, JUST IN CASE!
I TOOK MY OLD **SHORTWAVE RADIO** TO SCHOOL LAST MONTH TO SHOW THE **BOYS...**
...BUT I THINK...
OH! GREAT!
click click BZZZT
...THERE WE GO!
WE DEFINITELY WON'T LOSE TRACK OF EACH OTHER NOW.
OH! YES.
Ha ha!
SQUAAAWK
--YOU READ? REPEAT, DO YOU READ?

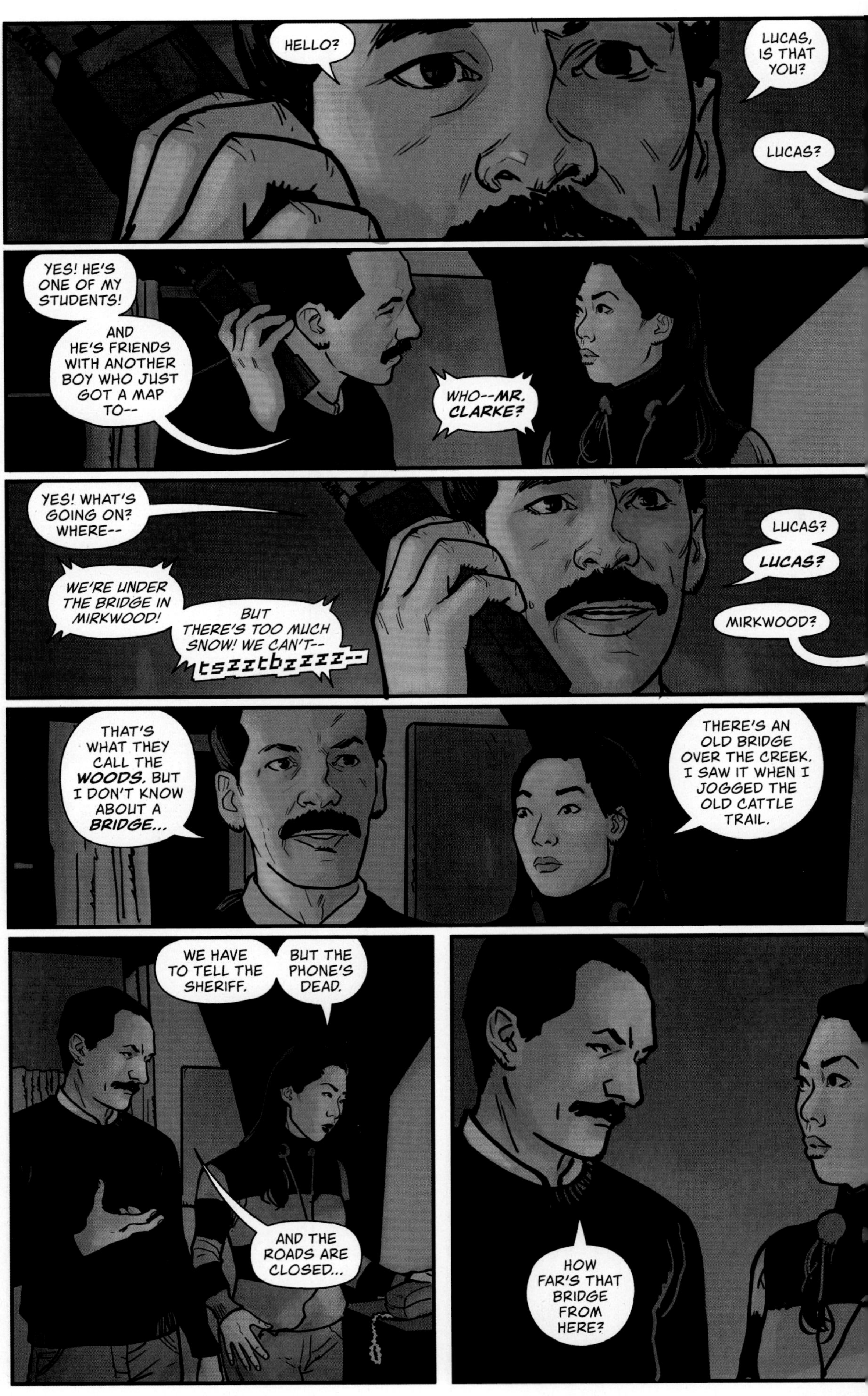

HELLO?
LUCAS, IS THAT YOU?
LUCAS?
YES! HE'S ONE OF MY STUDENTS!
AND HE'S FRIENDS WITH ANOTHER BOY WHO JUST GOT A MAP TO--
WHO--MR. CLARKE?
YES! WHAT'S GOING ON? WHERE--
WE'RE UNDER THE BRIDGE IN MIRKWOOD!
BUT THERE'S TOO MUCH SNOW! WE CAN'T--
tszztbzzzz--
LUCAS?
LUCAS?
MIRKWOOD?
THAT'S WHAT THEY CALL THE WOODS. BUT I DON'T KNOW ABOUT A BRIDGE...
THERE'S AN OLD BRIDGE OVER THE CREEK. I SAW IT WHEN I JOGGED THE OLD CATTLE TRAIL.
WE HAVE TO TELL THE SHERIFF.
BUT THE PHONE'S DEAD.
AND THE ROADS ARE CLOSED...
HOW FAR'S THAT BRIDGE FROM HERE?

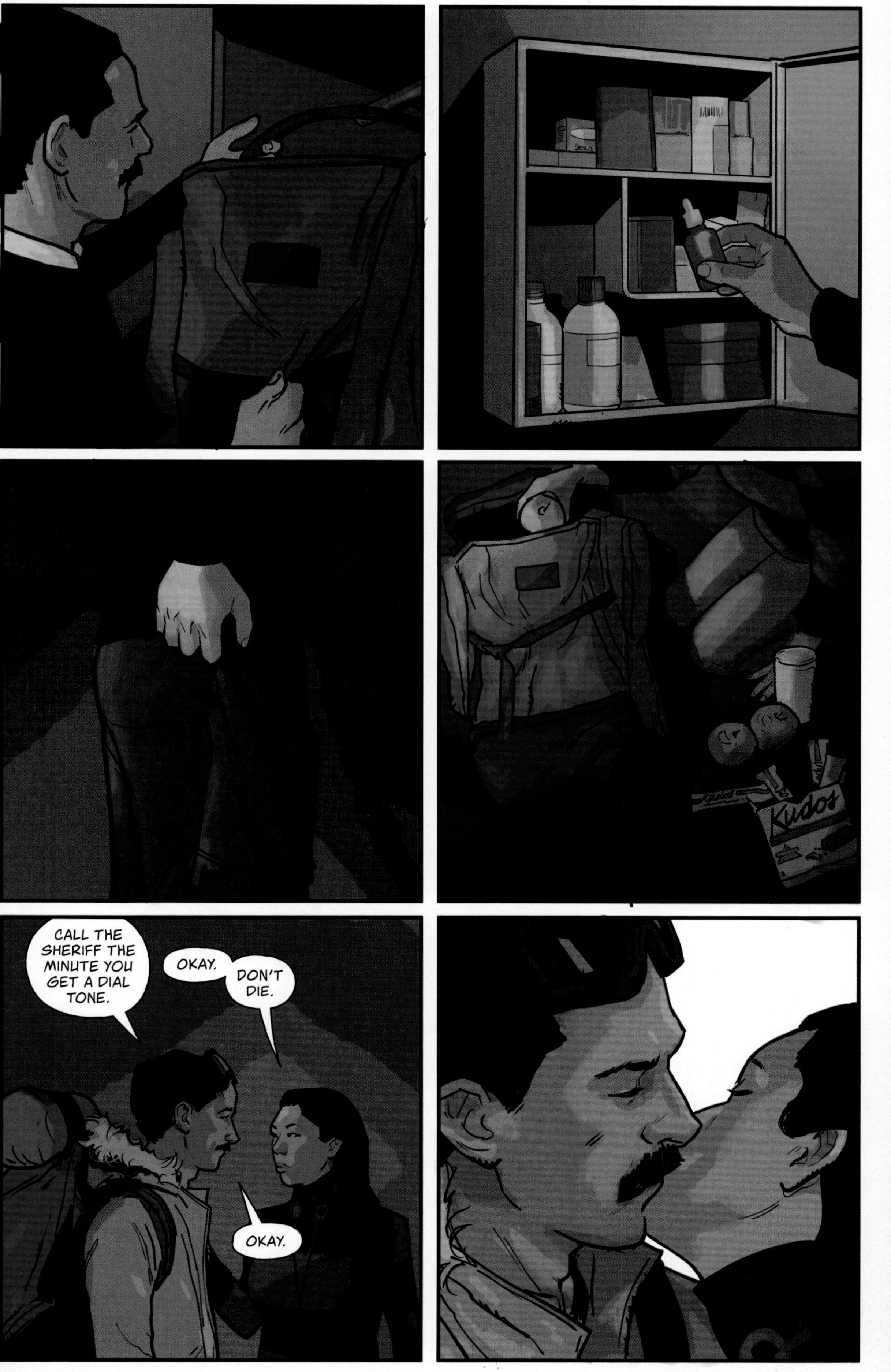
Kudos
Kudos
CALL THE SHERIFF THE MINUTE YOU GET A DIAL TONE.
OKAY.
DON'T DIE.
OKAY.

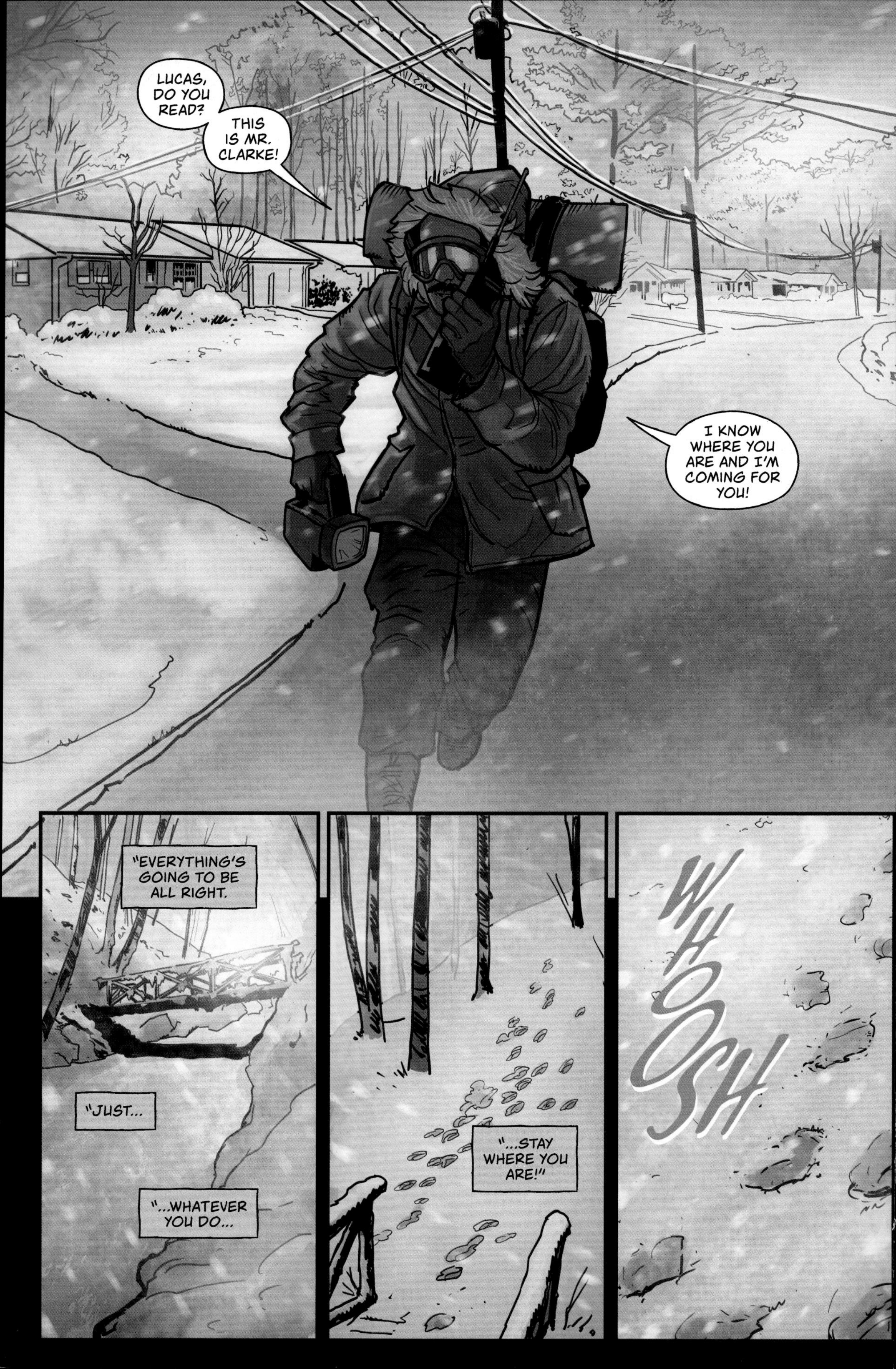
LUCAS, DO YOU READ?
THIS IS MR. CLARKE!
I KNOW WHERE YOU ARE AND I'M COMING FOR YOU!
"EVERYTHING'S GOING TO BE ALL RIGHT.
"JUST...
"...WHATEVER YOU DO...
"...STAY WHERE YOU ARE!"
WHOOSH

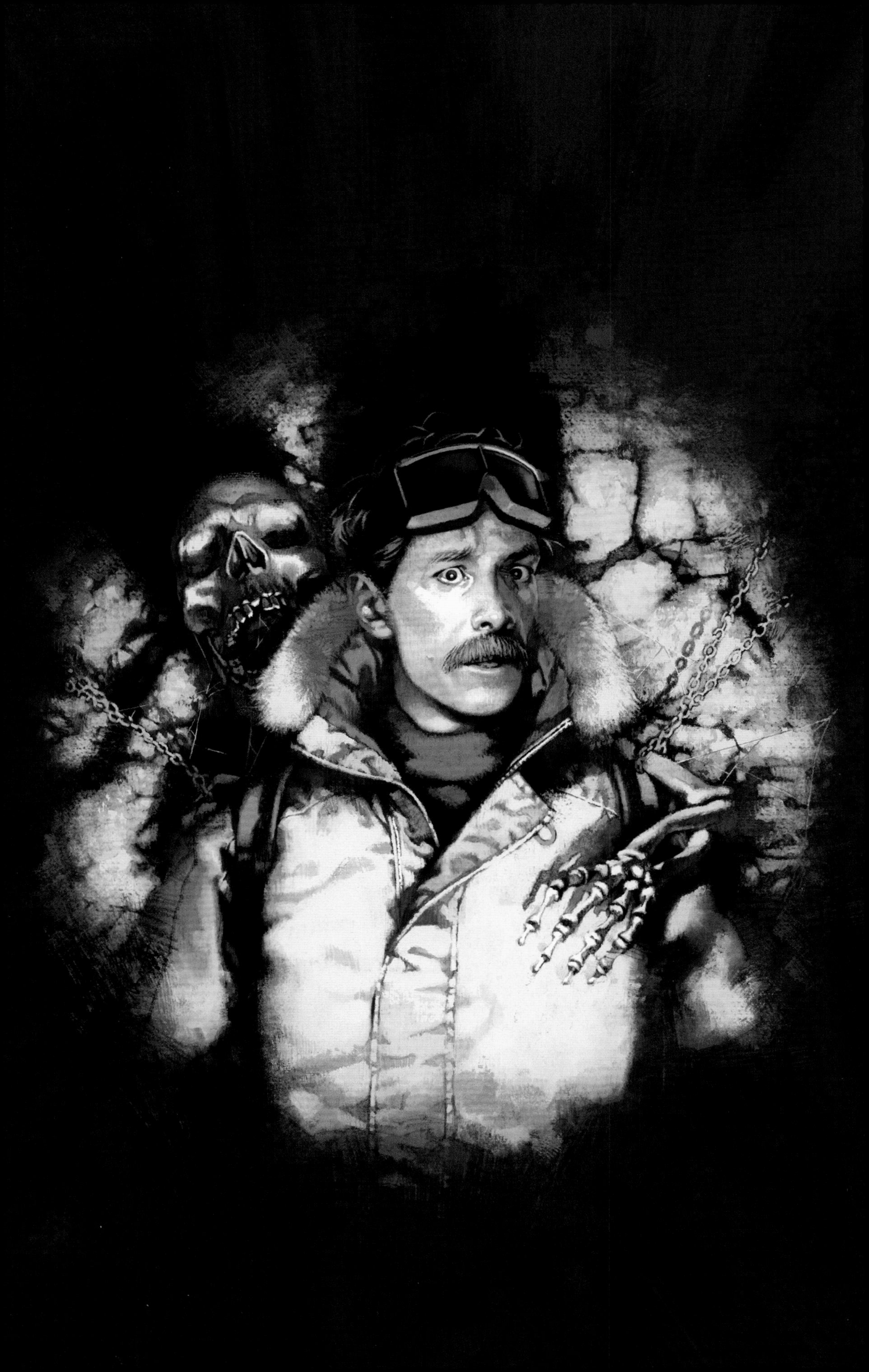

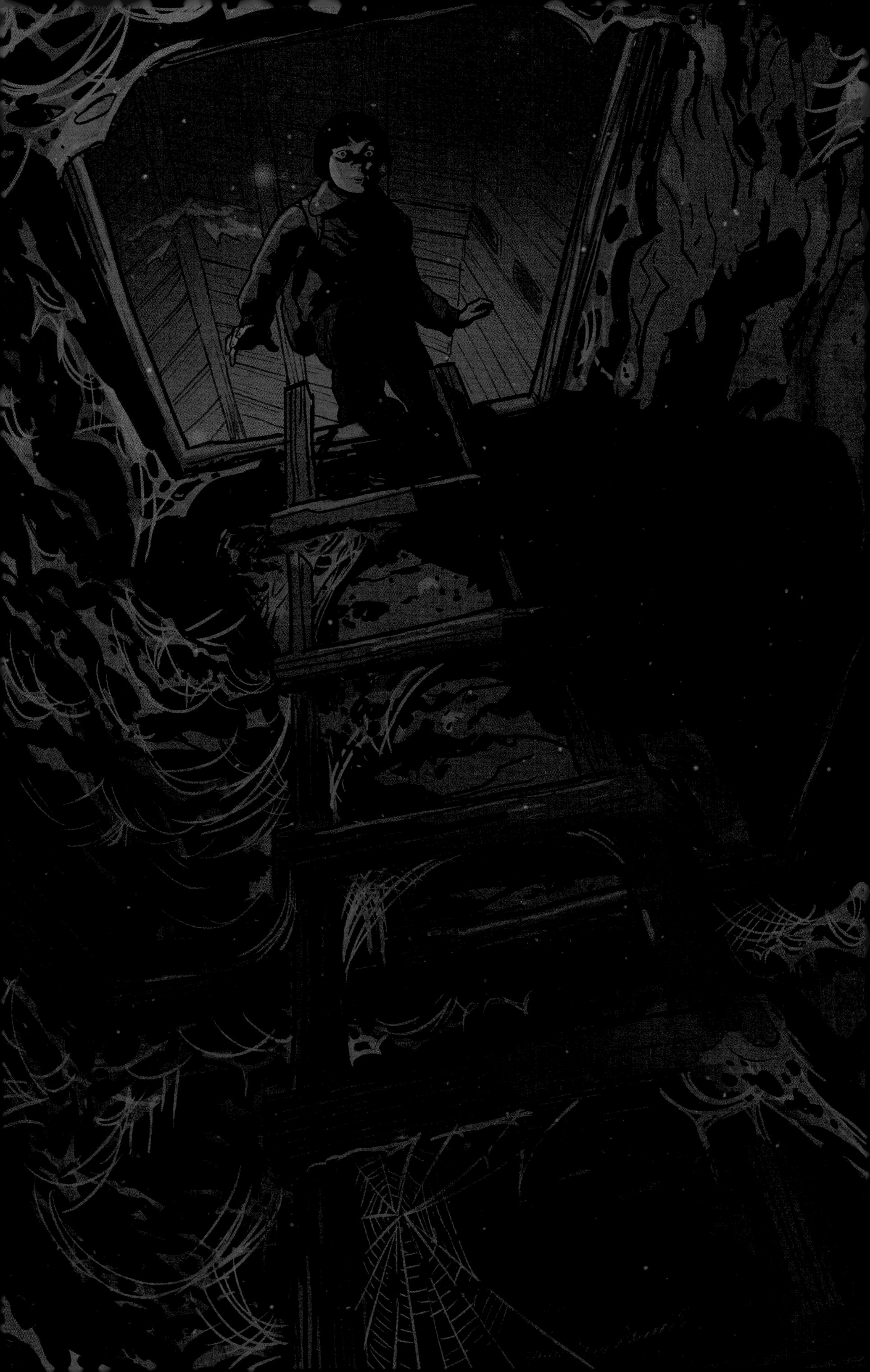

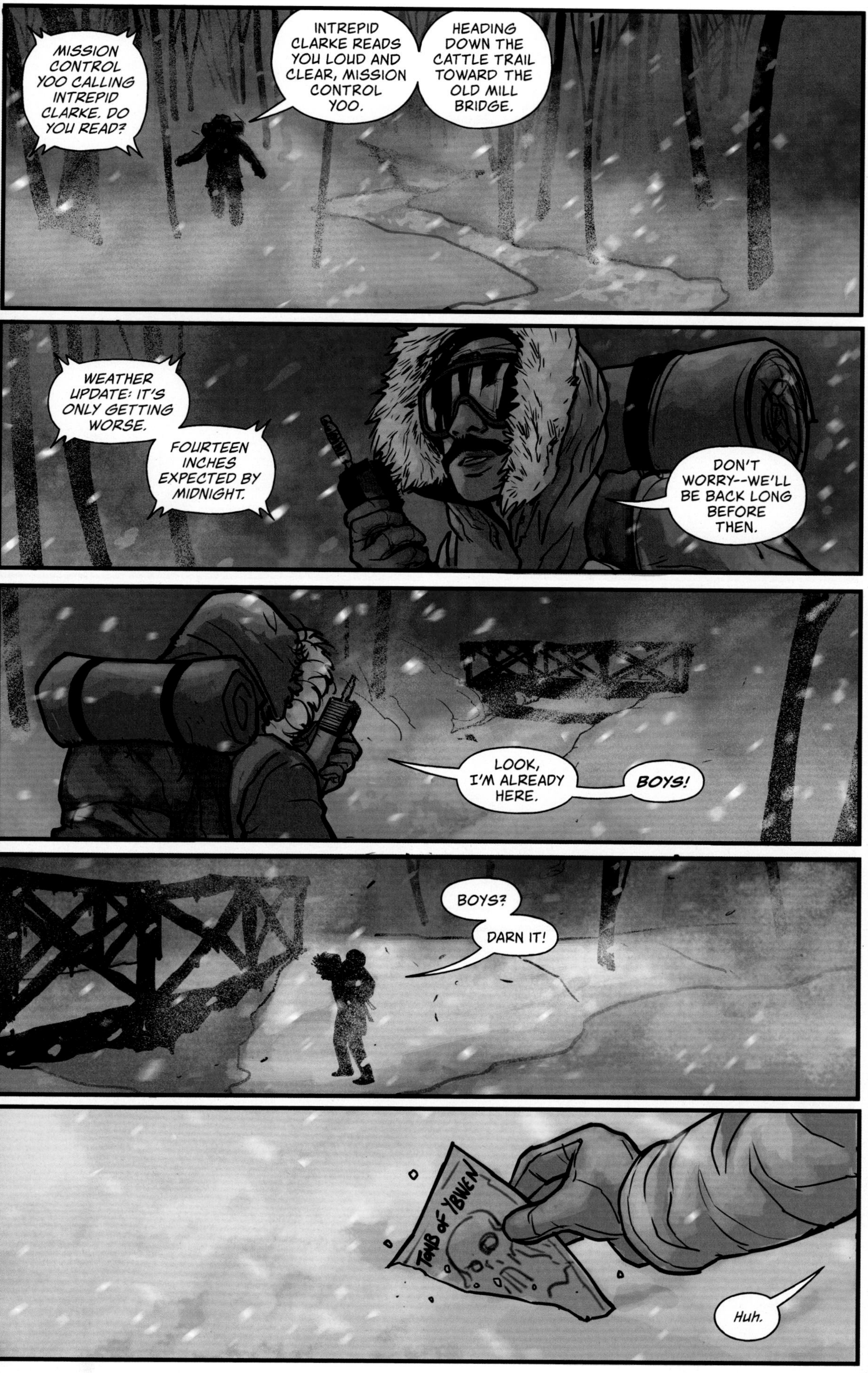
MISSION CONTROL YOO CALLING INTREPID CLARKE. DO YOU READ?
INTREPID CLARKE READS YOU LOUD AND CLEAR, MISSION CONTROL YOO.
HEADING DOWN THE CATTLE TRAIL TOWARD THE OLD MILL BRIDGE.
WEATHER UPDATE: IT'S ONLY GETTING WORSE.
FOURTEEN INCHES EXPECTED BY MIDNIGHT.
DON'T WORRY--WE'LL BE BACK LONG BEFORE THEN.
LOOK, I'M ALREADY HERE.
BOYS!
BOYS?
DARN IT!
TOMB OF YBWEN
Huh.

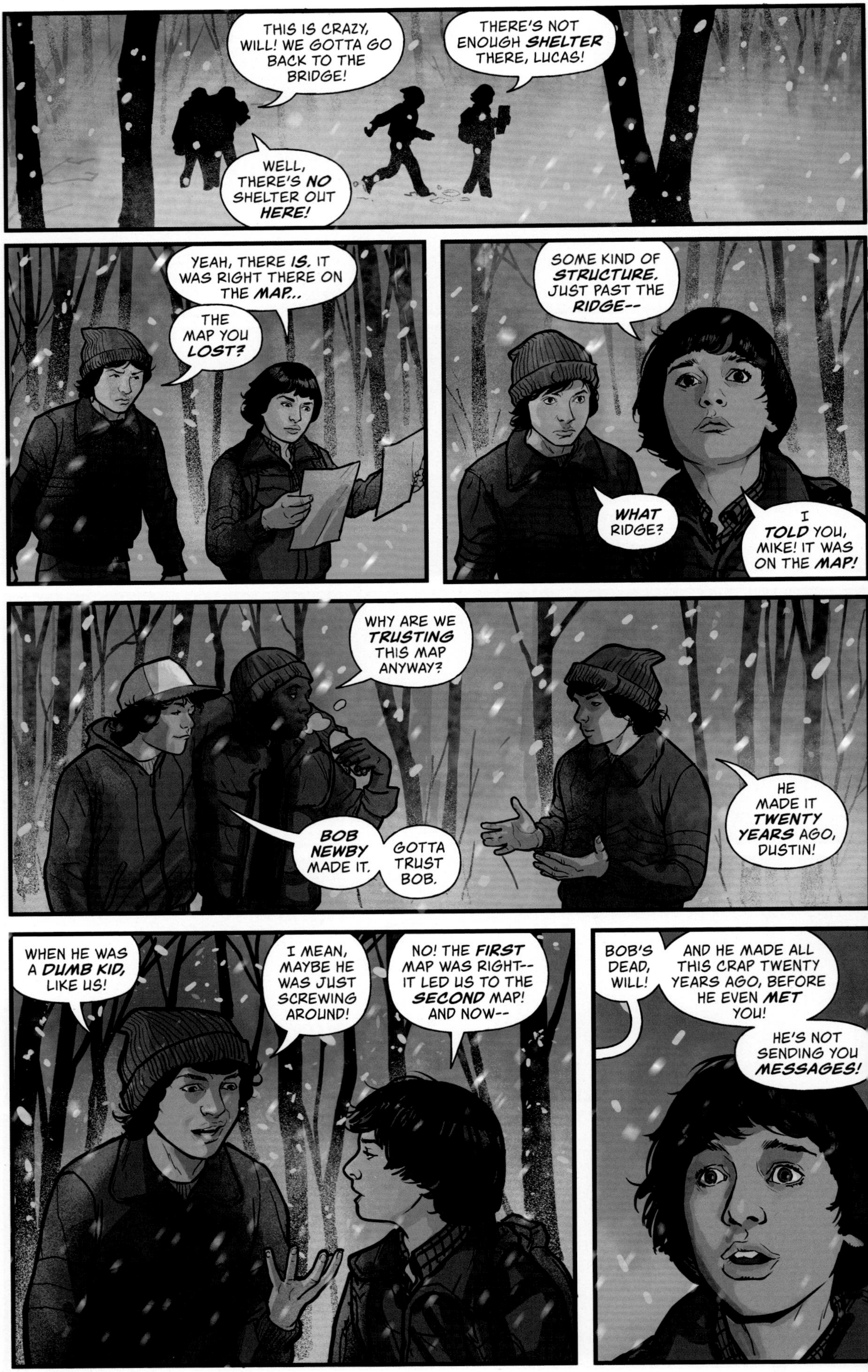
THIS IS CRAZY, WILL! WE GOTTA GO BACK TO THE BRIDGE!
THERE'S NOT ENOUGH SHELTER THERE, LUCAS!
WELL, THERE'S NO SHELTER OUT HERE!
YEAH, THERE IS. IT WAS RIGHT THERE ON THE MAP...
THE MAP YOU LOST?
SOME KIND OF STRUCTURE. JUST PAST THE RIDGE--
WHAT RIDGE?
I TOLD YOU, MIKE! IT WAS ON THE MAP!
WHY ARE WE TRUSTING THIS MAP ANYWAY?
BOB NEWBY MADE IT.
GOTTA TRUST BOB.
HE MADE IT TWENTY YEARS AGO, DUSTIN!
WHEN HE WAS A DUMB KID, LIKE US!
I MEAN, MAYBE HE WAS JUST SCREWING AROUND!
NO! THE FIRST MAP WAS RIGHT-- IT LED US TO THE SECOND MAP! AND NOW--
BOB'S DEAD, WILL!
AND HE MADE ALL THIS CRAP TWENTY YEARS AGO, BEFORE HE EVEN MET YOU!
HE'S NOT SENDING YOU MESSAGES!

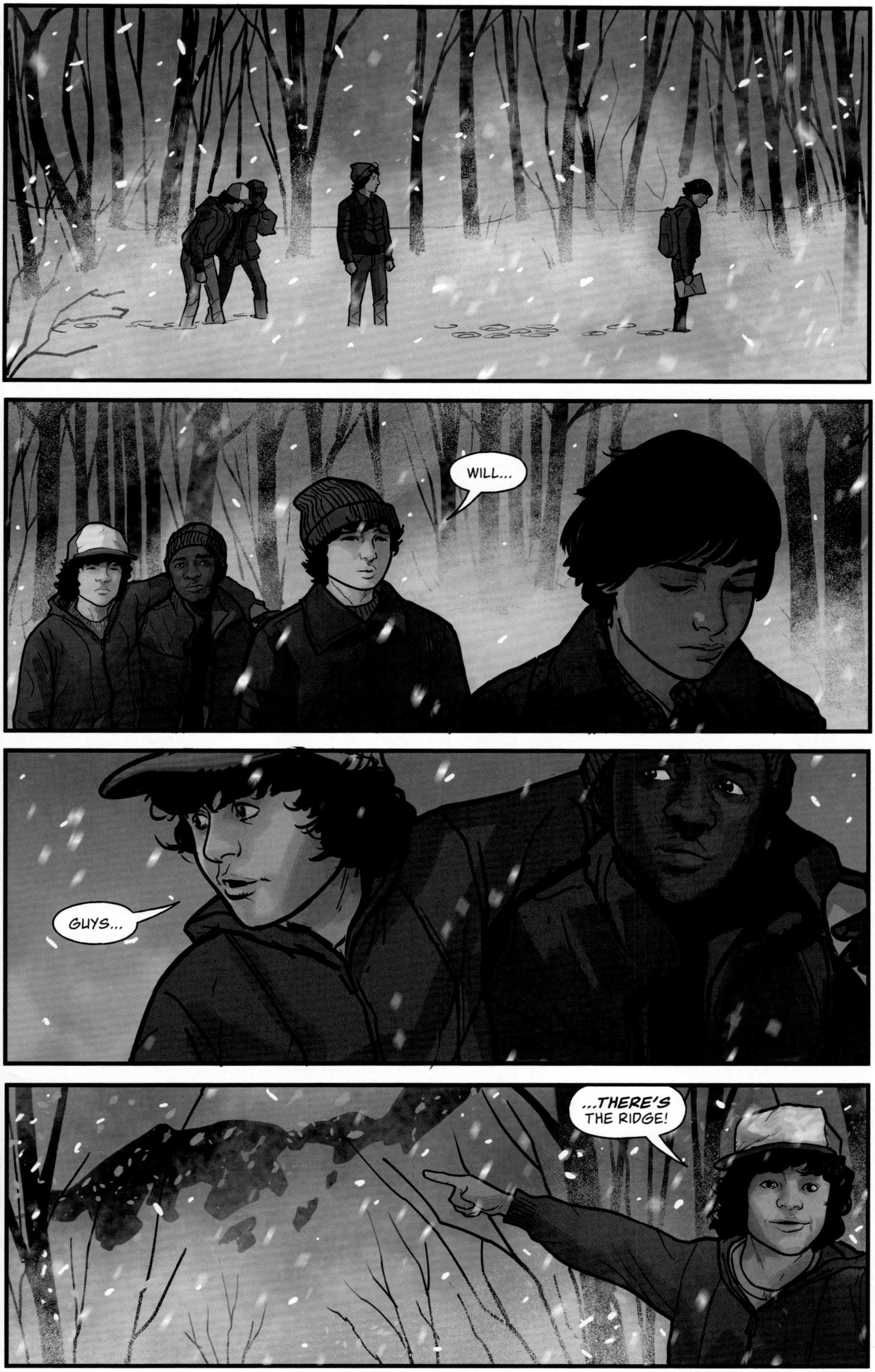
WILL...
GUYS...
...THERE'S THE RIDGE!

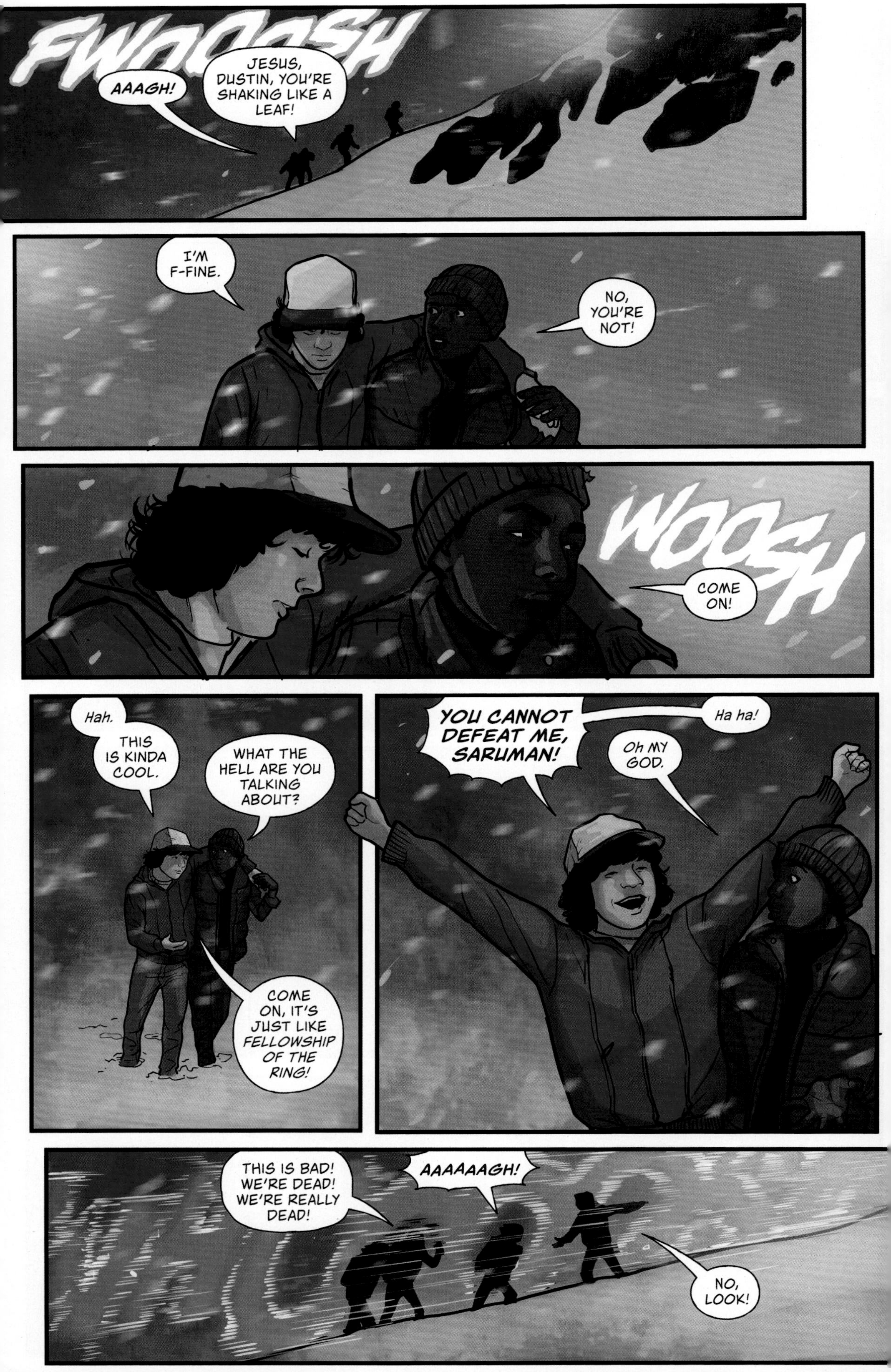
FWOOOSH
AAAGH!
JESUS, DUSTIN, YOU'RE SHAKING LIKE A LEAF!
I'M F-FINE.
NO, YOU'RE NOT!
WOOSH
COME ON!
Hah.
THIS IS KINDA COOL.
WHAT THE HELL ARE YOU TALKING ABOUT?
COME ON, IT'S JUST LIKE FELLOWSHIP OF THE RING!
YOU CANNOT DEFEAT ME, SARUMAN!
Ha ha!
Oh MY GOD.
THIS IS BAD! WE'RE DEAD! WE'RE REALLY DEAD!
AAAAAAGH!
NO, LOOK!

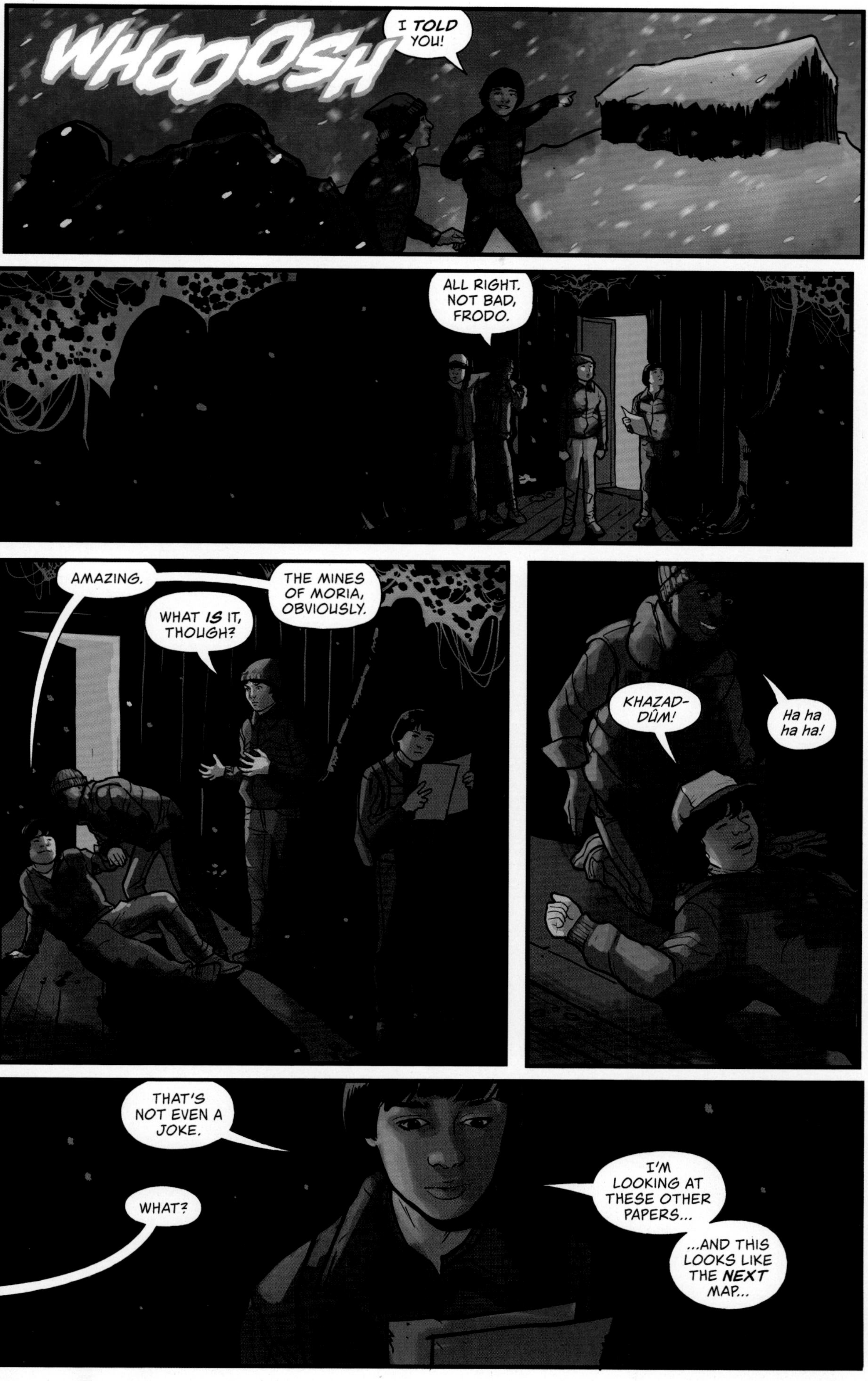
WHOOOOSH
I TOLD YOU!
ALL RIGHT. NOT BAD, FRODO.
AMAZING.
THE MINES OF MORIA, OBVIOUSLY.
WHAT IS IT, THOUGH?
KHAZAD-DÛM!
Ha ha ha ha!
THAT'S NOT EVEN A JOKE.
WHAT?
I'M LOOKING AT THESE OTHER PAPERS...
...AND THIS LOOKS LIKE THE NEXT MAP...

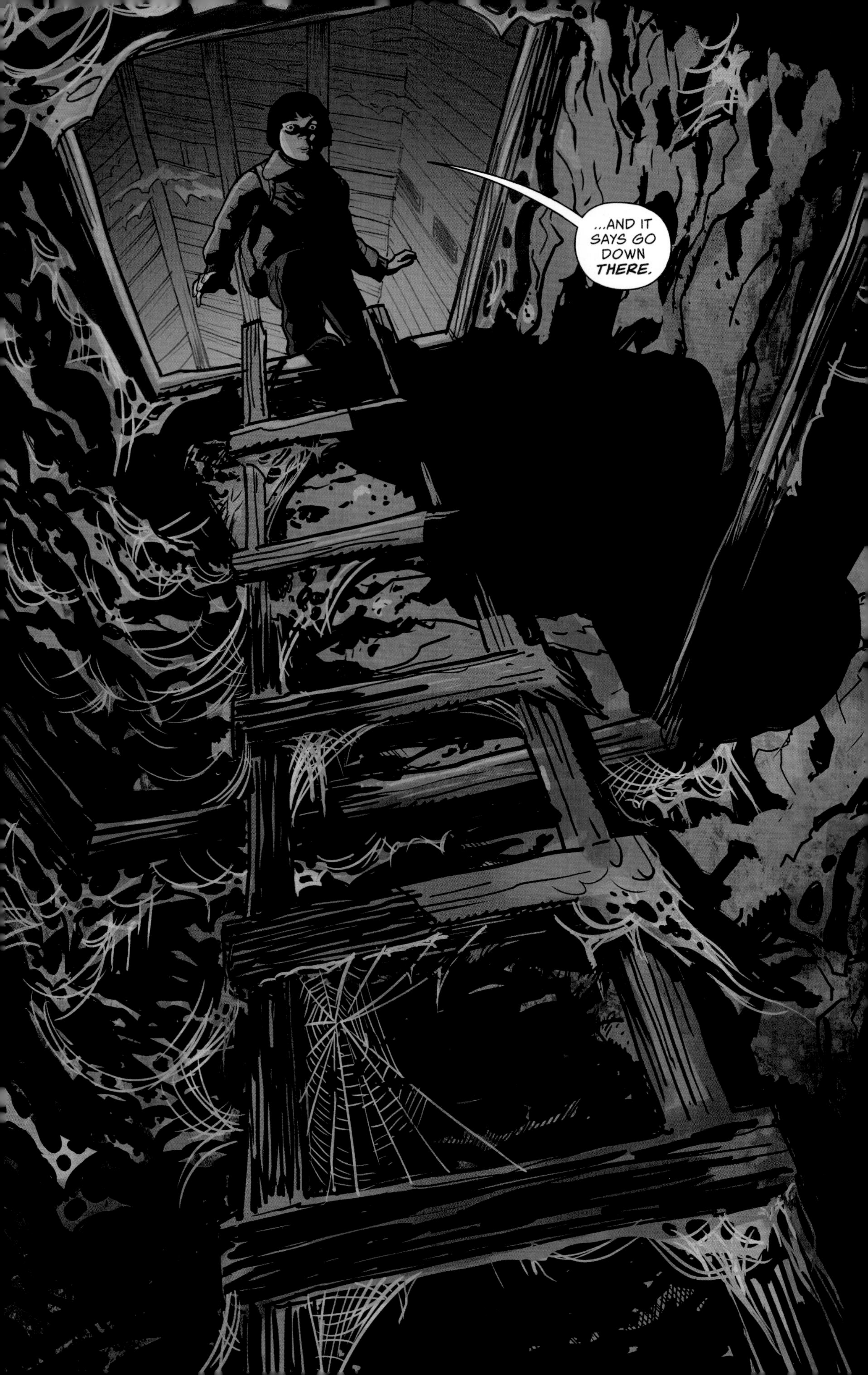
...AND IT SAYS GO DOWN *THERE.*

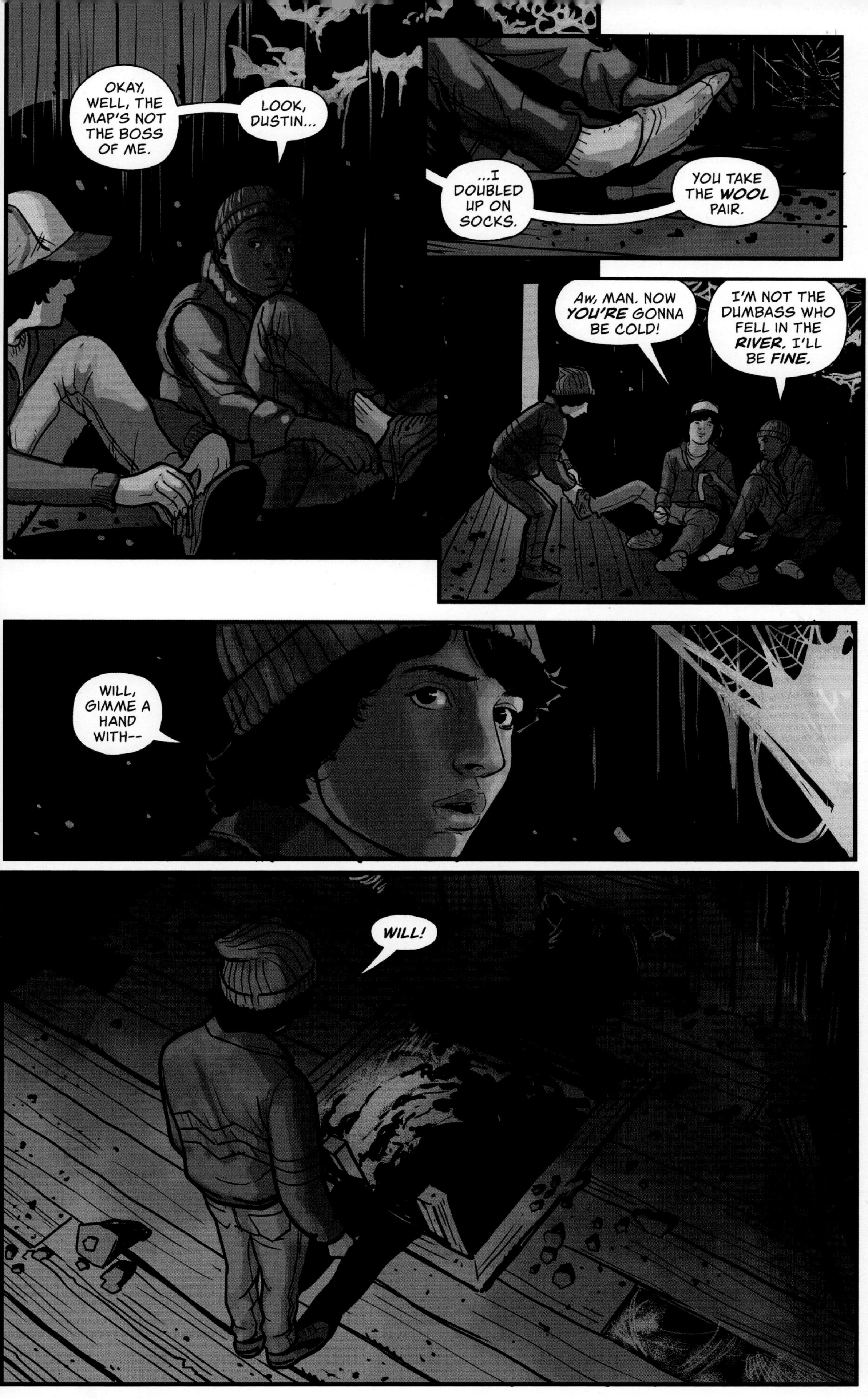
OKAY, WELL, THE MAP'S NOT THE BOSS OF ME.
LOOK, DUSTIN...
...I DOUBLED UP ON SOCKS.
YOU TAKE THE WOOL PAIR.
AW, MAN. NOW YOU'RE GONNA BE COLD!
I'M NOT THE DUMBASS WHO FELL IN THE RIVER. I'LL BE FINE.
WILL, GIMME A HAND WITH--
WILL!

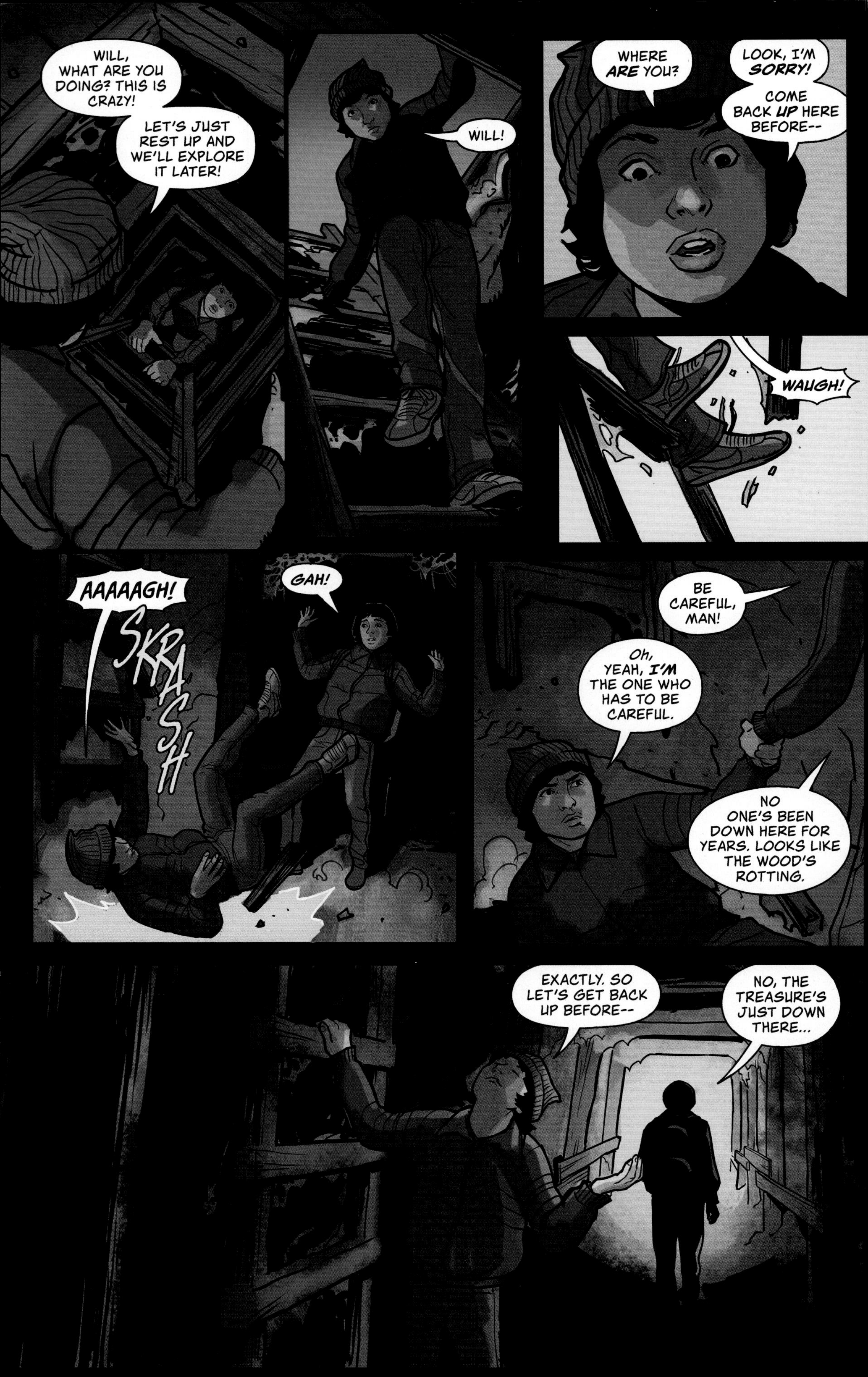
WILL, WHAT ARE YOU DOING? THIS IS CRAZY!
LET'S JUST REST UP AND WE'LL EXPLORE IT LATER!
WILL!
WHERE ARE YOU?
LOOK, I'M SORRY!
COME BACK UP HERE BEFORE--
WAUGH!
AAAAAGH!
SKRASH
GAH!
BE CAREFUL, MAN!
Oh, YEAH, I'M THE ONE WHO HAS TO BE CAREFUL.
NO ONE'S BEEN DOWN HERE FOR YEARS. LOOKS LIKE THE WOOD'S ROTTING.
EXACTLY. SO LET'S GET BACK UP BEFORE--
NO, THE TREASURE'S JUST DOWN THERE...

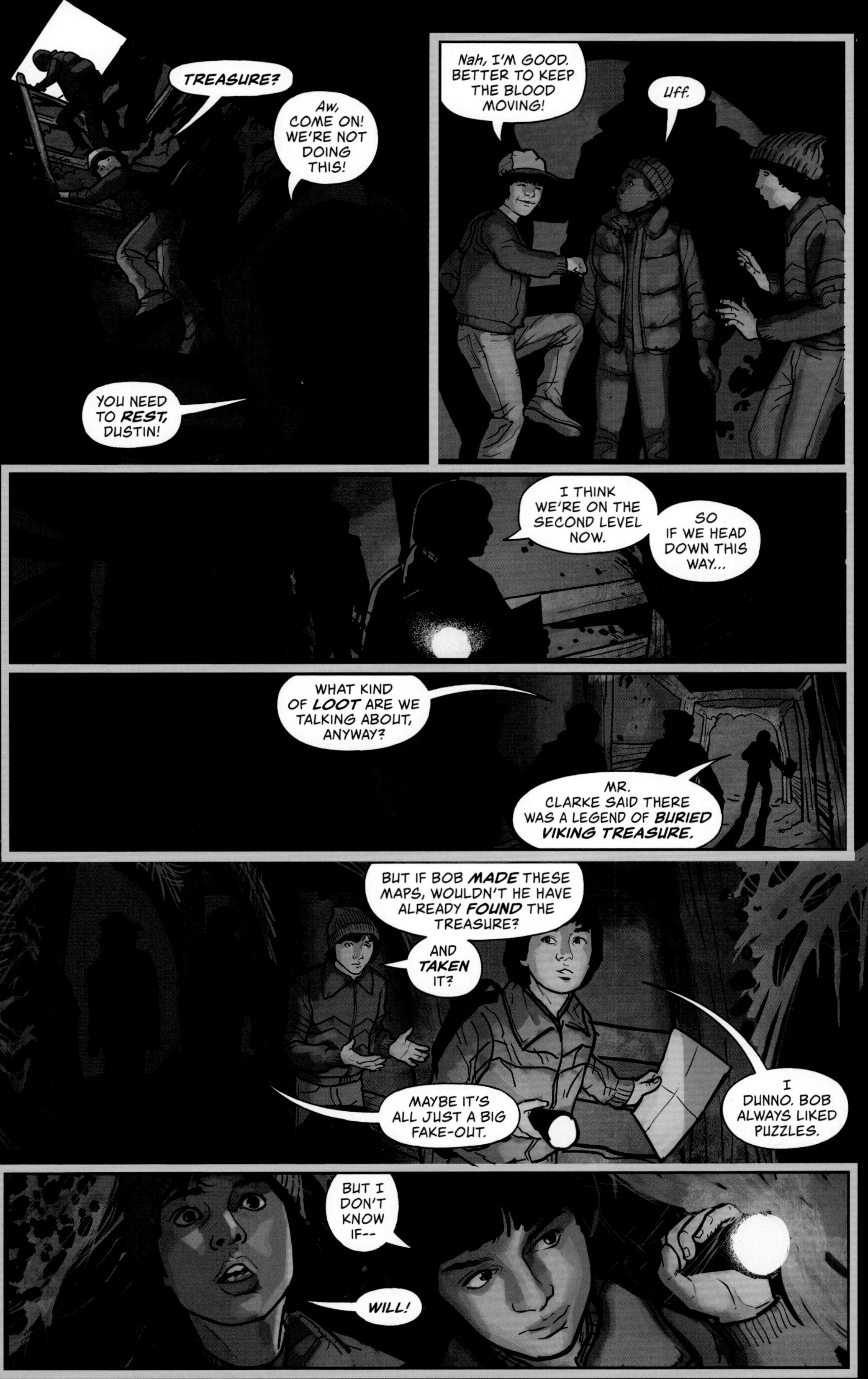
TREASURE?
Aw, COME ON! WE'RE NOT DOING THIS!
YOU NEED TO REST, DUSTIN!
Nah, I'M GOOD. BETTER TO KEEP THE BLOOD MOVING!
Uff.
I THINK WE'RE ON THE SECOND LEVEL NOW.
SO IF WE HEAD DOWN THIS WAY...
WHAT KIND OF LOOT ARE WE TALKING ABOUT, ANYWAY?
MR. CLARKE SAID THERE WAS A LEGEND OF BURIED VIKING TREASURE.
BUT IF BOB MADE THESE MAPS, WOULDN'T HE HAVE ALREADY FOUND THE TREASURE?
AND TAKEN IT?
MAYBE IT'S ALL JUST A BIG FAKE-OUT.
I DUNNO. BOB ALWAYS LIKED PUZZLES.
BUT I DON'T KNOW IF--
WILL!

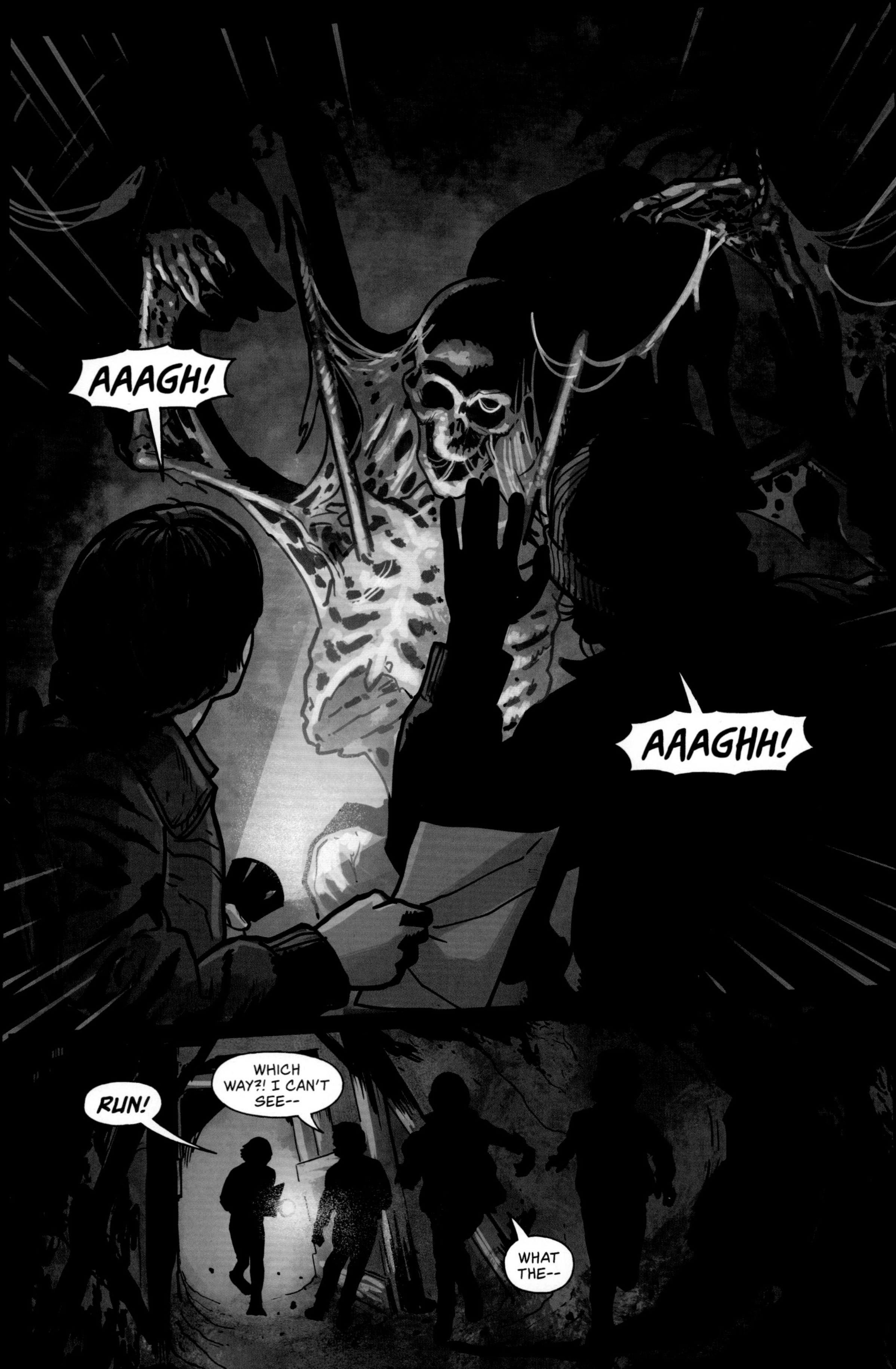
AAAGH!
AAAGHH!
RUN!
WHICH WAY?! I CAN'T SEE--
WHAT THE--

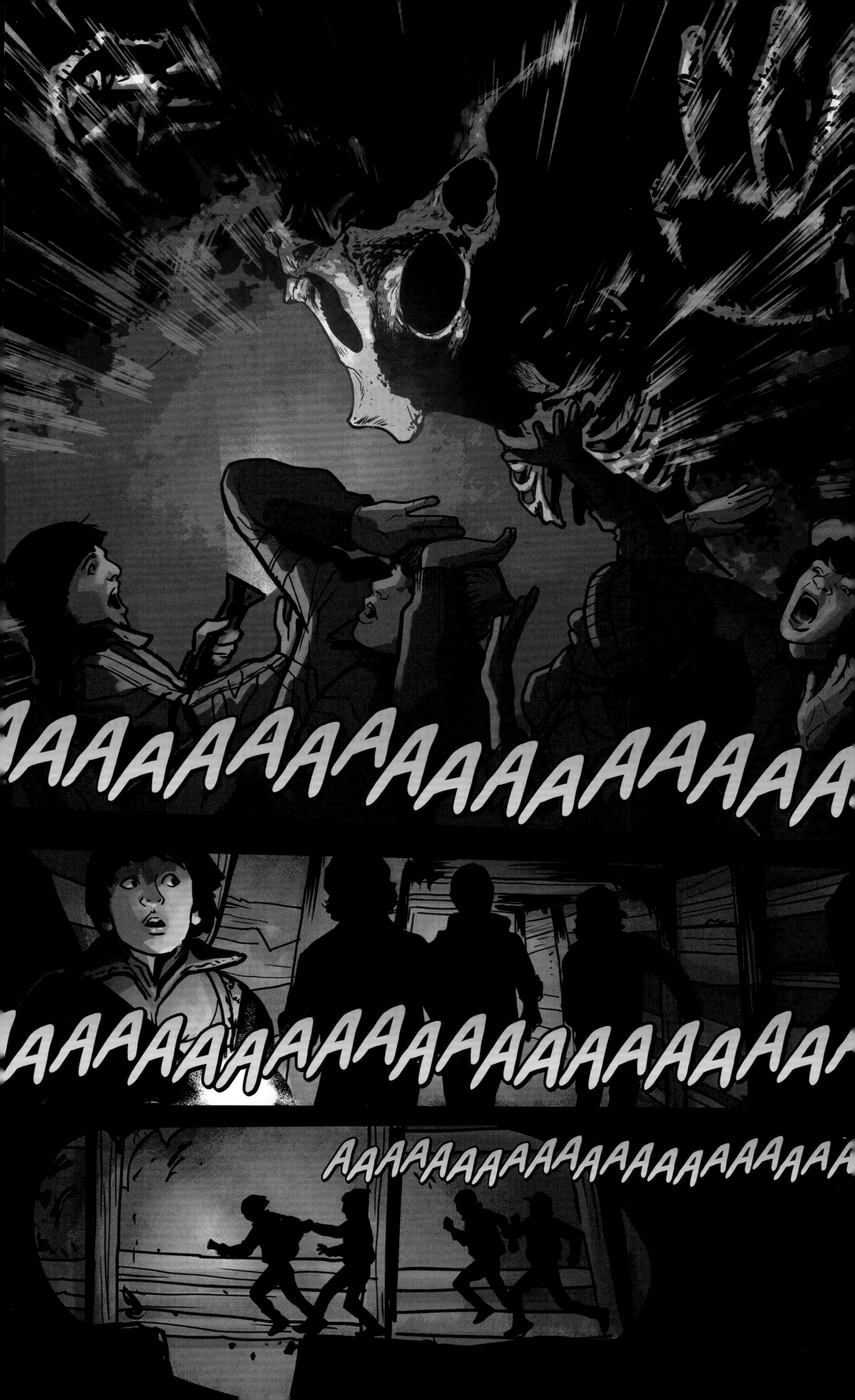
AAAAAAAAAAAAAAAAA
AAAAAAAAAAAAAAAAAAAA
AAAAAAAAAAAAAAAAAAAAA

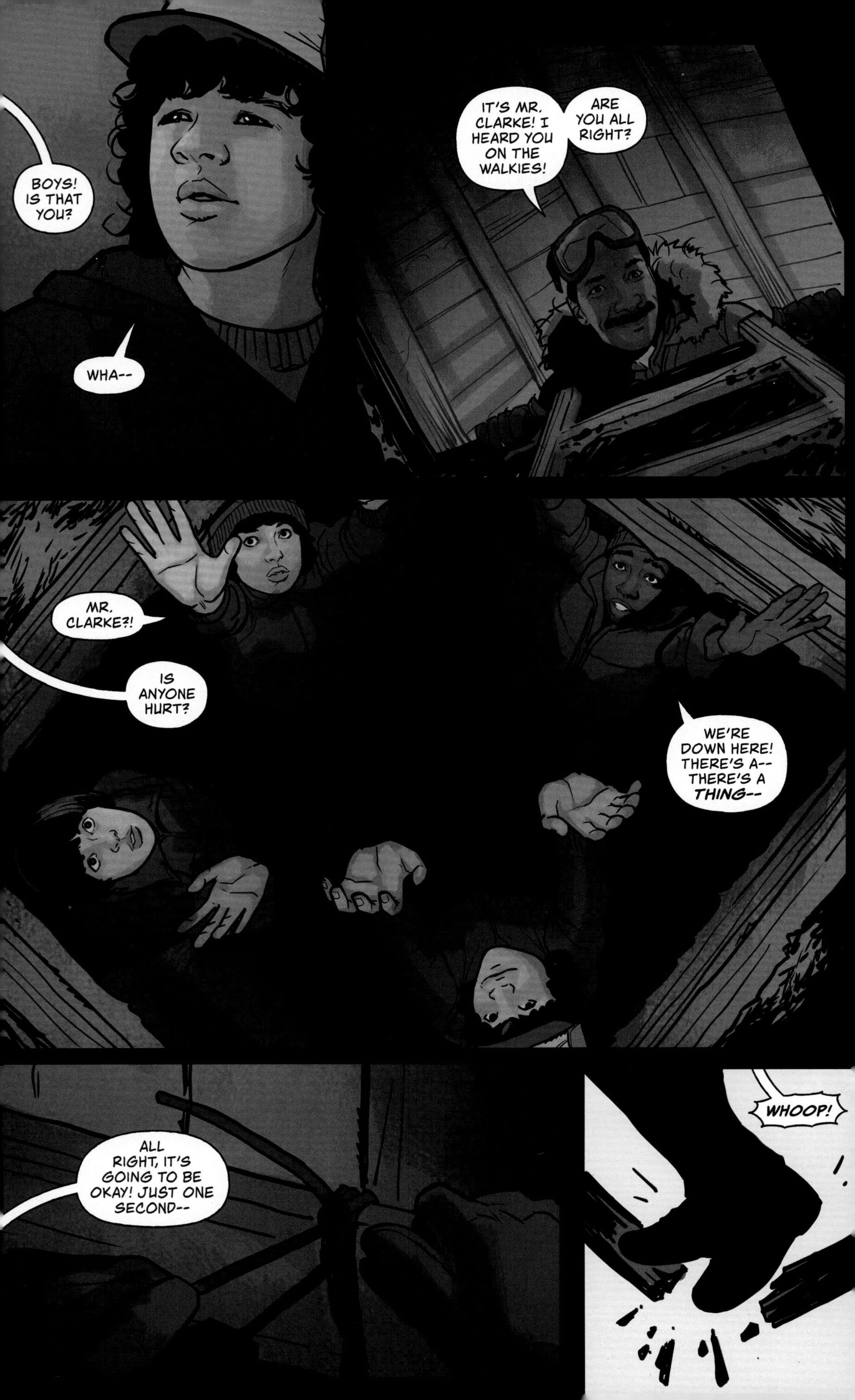
BOYS! IS THAT YOU?
WHA--
IT'S MR. CLARKE! I HEARD YOU ON THE WALKIES!
ARE YOU ALL RIGHT?
MR. CLARKE?!
IS ANYONE HURT?
WE'RE DOWN HERE! THERE'S A-- THERE'S A *THING*--
ALL RIGHT, IT'S GOING TO BE OKAY! JUST ONE SECOND--
WHOOP!

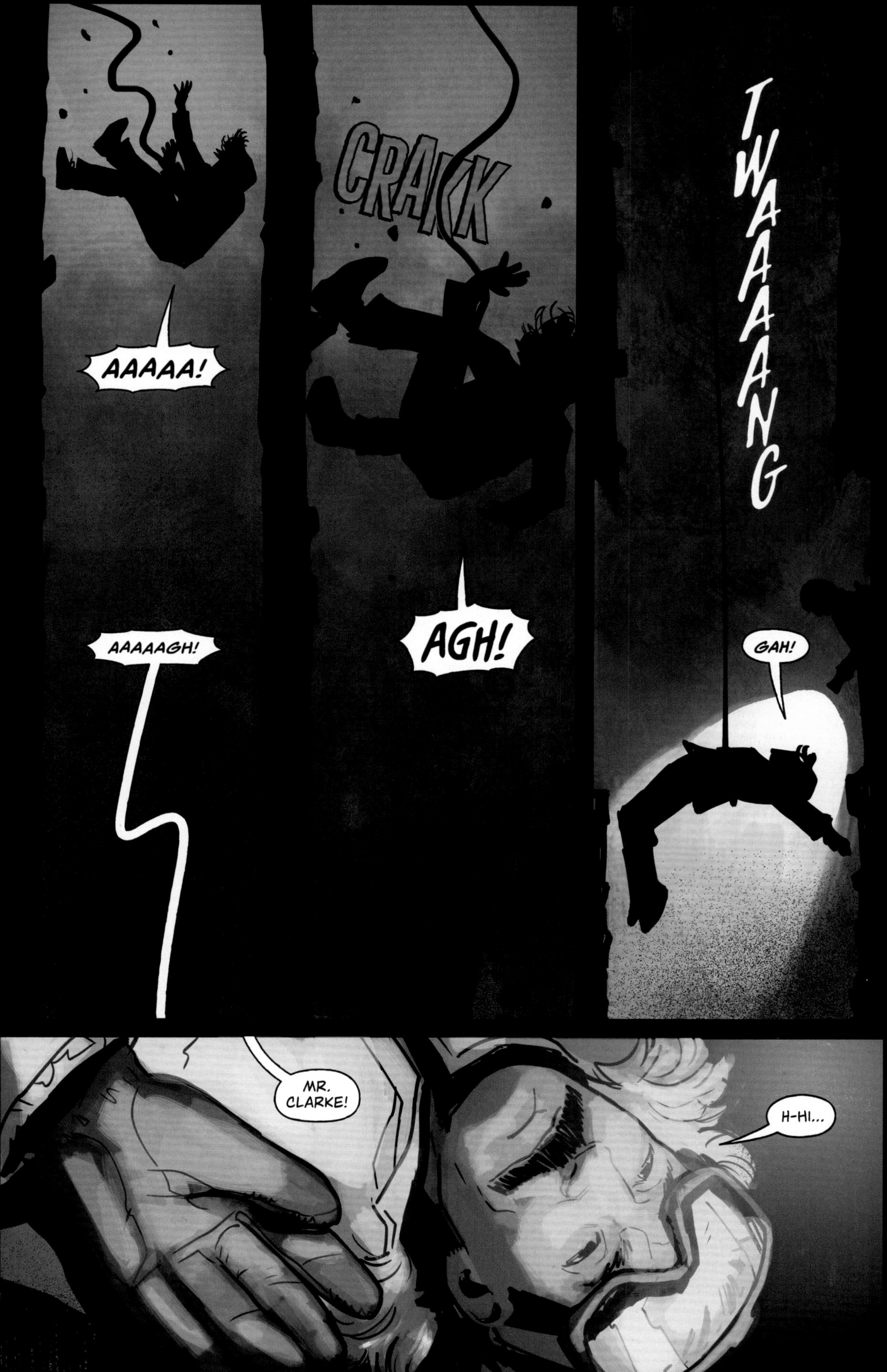
AAAAA!
CRAKK
AGH!
AAAAAGH!
TWAAAAANG
GAH!
MR. CLARKE!
H-HI...

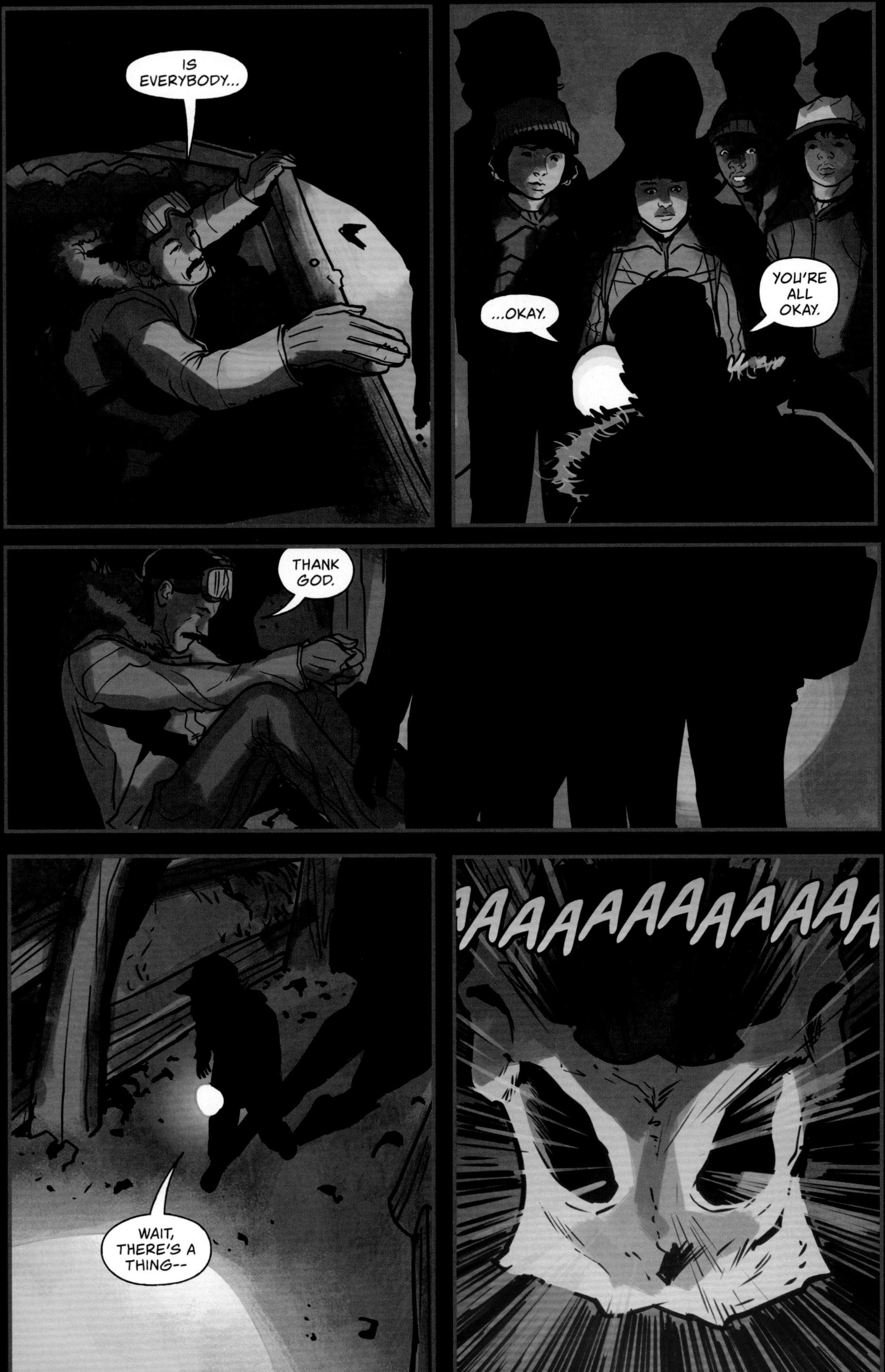
IS EVERYBODY...
...OKAY.
YOU'RE ALL OKAY.
THANK GOD.
WAIT, THERE'S A THING--
AAAAAAAAAAAA

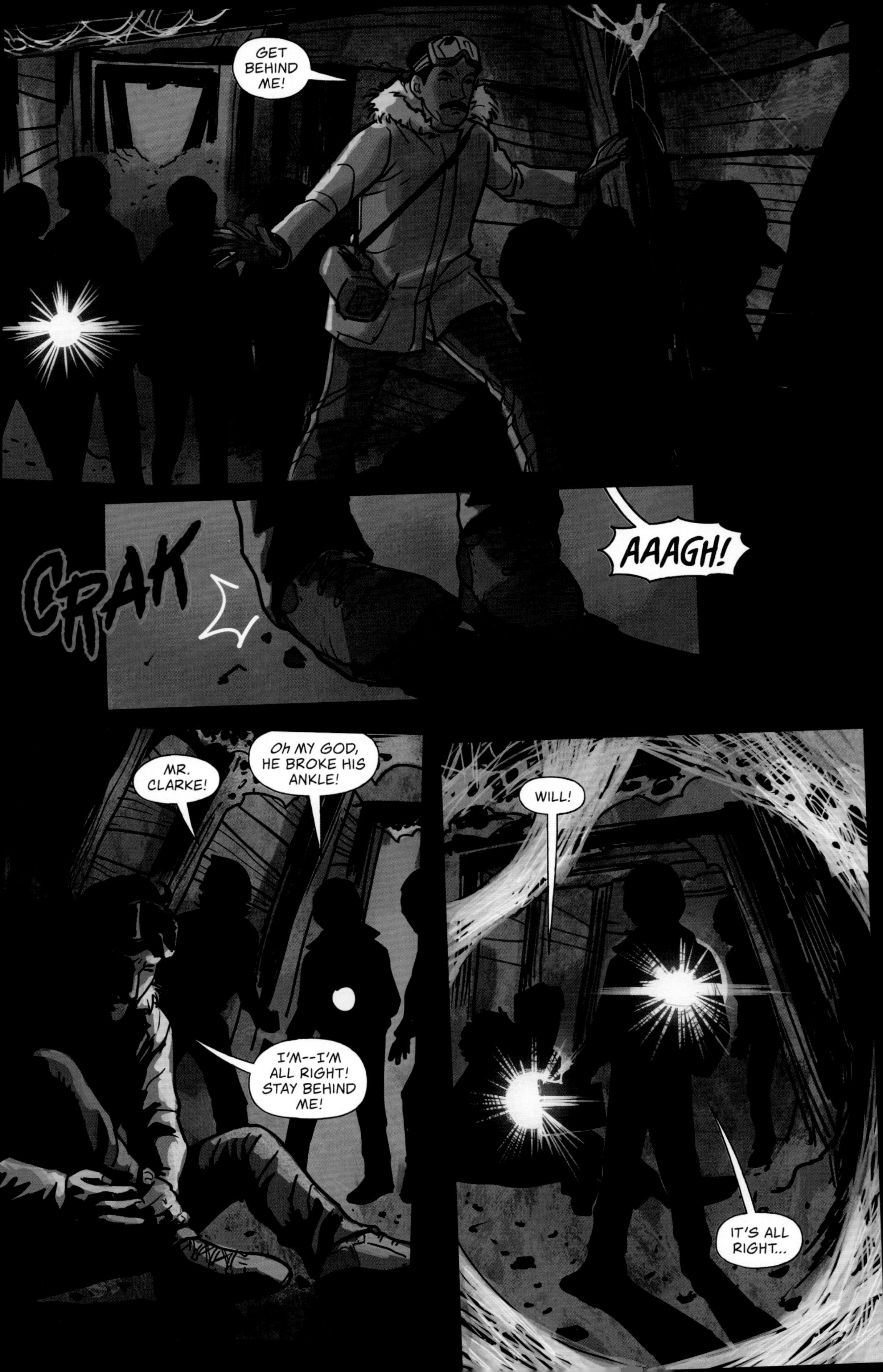
GET BEHIND ME!
CRAK
AAAGH!
MR. CLARKE!
Oh MY GOD, HE BROKE HIS ANKLE!
I'M--I'M ALL RIGHT! STAY BEHIND ME!
WILL!
IT'S ALL RIGHT...

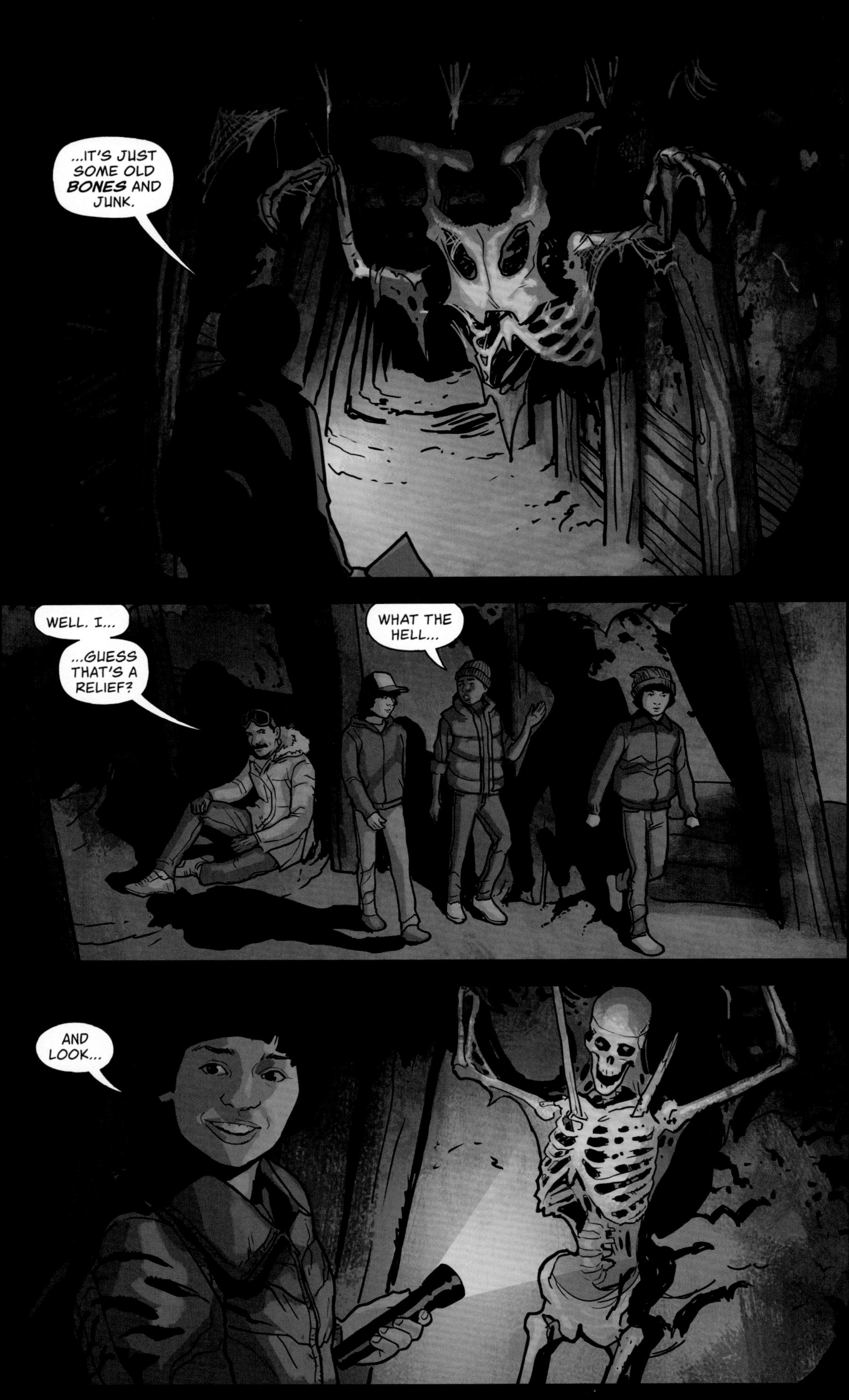
...IT'S JUST SOME OLD **BONES** AND JUNK.
WELL, I...
...GUESS THAT'S A RELIEF?
WHAT THE HELL...
AND LOOK...

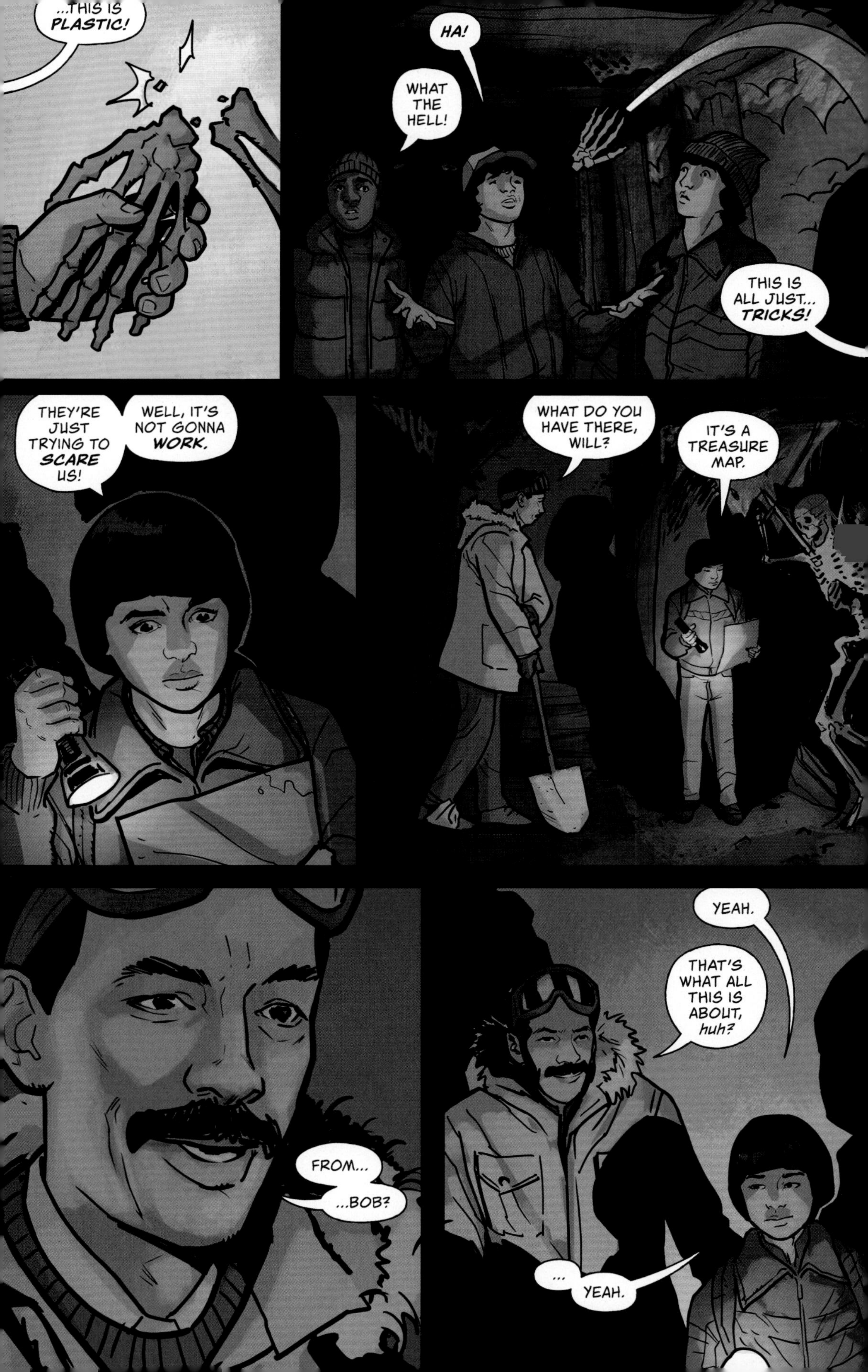

...THIS IS PLASTIC!
HA!
WHAT THE HELL!
THIS IS ALL JUST... TRICKS!
THEY'RE JUST TRYING TO SCARE US!
WELL, IT'S NOT GONNA WORK.
WHAT DO YOU HAVE THERE, WILL?
IT'S A TREASURE MAP.
FROM...
...BOB?
YEAH.
THAT'S WHAT ALL THIS IS ABOUT, huh?
... YEAH.

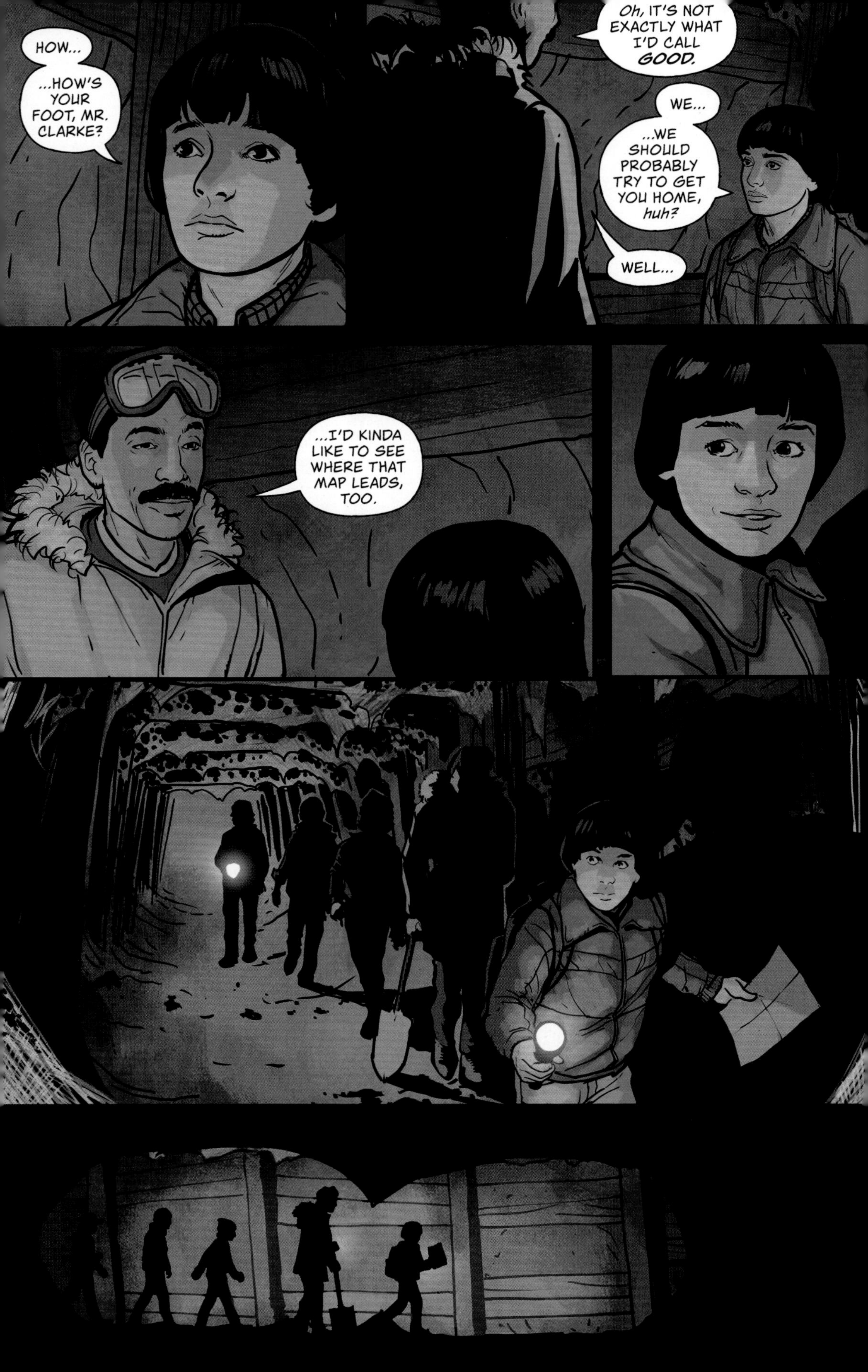
HOW...
...HOW'S YOUR FOOT, MR. CLARKE?
Oh, IT'S NOT EXACTLY WHAT I'D CALL ***GOOD.***
WE...
...WE SHOULD PROBABLY TRY TO GET YOU HOME, *huh?*
WELL...
...I'D KINDA LIKE TO SEE WHERE THAT MAP LEADS, TOO.

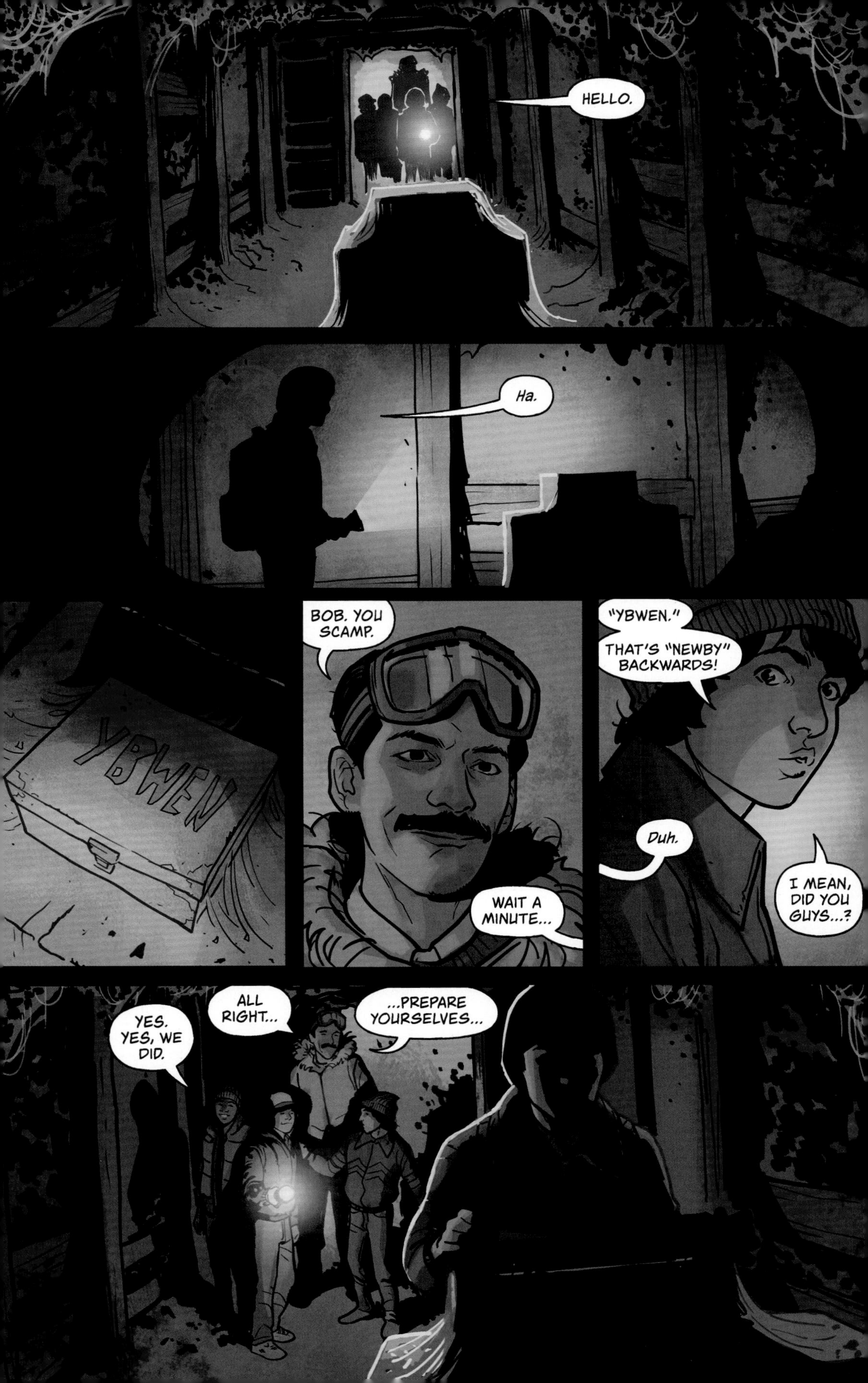
HELLO.
Ha.
YBWEN
BOB. YOU SCAMP.
WAIT A MINUTE...
"YBWEN."
THAT'S "NEWBY" BACKWARDS!
Duh.
I MEAN, DID YOU GUYS...?
YES. YES, WE DID.
ALL RIGHT...
...PREPARE YOURSELVES...

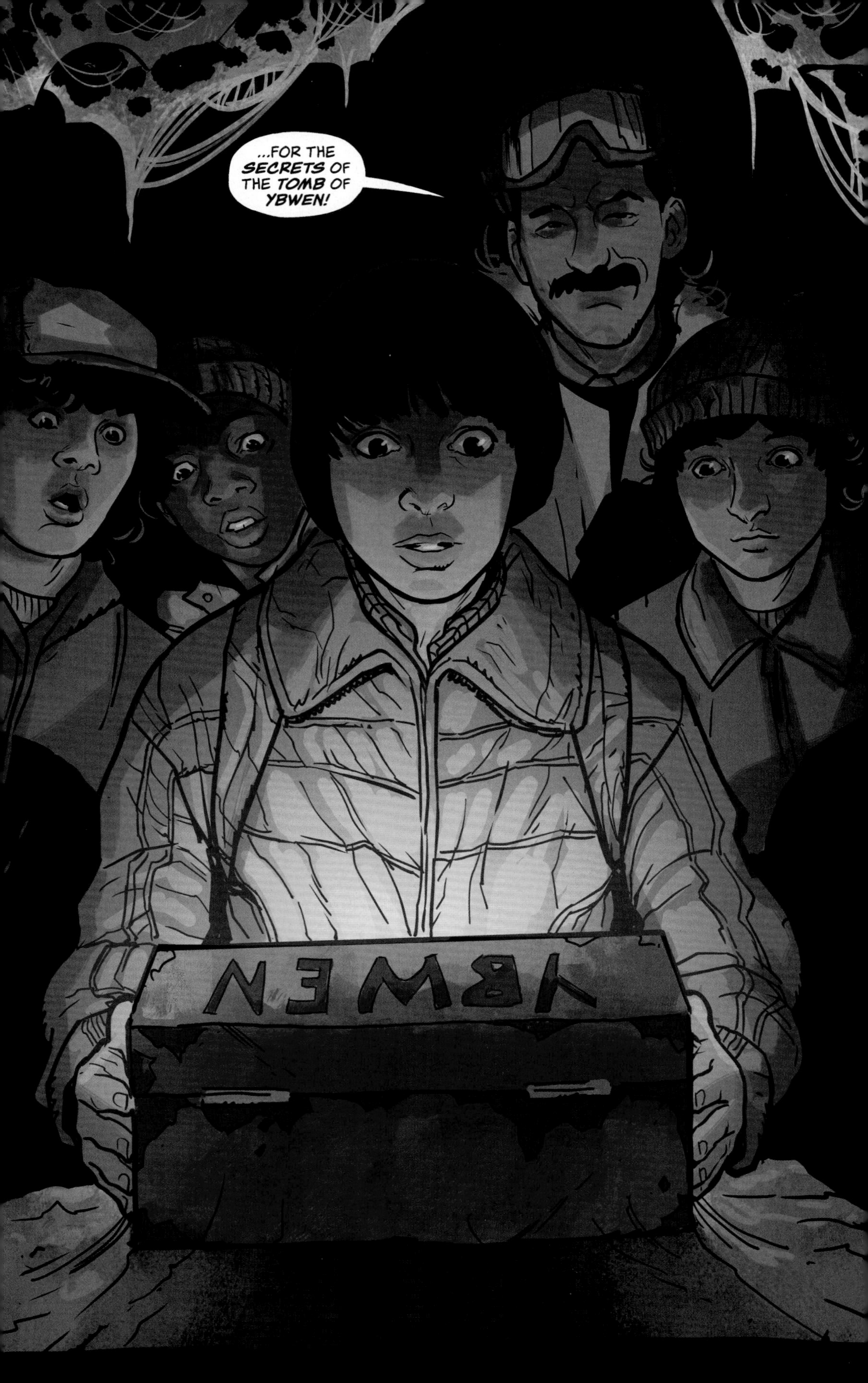
...FOR THE SECRETS OF THE TOMB OF YBWEN!

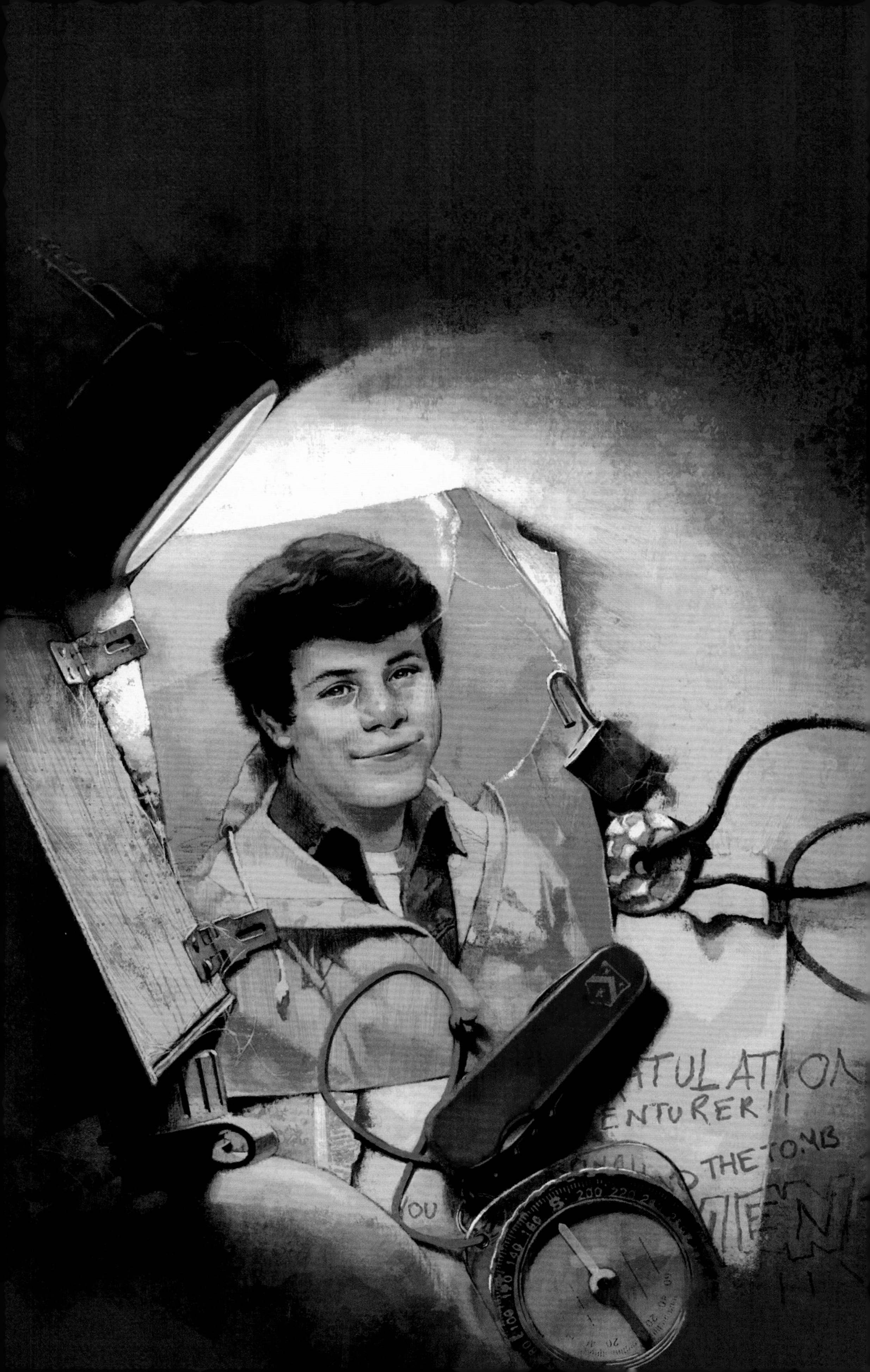
ATULATION
ENTURER!!
THE TOMB
YOU

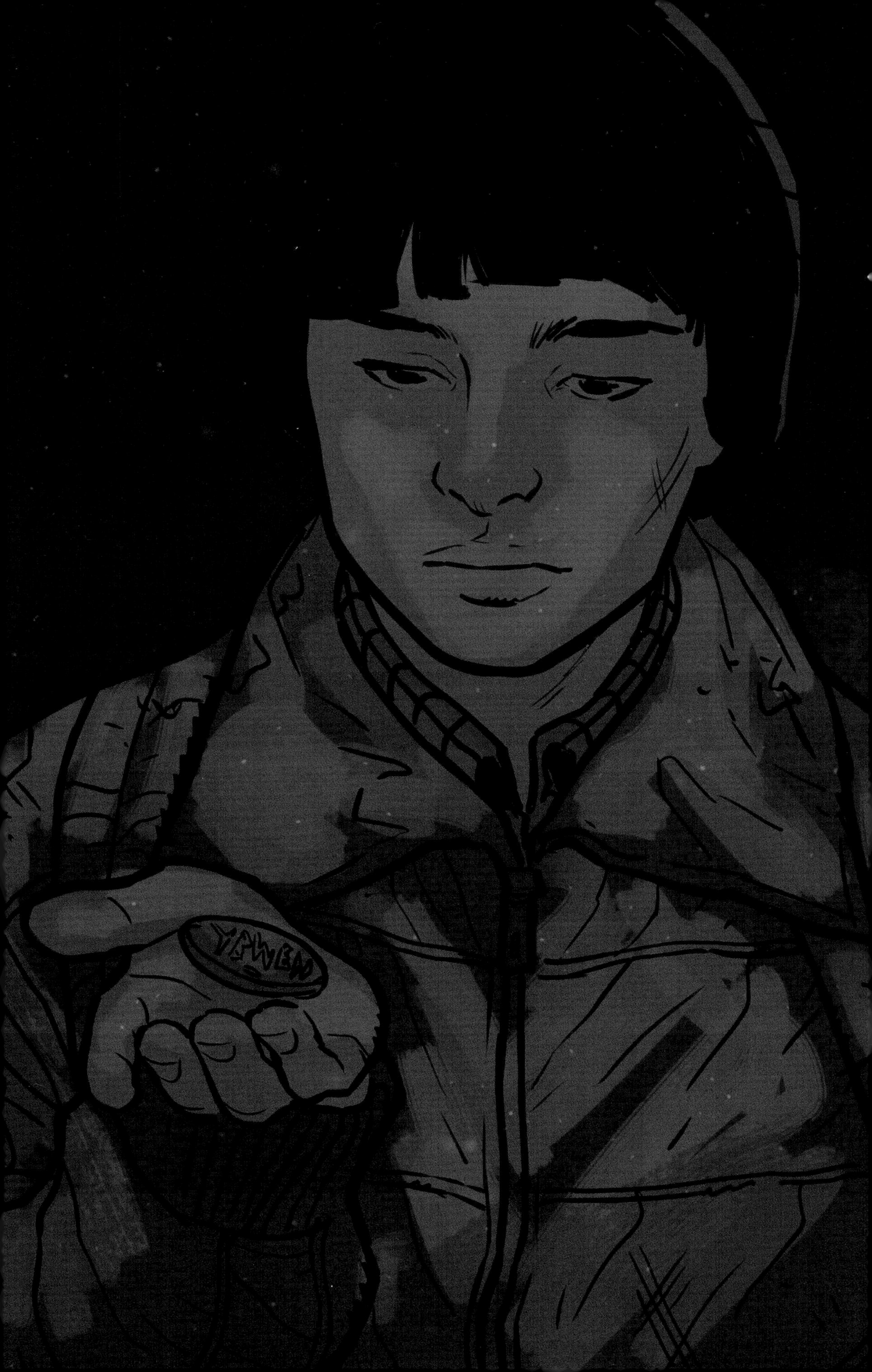

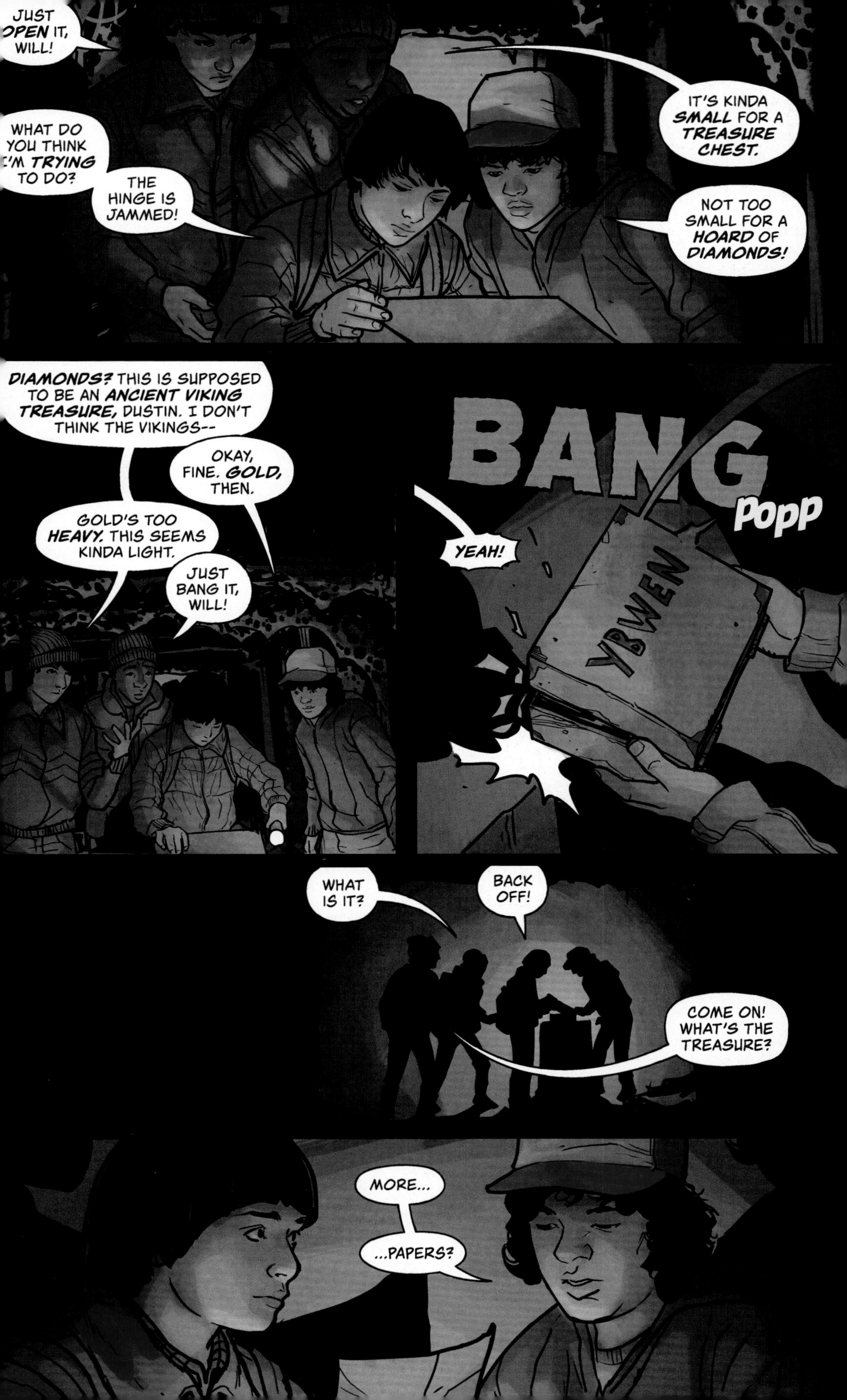
JUST OPEN IT, WILL!
IT'S KINDA SMALL FOR A TREASURE CHEST.
WHAT DO YOU THINK I'M TRYING TO DO?
THE HINGE IS JAMMED!
NOT TOO SMALL FOR A HOARD OF DIAMONDS!
DIAMONDS? THIS IS SUPPOSED TO BE AN ANCIENT VIKING TREASURE, DUSTIN. I DON'T THINK THE VIKINGS--
OKAY, FINE. GOLD, THEN.
GOLD'S TOO HEAVY. THIS SEEMS KINDA LIGHT.
JUST BANG IT, WILL!
BANG
POPP
YEAH!
YBWEN
WHAT IS IT?
BACK OFF!
COME ON! WHAT'S THE TREASURE?
MORE...
...PAPERS?

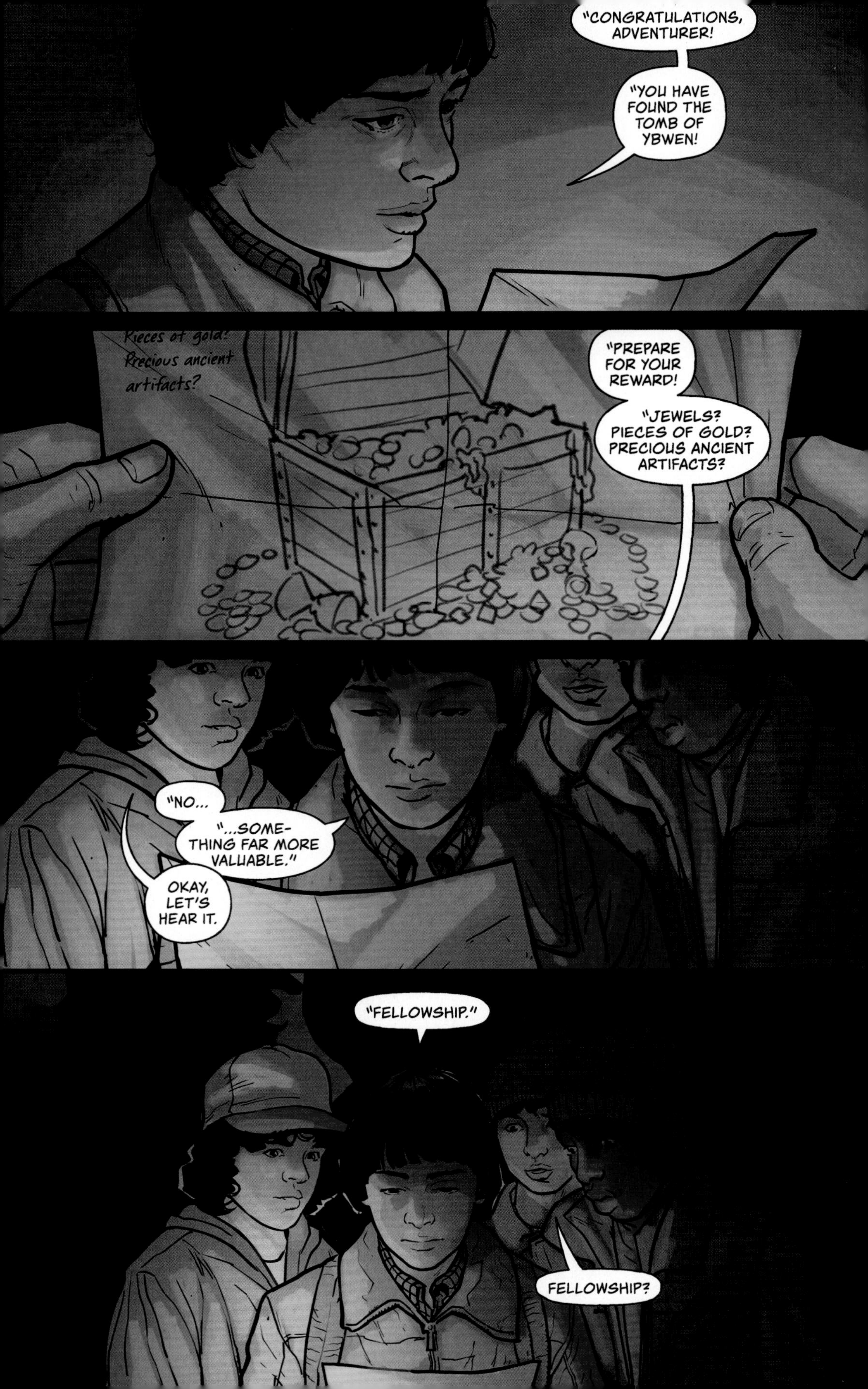
"CONGRATULATIONS, ADVENTURER!
"YOU HAVE FOUND THE TOMB OF YBWEN!
Pieces of gold? Precious ancient artifacts?
"PREPARE FOR YOUR REWARD!
"JEWELS? PIECES OF GOLD? PRECIOUS ANCIENT ARTIFACTS?
"NO...
"...SOME-THING FAR MORE VALUABLE."
OKAY, LET'S HEAR IT.
"FELLOWSHIP."
FELLOWSHIP?

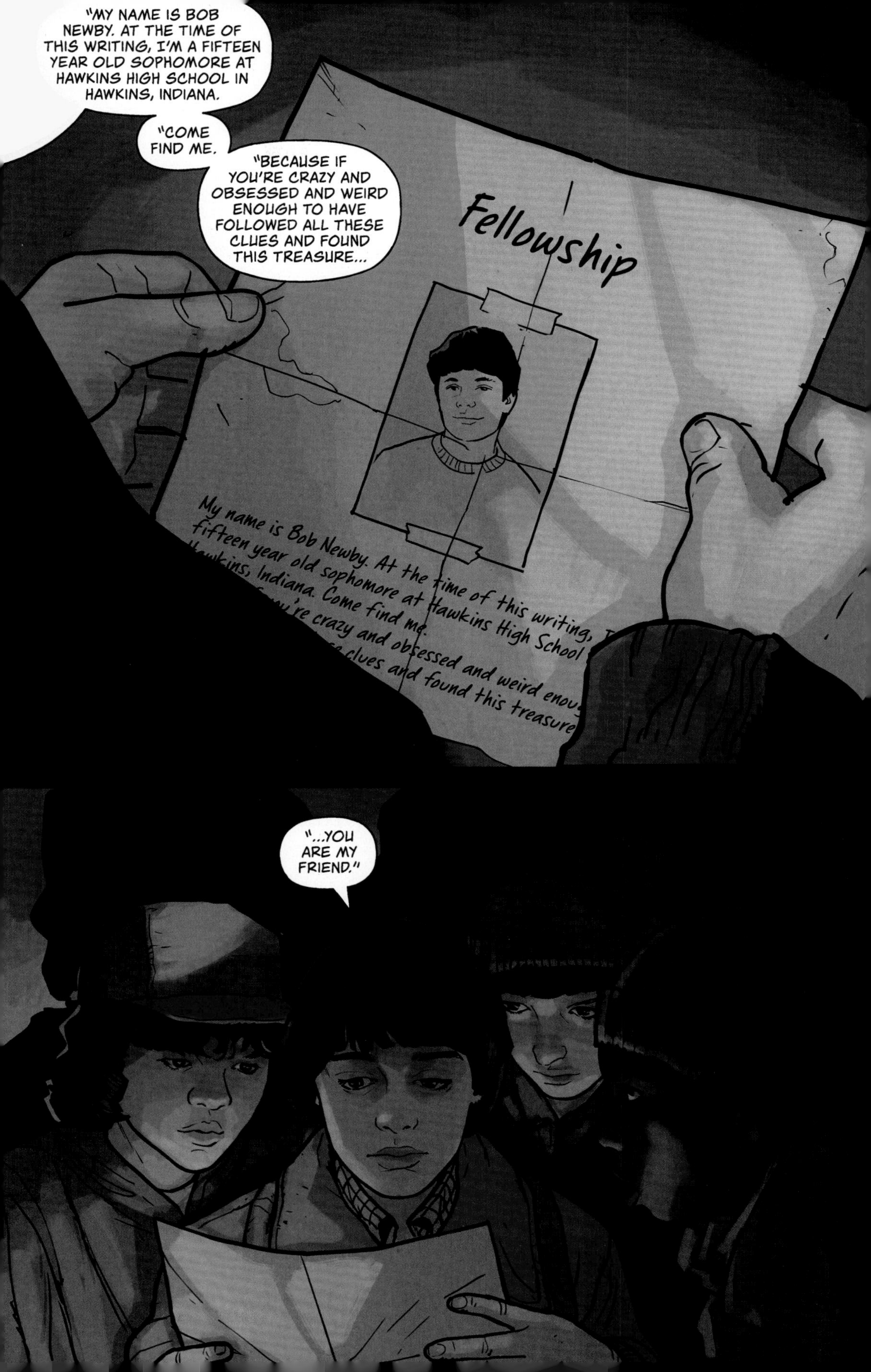
"MY NAME IS BOB NEWBY. AT THE TIME OF THIS WRITING, I'M A FIFTEEN YEAR OLD SOPHOMORE AT HAWKINS HIGH SCHOOL IN HAWKINS, INDIANA.
"COME FIND ME.
"BECAUSE IF YOU'RE CRAZY AND OBSESSED AND WEIRD ENOUGH TO HAVE FOLLOWED ALL THESE CLUES AND FOUND THIS TREASURE...
Fellowship
My name is Bob Newby. At the time of this writing,
fifteen year old sophomore at Hawkins High School
Indiana. Come find me.
crazy and obsessed and weird
clues and found this treasure
"...YOU ARE MY FRIEND."

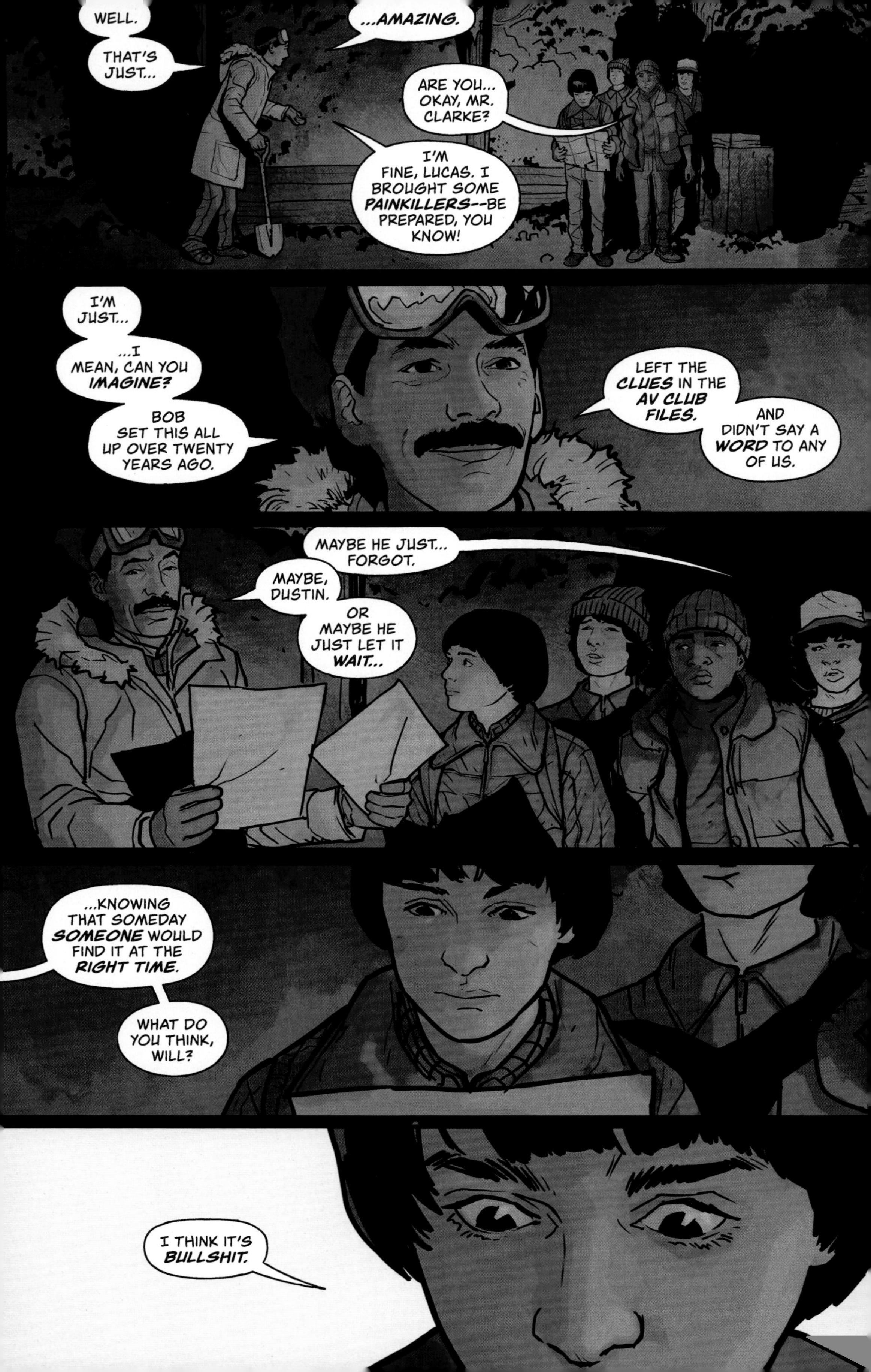
WELL.
THAT'S JUST...
...AMAZING.
ARE YOU... OKAY, MR. CLARKE?
I'M FINE, LUCAS. I BROUGHT SOME PAINKILLERS--BE PREPARED, YOU KNOW!
I'M JUST...
...I MEAN, CAN YOU IMAGINE?
BOB SET THIS ALL UP OVER TWENTY YEARS AGO.
LEFT THE CLUES IN THE AV CLUB FILES.
AND DIDN'T SAY A WORD TO ANY OF US.
MAYBE HE JUST... FORGOT.
MAYBE, DUSTIN.
OR MAYBE HE JUST LET IT WAIT...
...KNOWING THAT SOMEDAY SOMEONE WOULD FIND IT AT THE RIGHT TIME.
WHAT DO YOU THINK, WILL?
I THINK IT'S BULLSHIT.

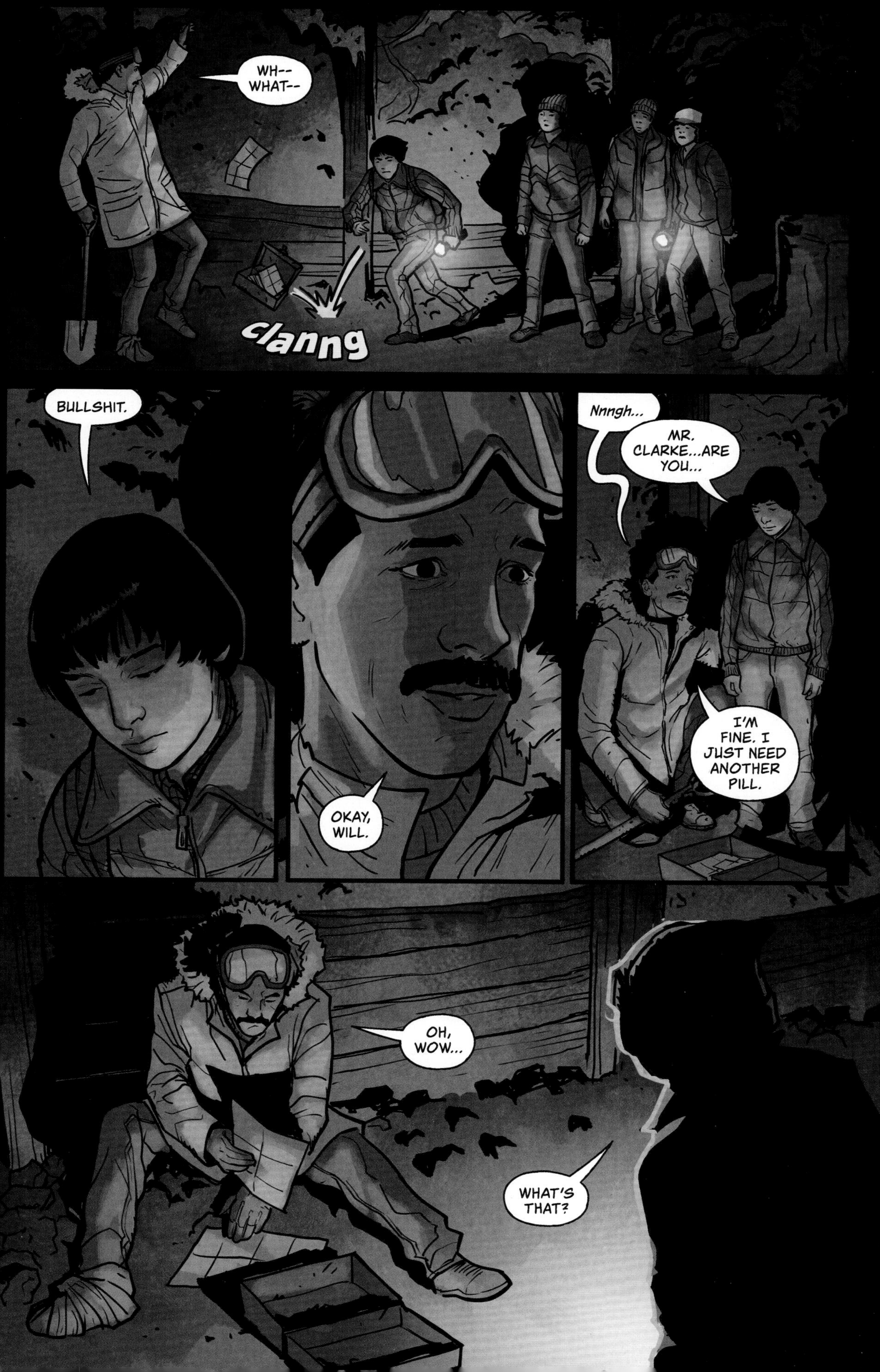
WH--
WHAT--
clanng
BULLSHIT.
OKAY, WILL.
Nnngh...
MR. CLARKE...ARE YOU...
I'M FINE. I JUST NEED ANOTHER PILL.
OH, WOW...
WHAT'S THAT?

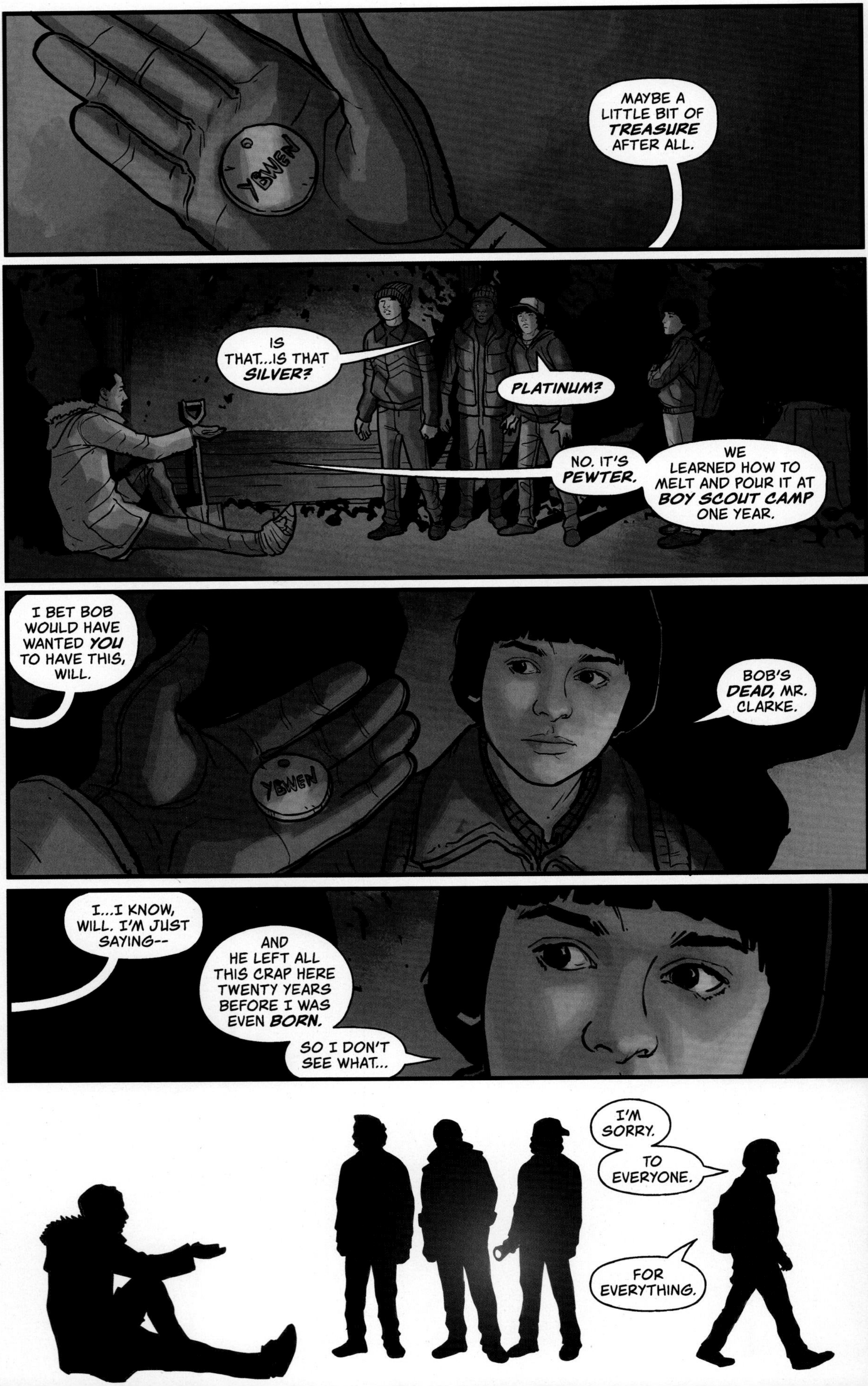
YBWEN
MAYBE A LITTLE BIT OF *TREASURE* AFTER ALL.
IS THAT...IS THAT *SILVER?*
PLATINUM?
NO. IT'S *PEWTER.*
WE LEARNED HOW TO MELT AND POUR IT AT *BOY SCOUT CAMP* ONE YEAR.
I BET BOB WOULD HAVE WANTED *YOU* TO HAVE THIS, WILL.
YBWEN
BOB'S *DEAD,* MR. CLARKE.
I...I KNOW, WILL. I'M JUST SAYING--
AND HE LEFT ALL THIS CRAP HERE TWENTY YEARS BEFORE I WAS EVEN *BORN.*
SO I DON'T SEE WHAT...
I'M SORRY.
TO EVERYONE.
FOR EVERYTHING.

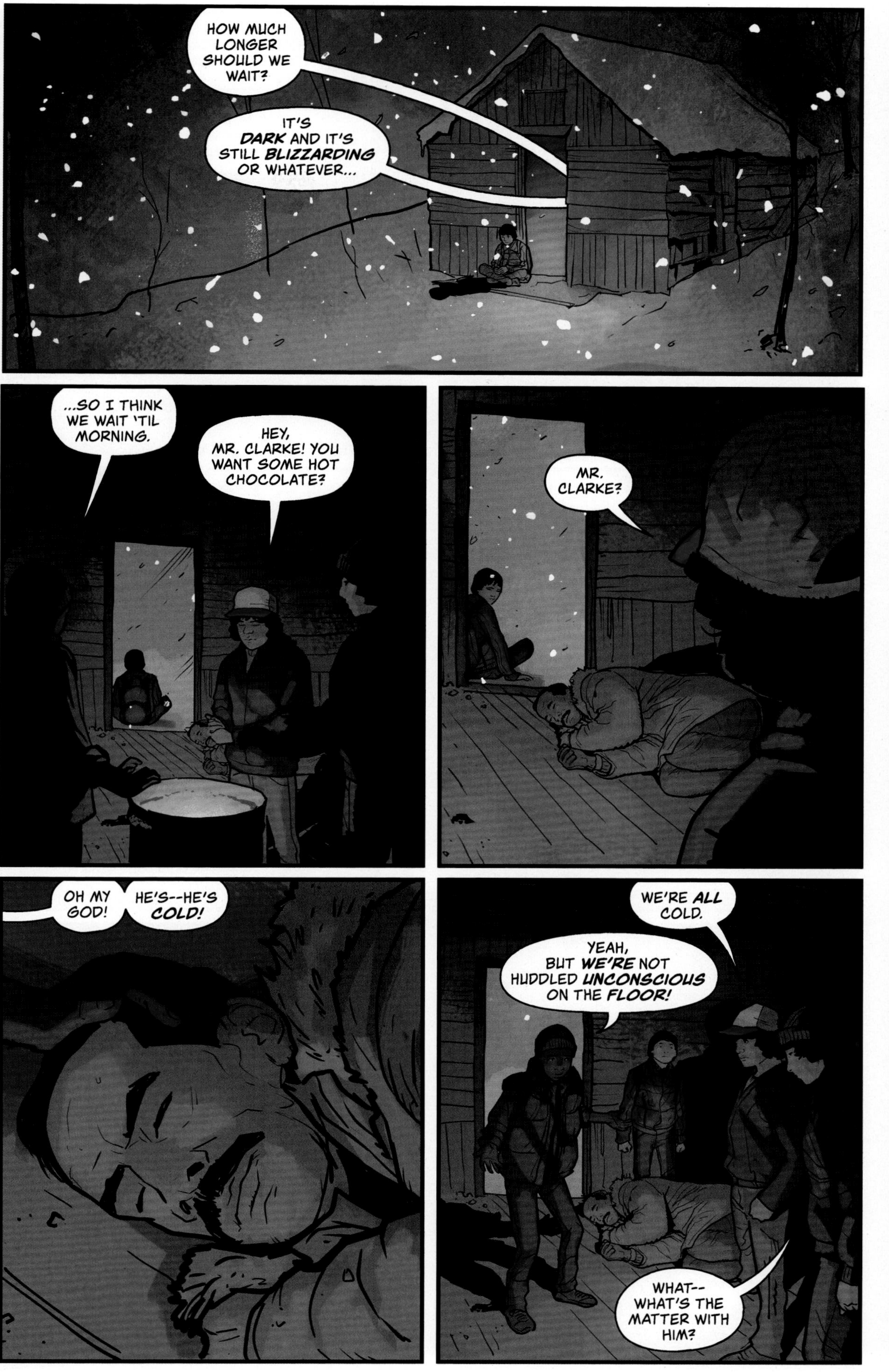
HOW MUCH LONGER SHOULD WE WAIT?
IT'S DARK AND IT'S STILL BLIZZARDING OR WHATEVER...
...SO I THINK WE WAIT 'TIL MORNING.
HEY, MR. CLARKE! YOU WANT SOME HOT CHOCOLATE?
MR. CLARKE?
OH MY GOD!
HE'S--HE'S COLD!
WE'RE ALL COLD.
YEAH, BUT WE'RE NOT HUDDLED UNCONSCIOUS ON THE FLOOR!
WHAT-- WHAT'S THE MATTER WITH HIM?

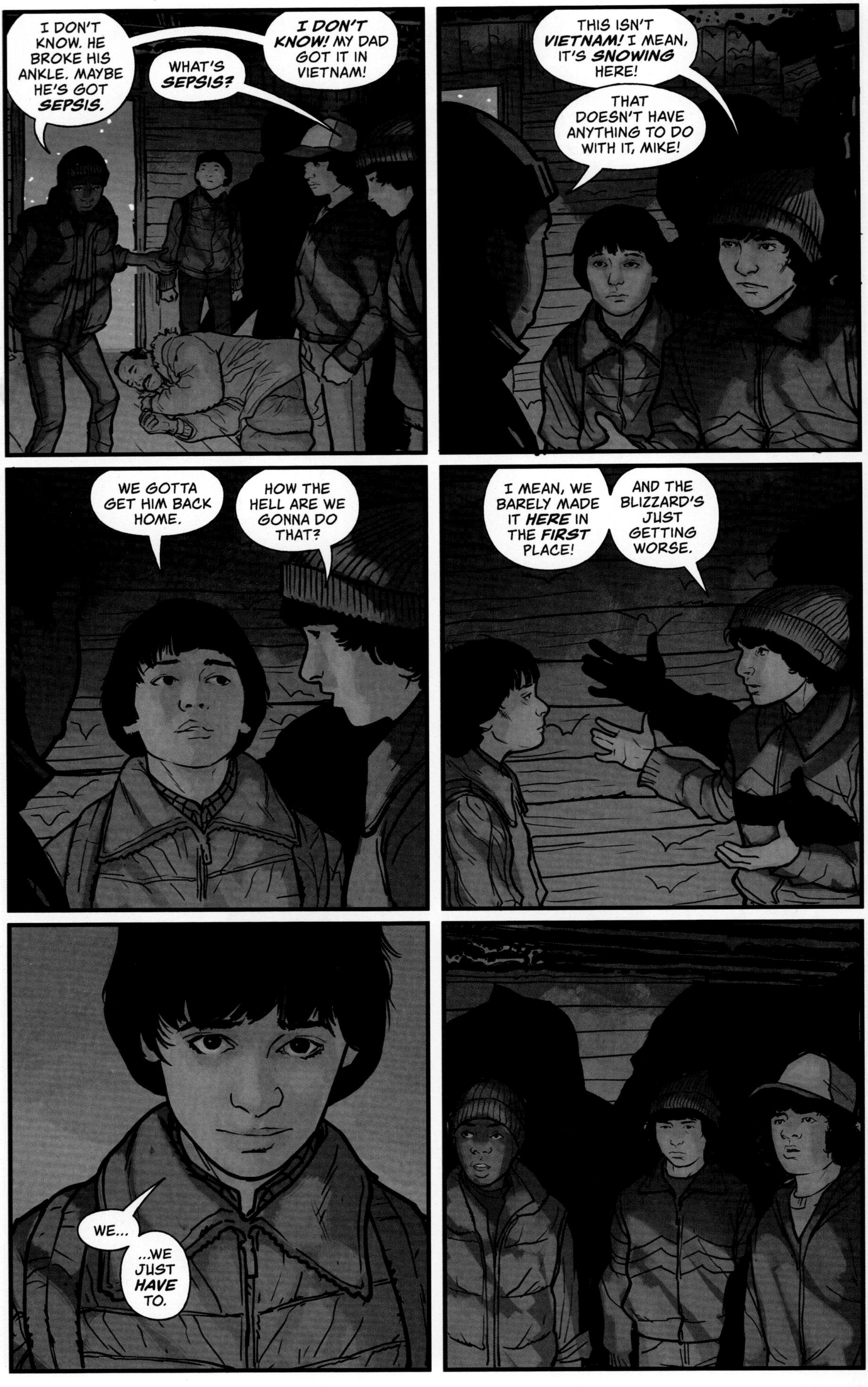
I DON'T KNOW. HE BROKE HIS ANKLE. MAYBE HE'S GOT SEPSIS.
WHAT'S SEPSIS?
I DON'T KNOW! MY DAD GOT IT IN VIETNAM!
THIS ISN'T VIETNAM! I MEAN, IT'S SNOWING HERE!
THAT DOESN'T HAVE ANYTHING TO DO WITH IT, MIKE!
WE GOTTA GET HIM BACK HOME.
HOW THE HELL ARE WE GONNA DO THAT?
I MEAN, WE BARELY MADE IT HERE IN THE FIRST PLACE!
AND THE BLIZZARD'S JUST GETTING WORSE.
WE...
...WE JUST HAVE TO.

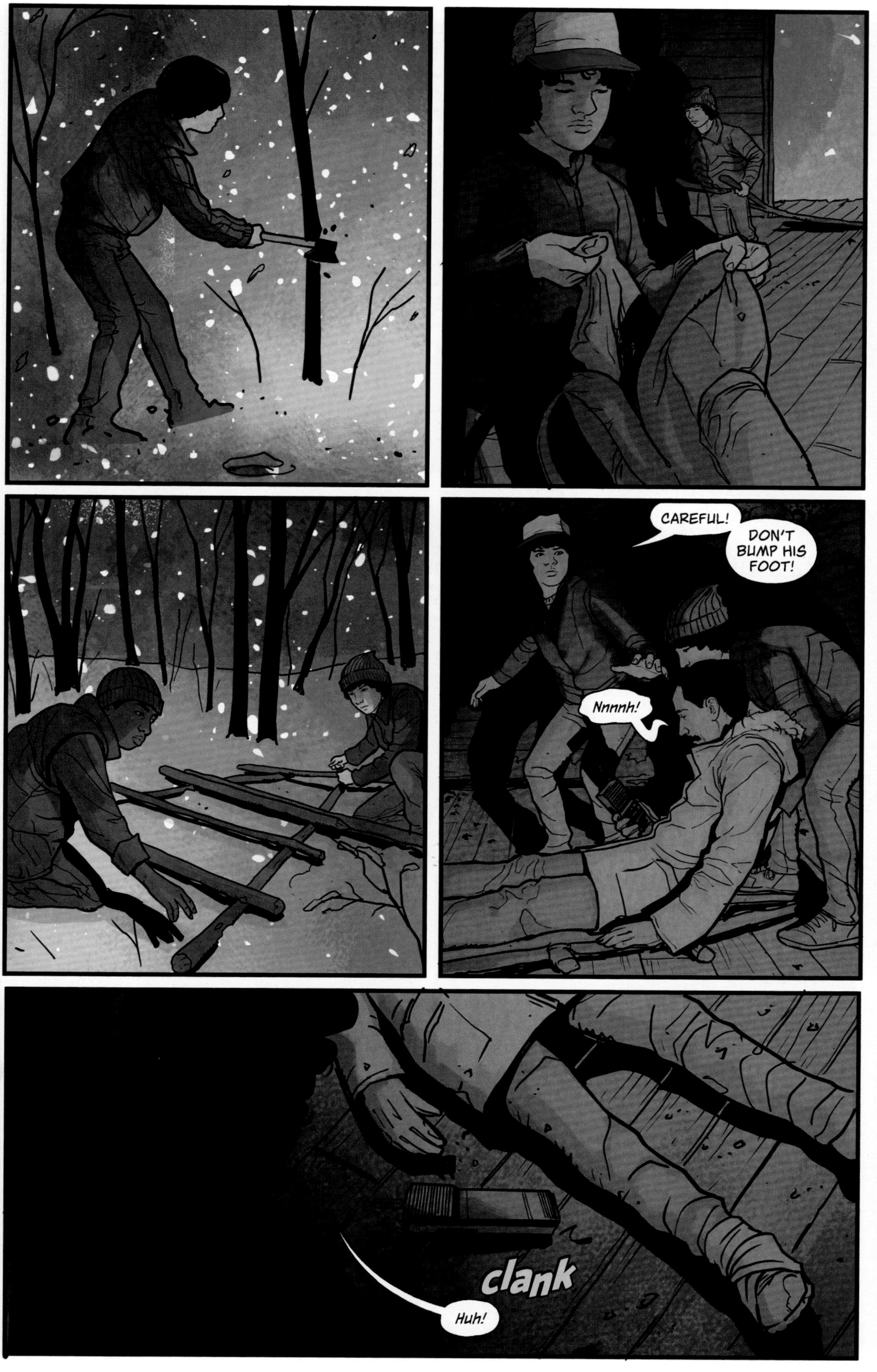
CAREFUL!
DON'T BUMP HIS FOOT!
Nnnnh!
clank
Huh!

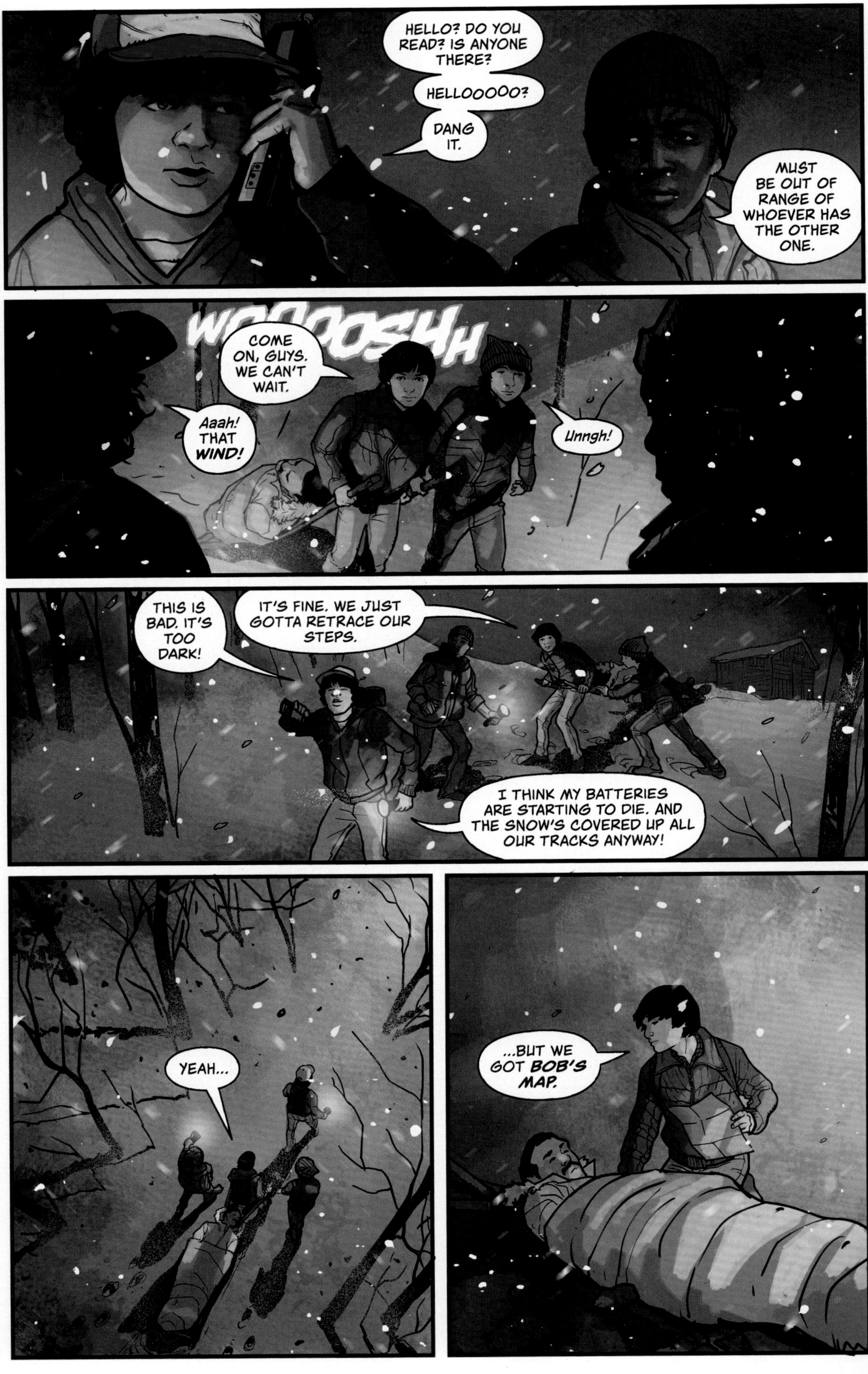
HELLO? DO YOU READ? IS ANYONE THERE?
HELLOOOOO?
DANG IT.
MUST BE OUT OF RANGE OF WHOEVER HAS THE OTHER ONE.
WOOOOSHH
COME ON, GUYS. WE CAN'T WAIT.
Aaah! THAT WIND!
Unngh!
THIS IS BAD. IT'S TOO DARK!
IT'S FINE. WE JUST GOTTA RETRACE OUR STEPS.
I THINK MY BATTERIES ARE STARTING TO DIE. AND THE SNOW'S COVERED UP ALL OUR TRACKS ANYWAY!
YEAH...
...BUT WE GOT BOB'S MAP.

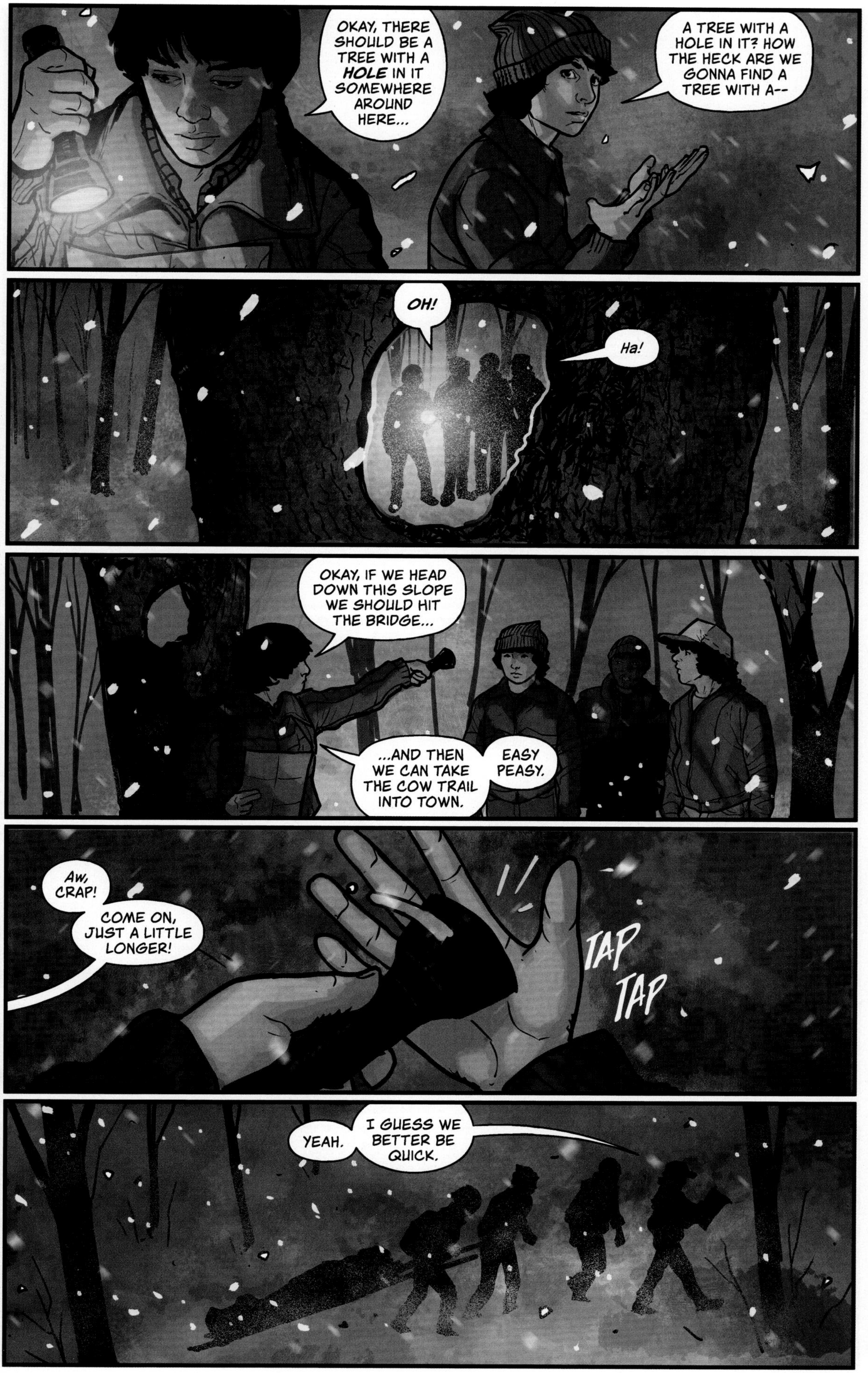
OKAY, THERE SHOULD BE A TREE WITH A HOLE IN IT SOMEWHERE AROUND HERE...
A TREE WITH A HOLE IN IT? HOW THE HECK ARE WE GONNA FIND A TREE WITH A--
OH!
Ha!
OKAY, IF WE HEAD DOWN THIS SLOPE WE SHOULD HIT THE BRIDGE...
...AND THEN WE CAN TAKE THE COW TRAIL INTO TOWN.
EASY PEASY.
AW, CRAP!
COME ON, JUST A LITTLE LONGER!
TAP TAP
YEAH.
I GUESS WE BETTER BE QUICK.

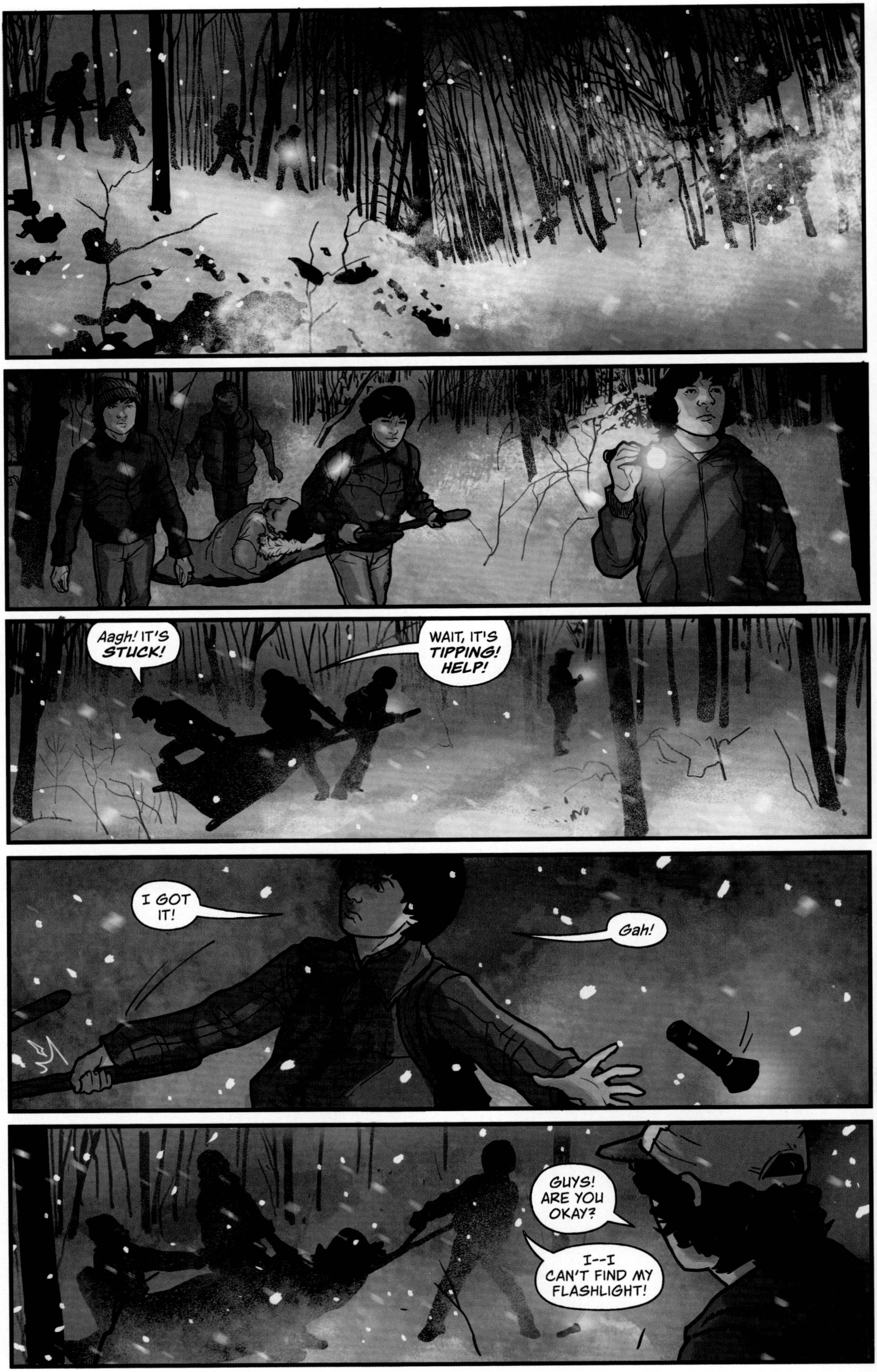
Aagh! IT'S STUCK!
WAIT, IT'S TIPPING! HELP!
I GOT IT!
Gah!
GUYS! ARE YOU OKAY?
I--I CAN'T FIND MY FLASHLIGHT!

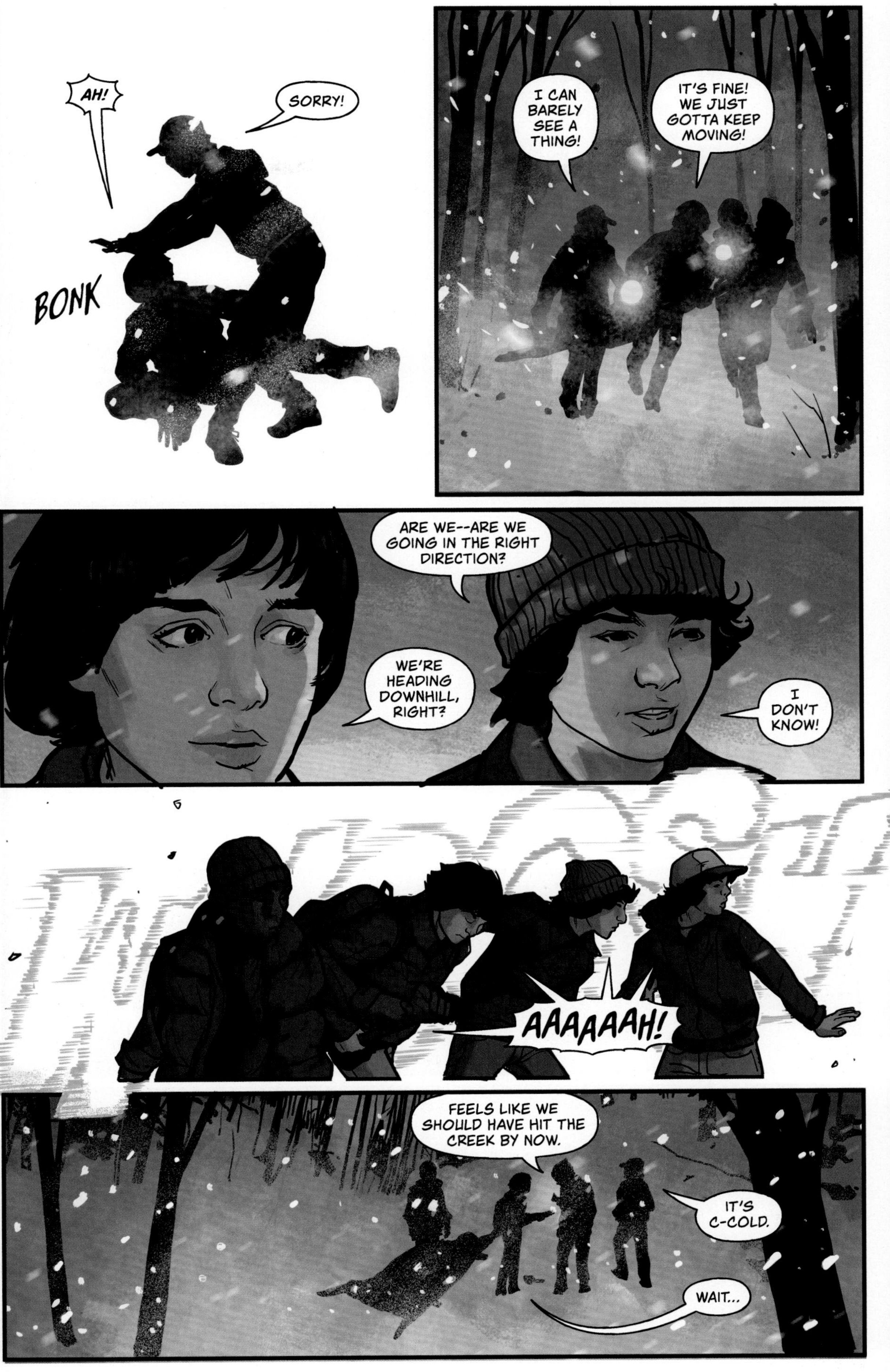
AH!
SORRY!
BONK
I CAN BARELY SEE A THING!
IT'S FINE! WE JUST GOTTA KEEP MOVING!
ARE WE--ARE WE GOING IN THE RIGHT DIRECTION?
WE'RE HEADING DOWNHILL, RIGHT?
I DON'T KNOW!
AAAAAAH!
FEELS LIKE WE SHOULD HAVE HIT THE CREEK BY NOW.
IT'S C-COLD.
WAIT...

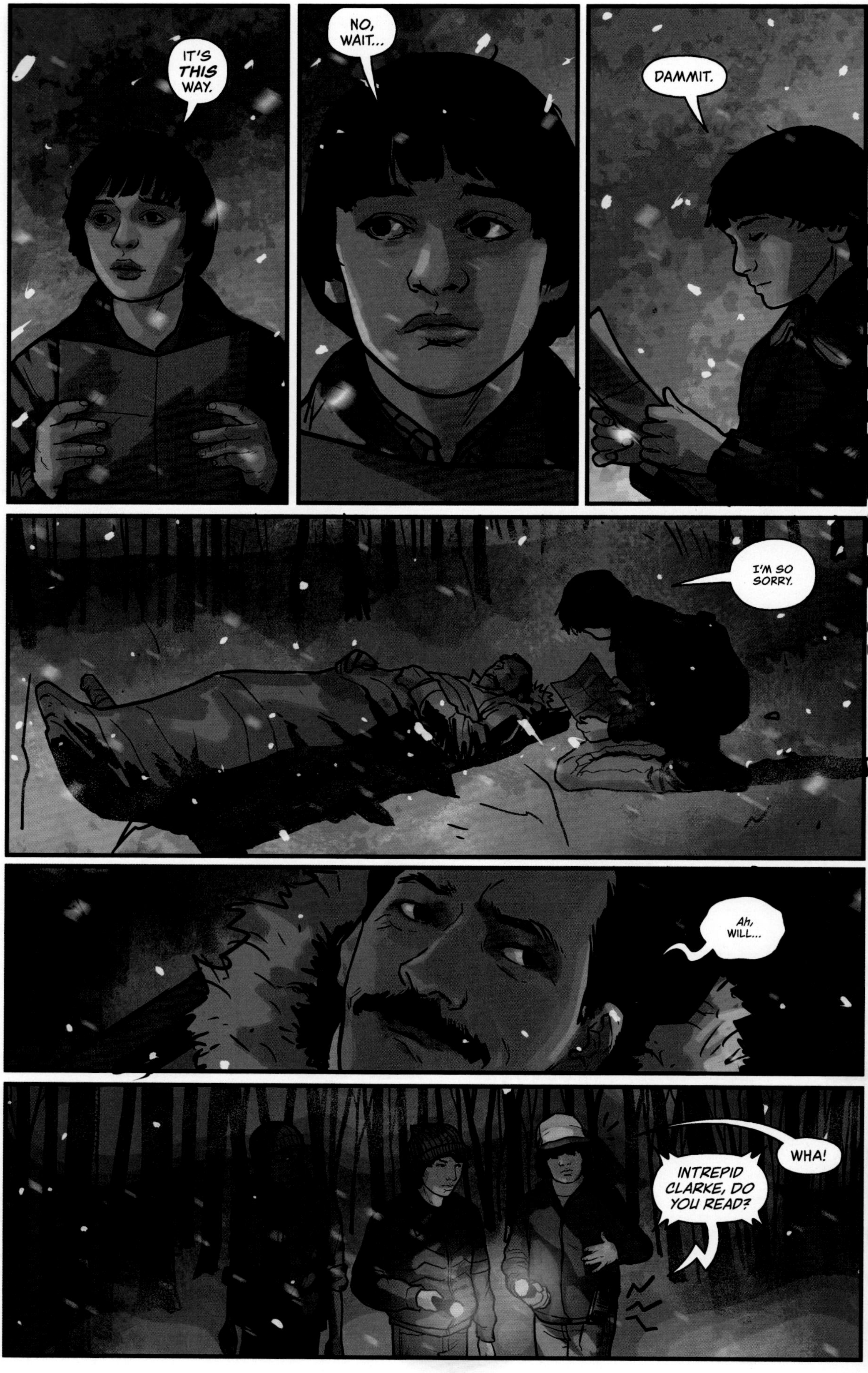
IT'S THIS WAY.
NO, WAIT...
DAMMIT.
I'M SO SORRY.
Ah, WILL...
WHA!
INTREPID CLARKE, DO YOU READ?

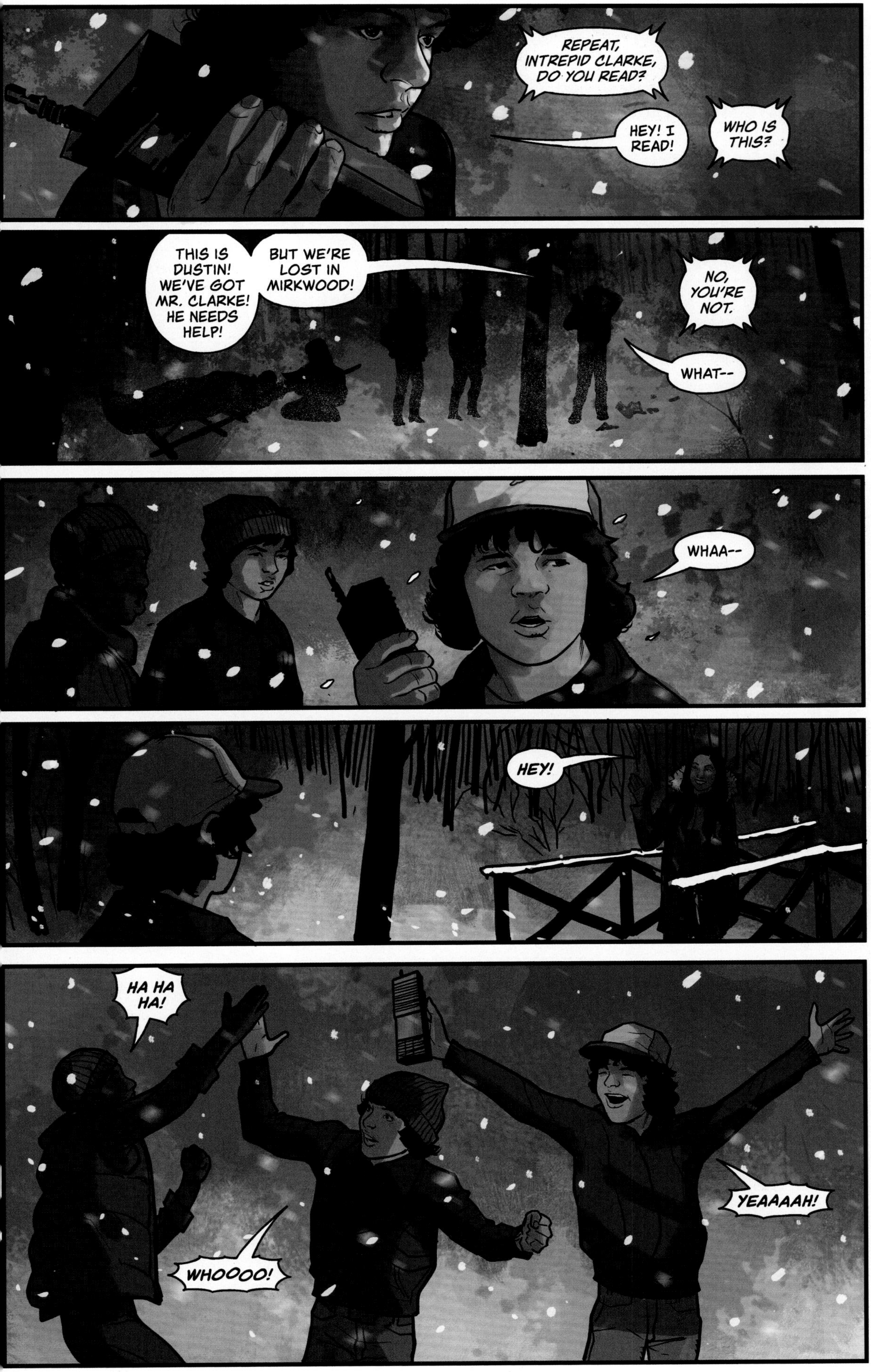
REPEAT, INTREPID CLARKE, DO YOU READ?
HEY! I READ!
WHO IS THIS?
THIS IS DUSTIN! WE'VE GOT MR. CLARKE! HE NEEDS HELP!
BUT WE'RE LOST IN MIRKWOOD!
NO, YOU'RE NOT.
WHAT--
WHAA--
HEY!
HA HA HA!
YEAAAAH!
WHOOOO!

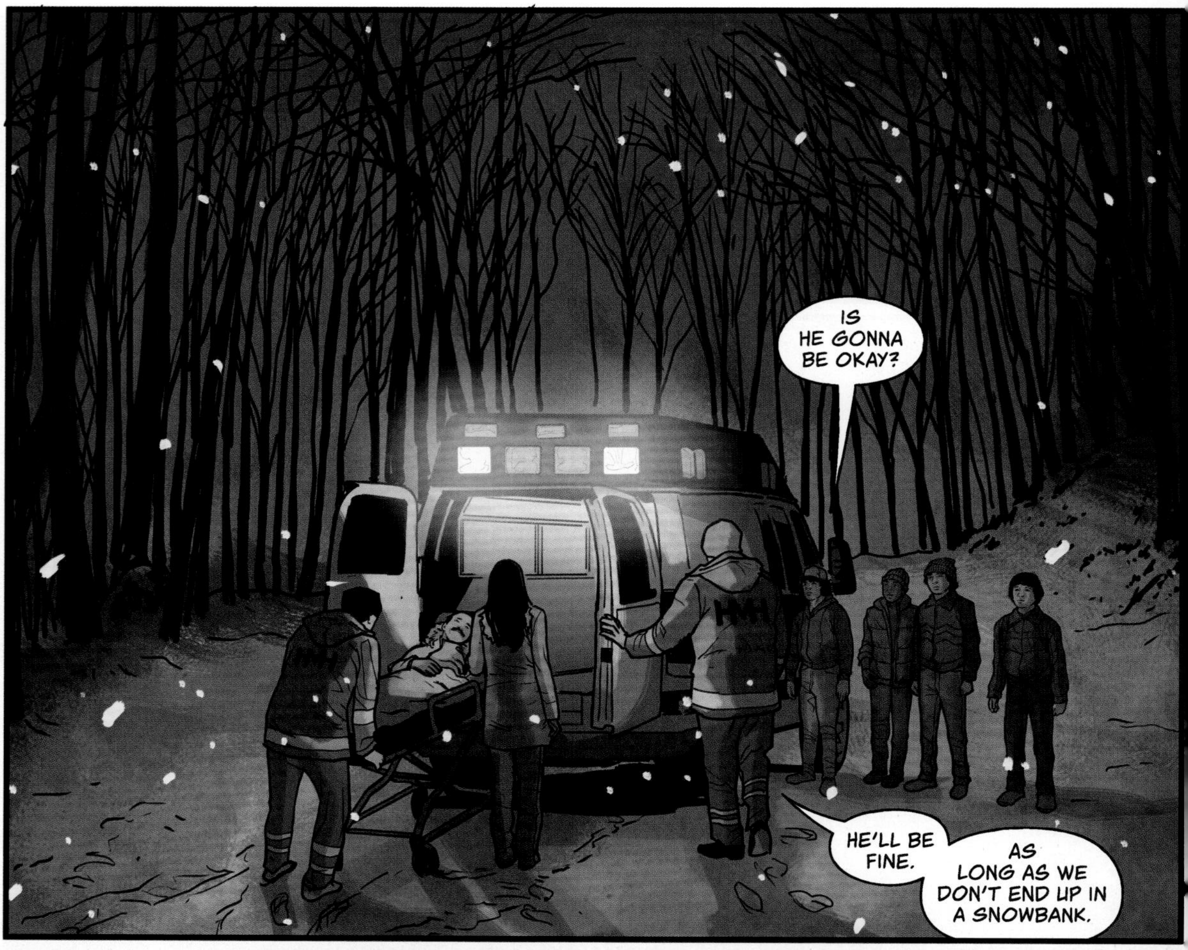
IS HE GONNA BE OKAY?
HE'LL BE FINE.
AS LONG AS WE DON'T END UP IN A SNOWBANK.

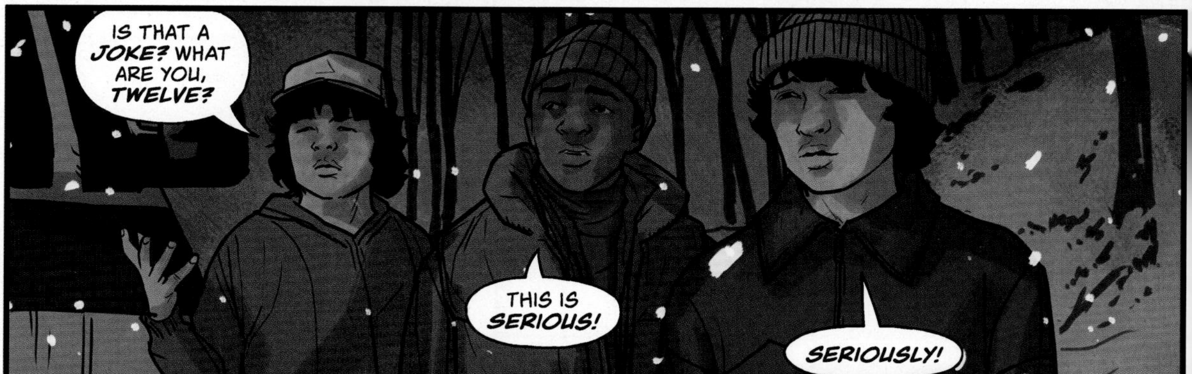
IS THAT A JOKE? WHAT ARE YOU, TWELVE?
THIS IS SERIOUS!
SERIOUSLY!

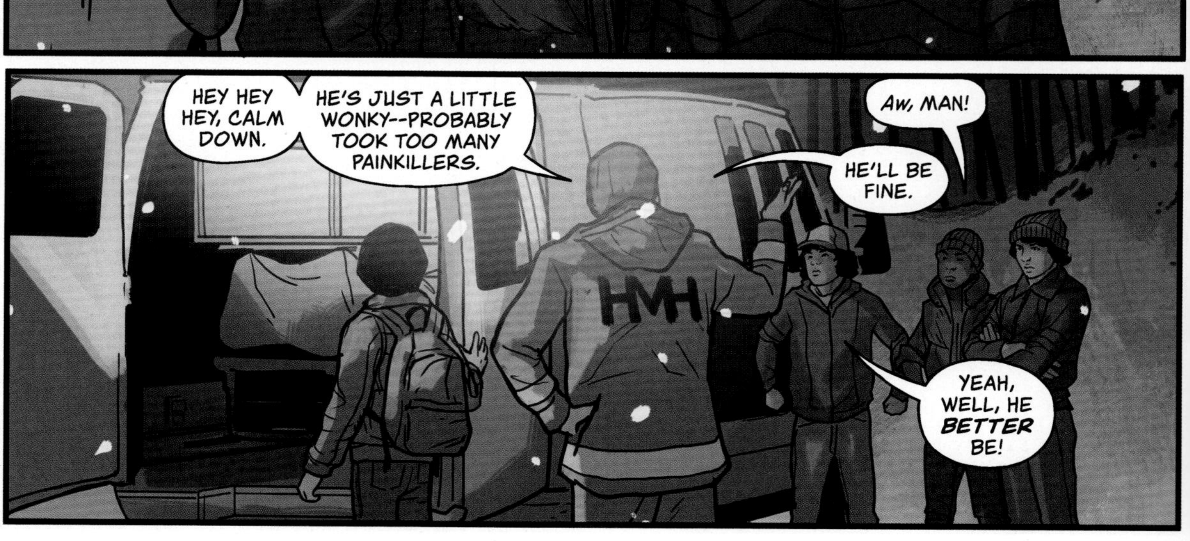
HEY HEY HEY, CALM DOWN.
HE'S JUST A LITTLE WONKY--PROBABLY TOOK TOO MANY PAINKILLERS.
AW, MAN!
HE'LL BE FINE.
YEAH, WELL, HE BETTER BE!

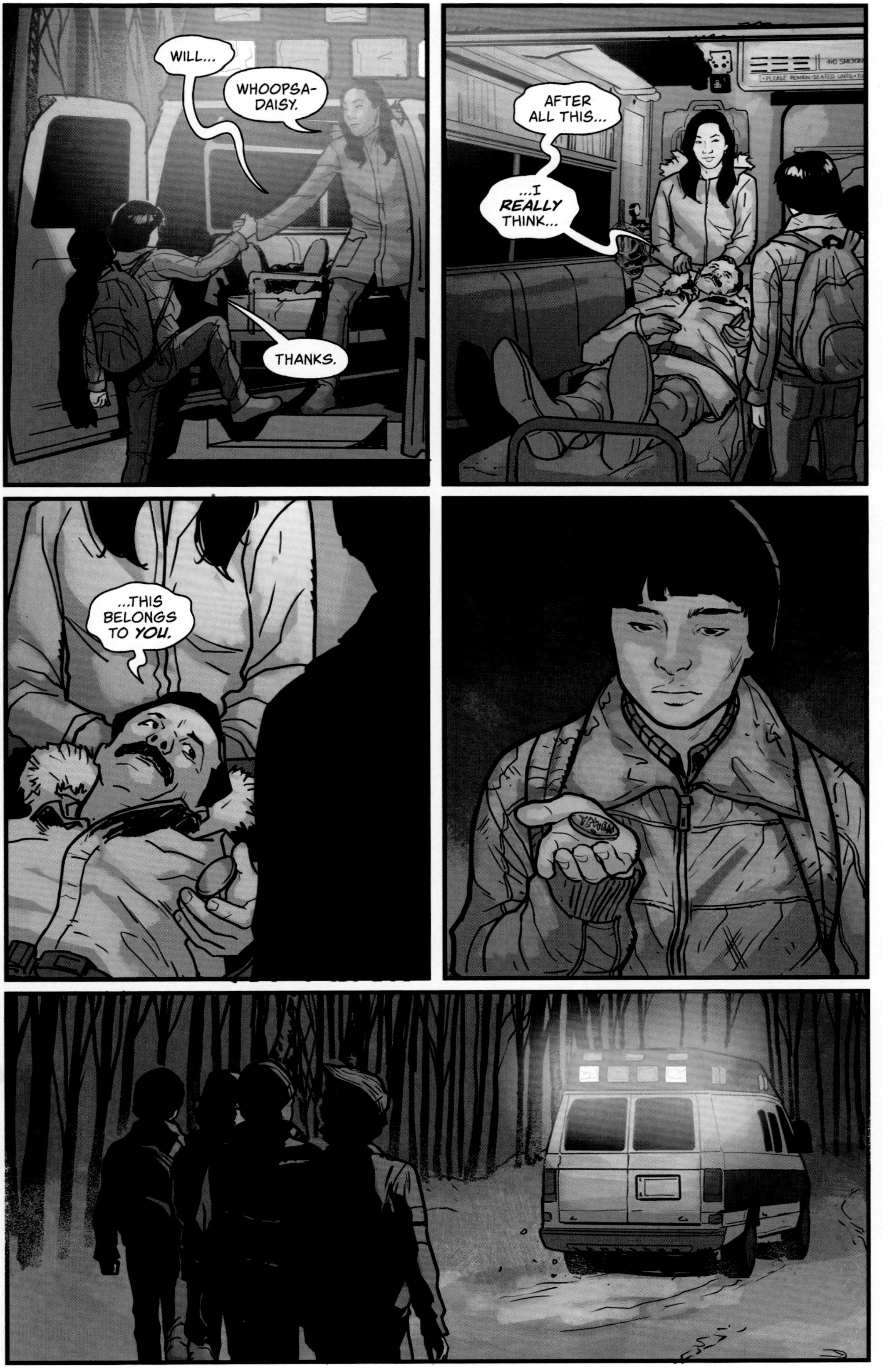
WILL...
WHOOPSA-DAISY.
THANKS.
-NO SMOKING-
-PLEASE REMAIN SEATED UNTIL-
AFTER ALL THIS...
...I REALLY THINK...
...THIS BELONGS TO YOU.

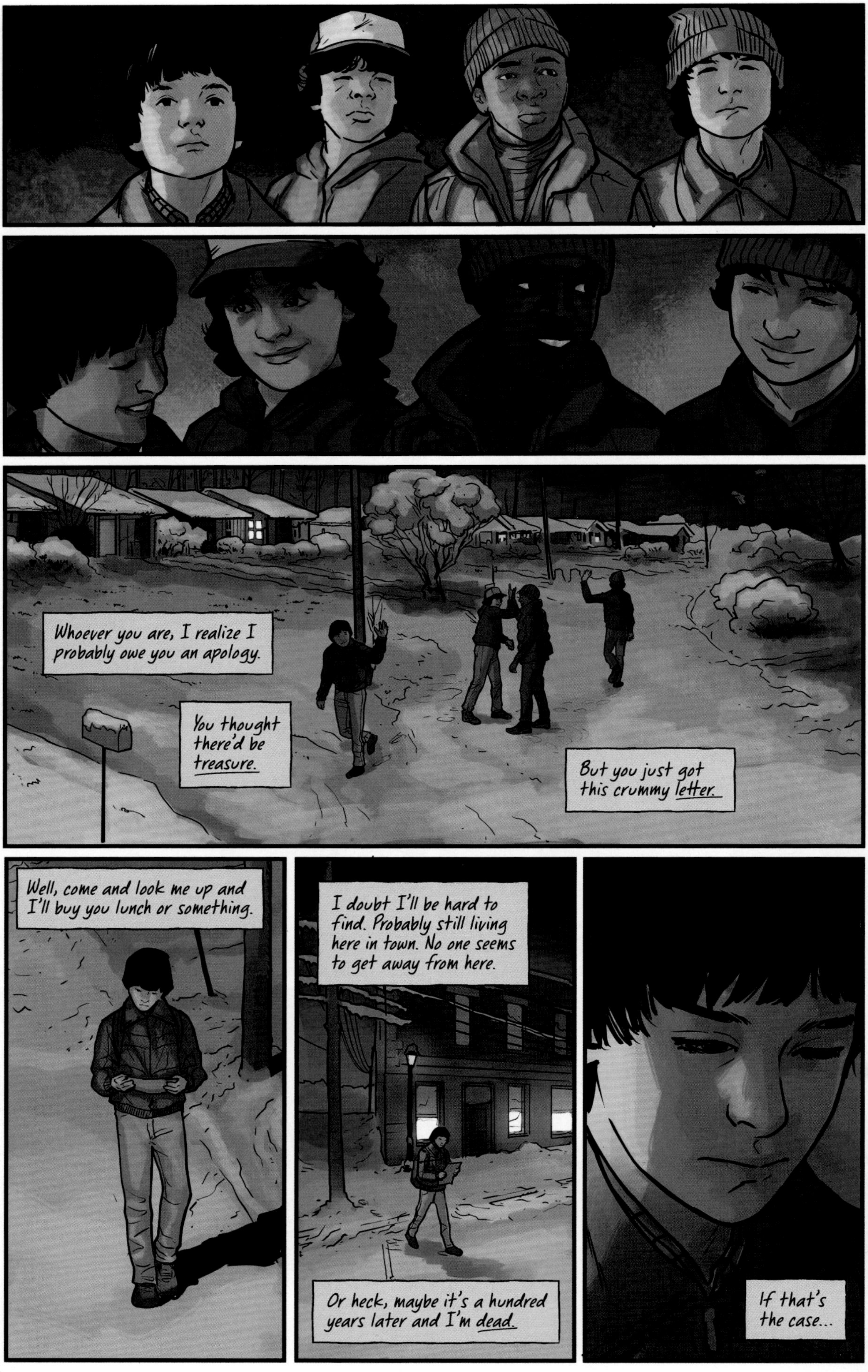
Whoever you are, I realize I probably owe you an apology.
You thought there'd be treasure.
But you just got this crummy letter.
Well, come and look me up and I'll buy you lunch or something.
I doubt I'll be hard to find. Probably still living here in town. No one seems to get away from here.
Or heck, maybe it's a hundred years later and I'm dead.
If that's the case...

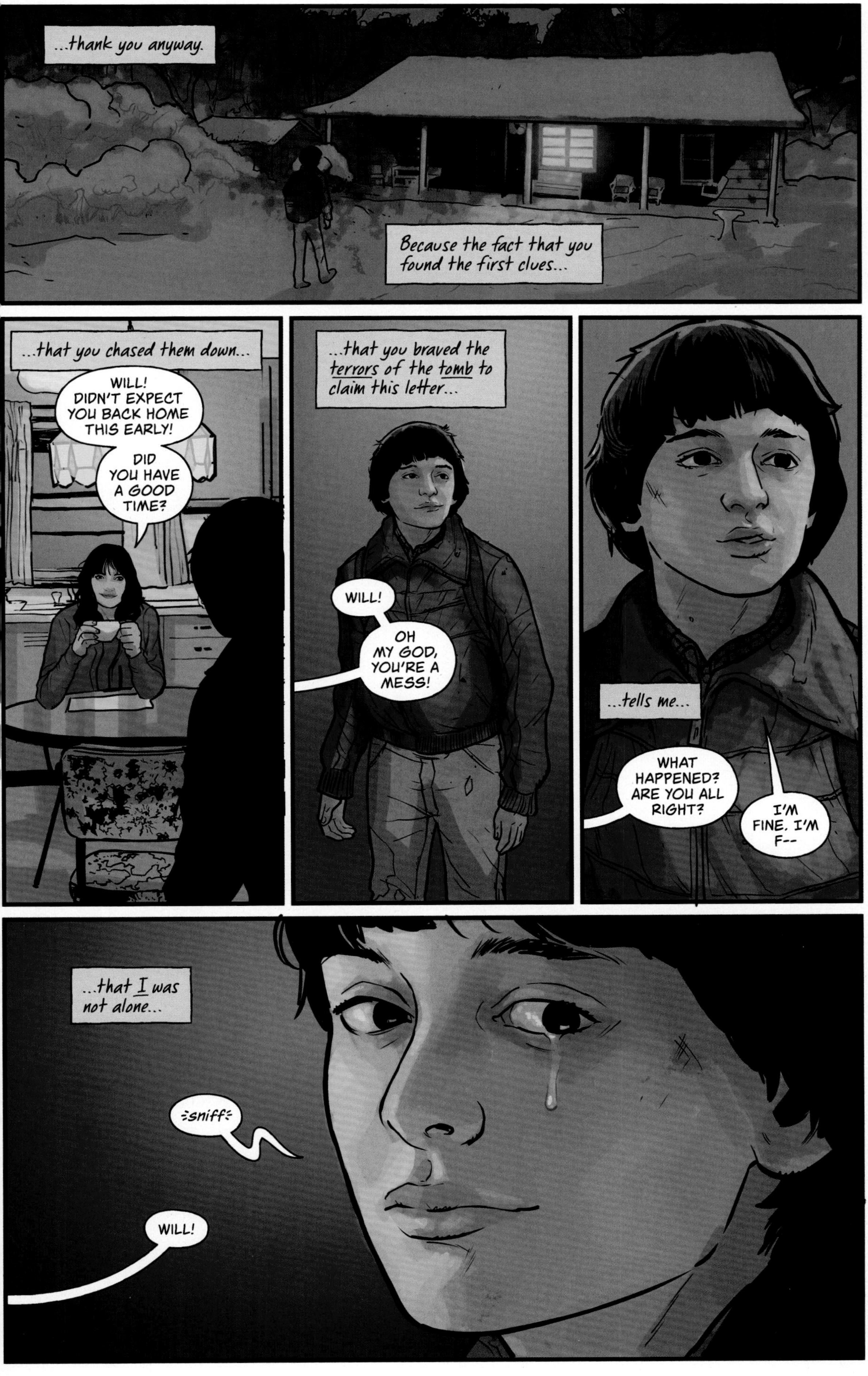
...thank you anyway.
Because the fact that you found the first clues...
...that you chased them down...
WILL! DIDN'T EXPECT YOU BACK HOME THIS EARLY!
DID YOU HAVE A GOOD TIME?
...that you braved the terrors of the tomb to claim this letter...
WILL!
OH MY GOD, YOU'RE A MESS!
...tells me...
WHAT HAPPENED? ARE YOU ALL RIGHT?
I'M FINE. I'M F--
...that I was not alone...
sniff
WILL!

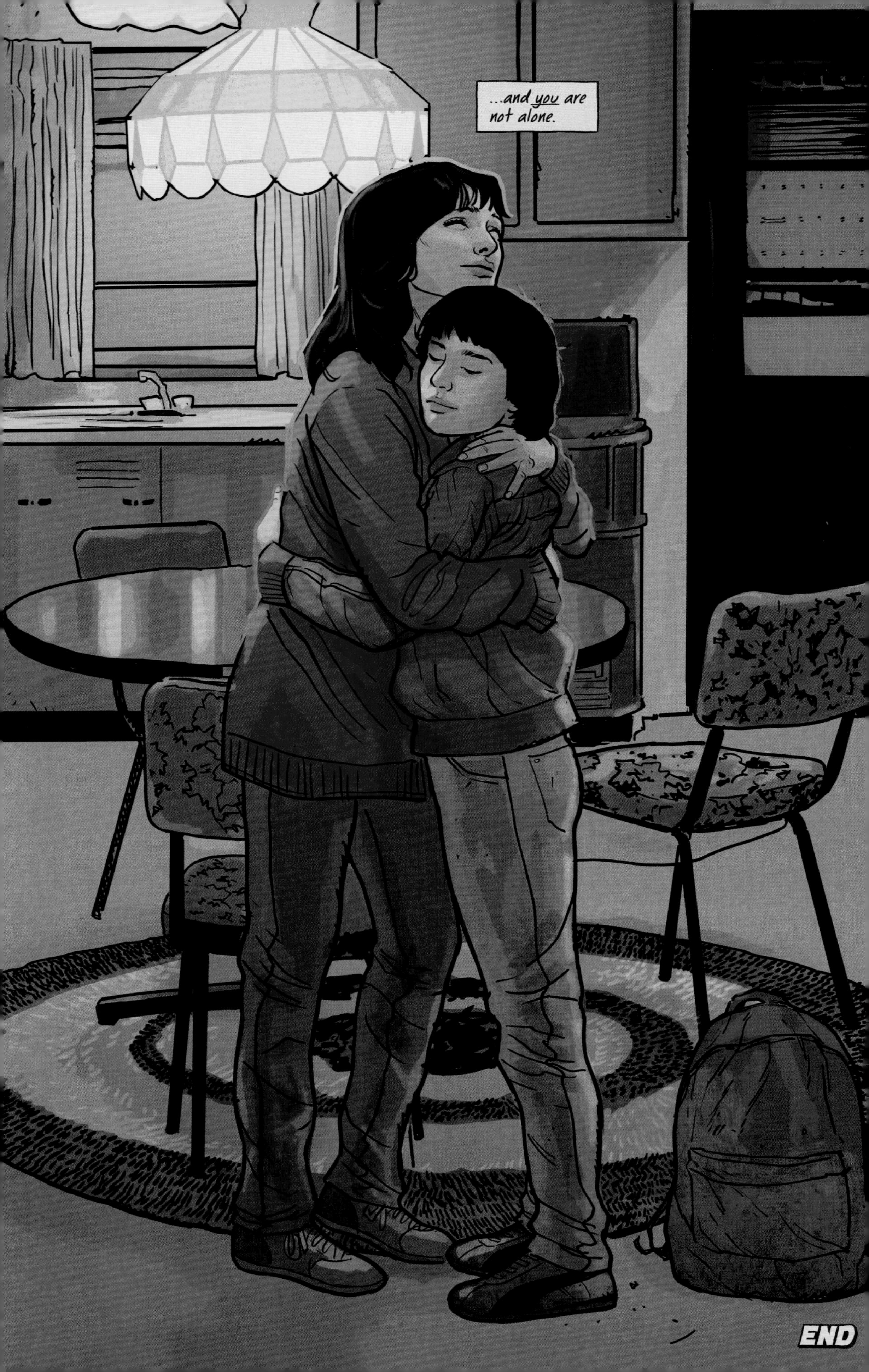
...and you are not alone.
END

Art by DIEGO GALINDO

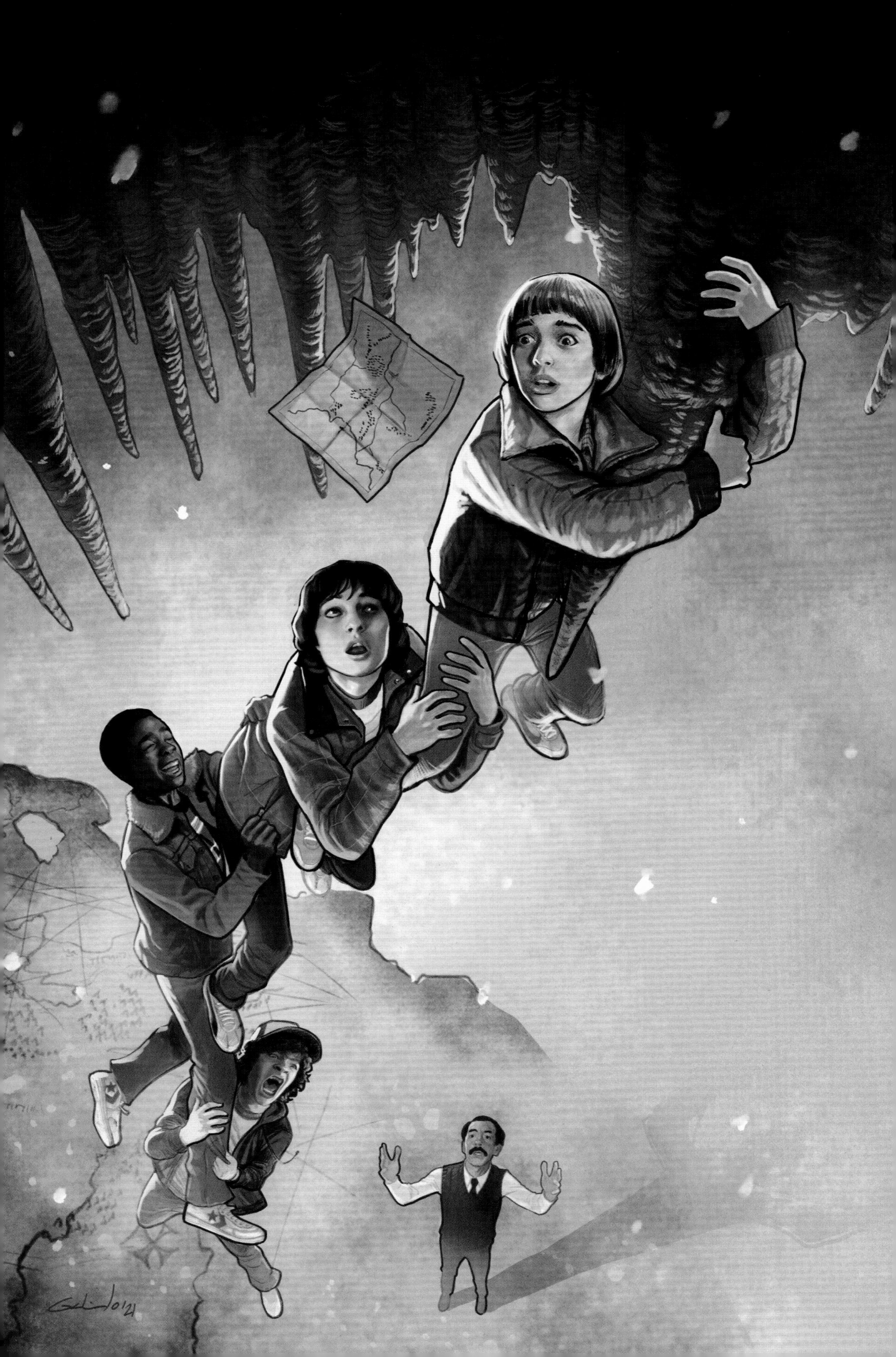

Art by CASPAR WIJNGAARD

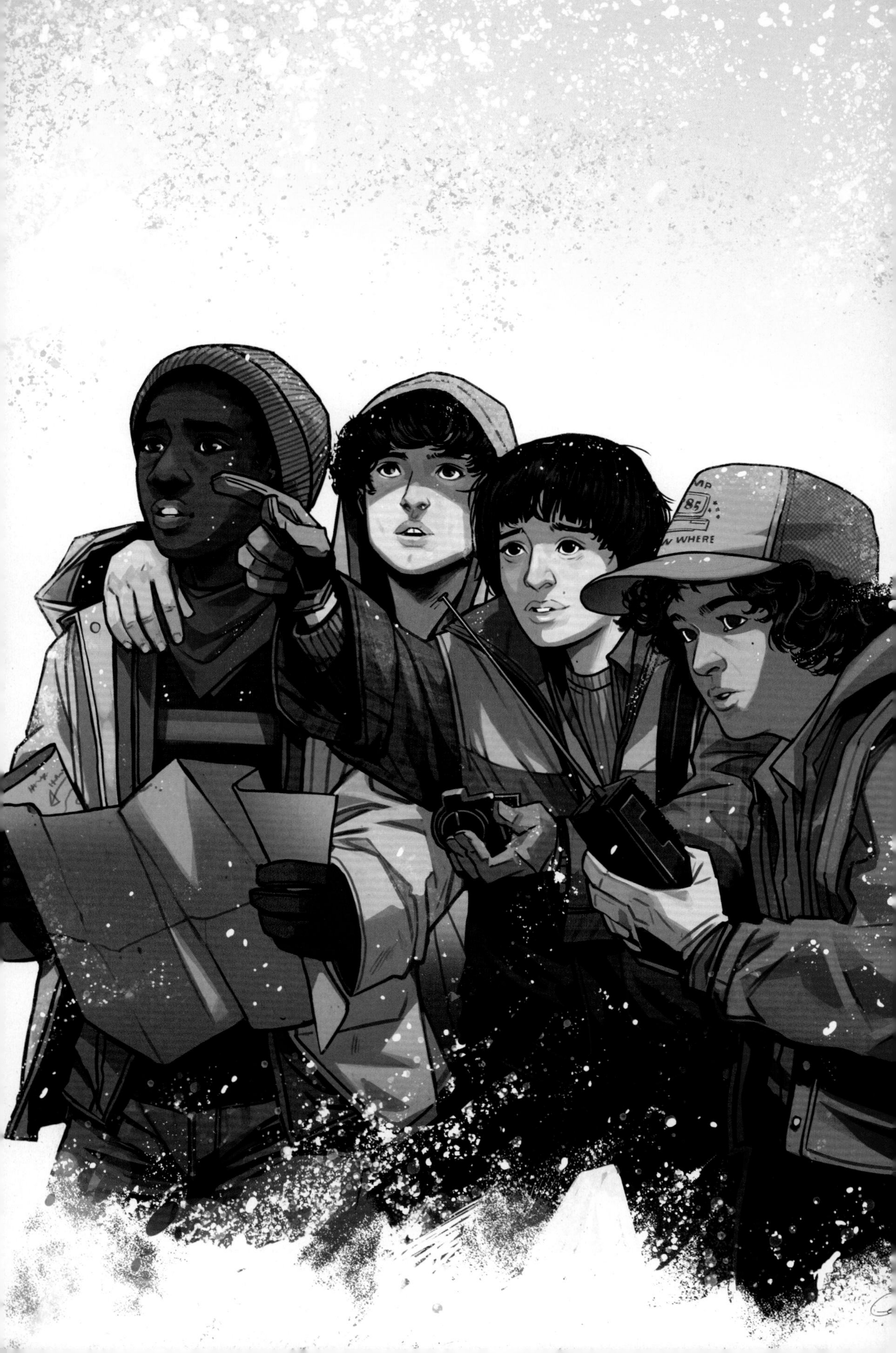

NETFLIX

THE NOSTALGIA-IGNITING HIT NETFLIX
ORIGINAL SERIES COMES TO COMICS!

**STRANGER THINGS AND
DUNGEONS & DRAGONS**
Jody Houser, Jim Zub,
Diego Galindo, MsssyK
ISBN 978-1-50672-107-1 • $19.99
COMING JUNE 2021!

**STRANGER THINGS:
ZOMBIE BOYS**
Greg Pak, Valeria Favoccia,
Dan Jackson
ISBN 978-1-50671-309-0 • $10.99

STRANGER THINGS: THE BULLY
Greg Pak, Valeria Favoccia,
Dan Jackson, Nate Piekos
ISBN 978-1-50671-453-0 • $12.99

VOLUME 4: SCIENCE CAMP
Jody Houser, Edgar Salazar,
Keith Champagne, Marissa Louise
ISBN 978-1-50671-576-6 • $19.99
COMING MAY 2021!

VOLUME 3: INTO THE FIRE
Jody Houser, Ryan Kelly,
Le Beau Underwood, Triona Farrell
ISBN 978-1-50671-308-3 • $19.99

VOLUME 2: SIX
Jody Houser, Edgar Salazar,
Keith Champagne, Marissa Louise
ISBN 978-1-50671-232-1 • $17.99

VOLUME 1: THE OTHER SIDE
Jody Houser, Stefano Martino,
Keith Champagne, Lauren Affe
ISBN 978-1-50670-976-5 • $17.99

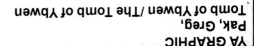

YA GRAPHIC
Pak, Greg,
Tomb of Ybwen /The Tomb of Ybwen
05/2022

Art by TODOR HRISTOV

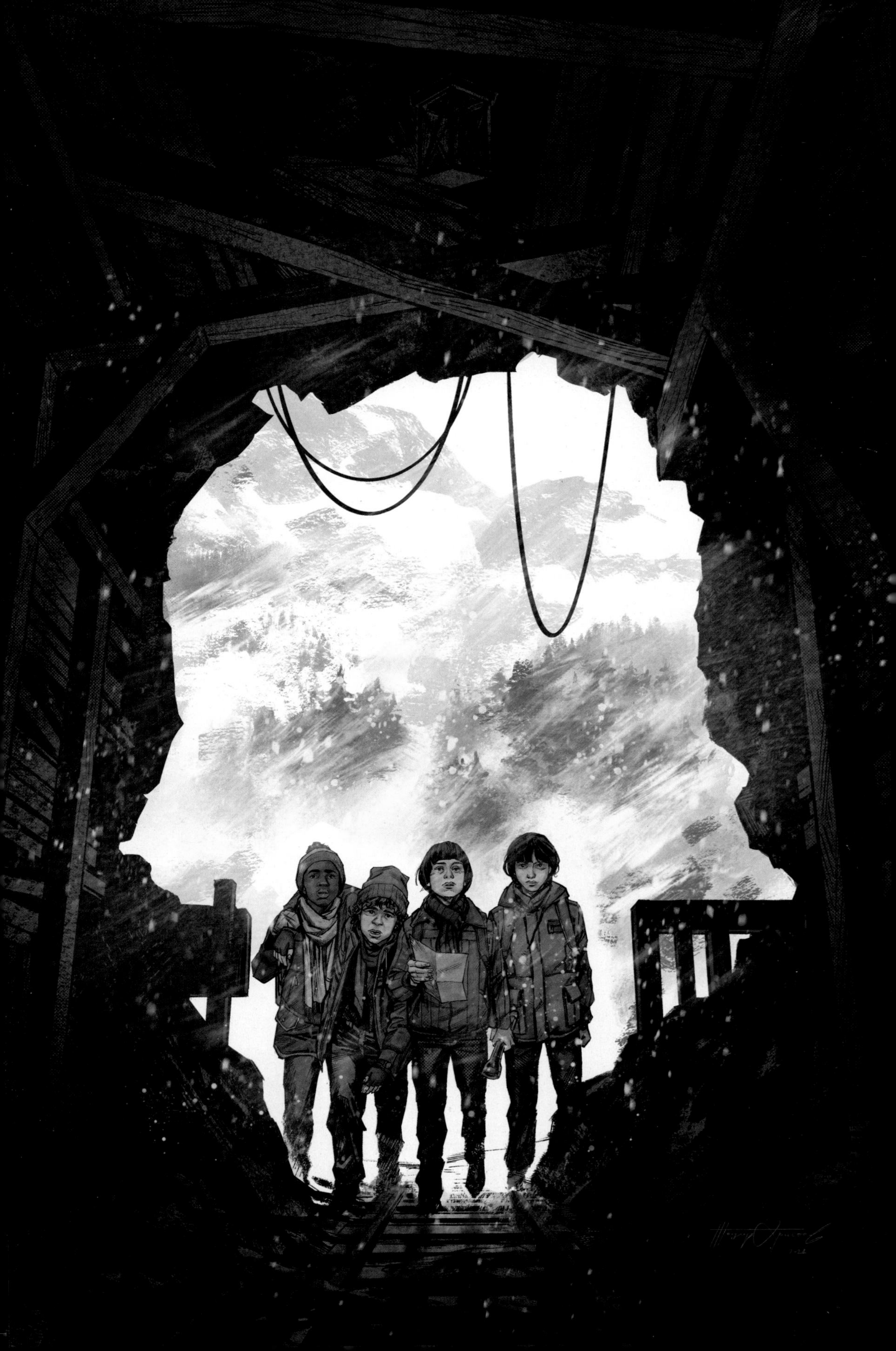